DP|13

WESKER'S SOCIAL PLAYS

D1635082

Arnold Wesker's
SOCIAL PLAYS

THE KITCHEN

VOICES ON THE WIND

DENIAL

THE ROCKING HORSE KID

WHEN GOD WANTED A SON

OBERON BOOKS
LONDON

First published in this collection in 2009 by Oberon Books Ltd
521 Caledonian Road, London N7 9RH
Tel: 020 7607 3637 / Fax: 020 7607 3629
email: info@oberonbooks.com
www.oberonbooks.com

A catalogue record for this book is available from the British Library.

Cover photograph by Nobby Clark

ISBN 978-1-84002-889-8

Printed in Great Britain by CPI Antony Rowe, Chippenham

Contents

THE KITCHEN

A play in two parts with an Interlude

Characters

		Waitresses
MAGI	Night porter	
MAX	Butcher	MONIQUE
BERTHA	Vegetable cook	MOLLY
FRANK	Second chef poultry	WINNIE
		HETTIE
ALFREDO	Roast	VIOLET
HANS	Fry	GWEN
PETER	Boiled fish	DAPHNE
KEVIN	Fried fish	CYNTHIA
GASTON	Grill	BETTY
MICHAEL	Eggs	JACKIE
NICHOLAS	Cold buffet	
PAUL	Pastry chef	
RAYMONDO	Assistant pastry chef	
CHEF	Head	
MARANGO	Proprietor	
ANNE	Desserts and coffee	
MANGOLIS	Kitchen porter	
DIMITRI	Kitchen porter	
HEAD WAITER		
TRAMP		

The original, shorter, version of *The Kitchen* was first presented by the English Stage Society at The Royal Court Theatre for two Sunday night 'Productions without Decor' on 13 and 20 September 1959.

A full-length version was later presented by the English Stage Company at The Royal Court Theatre for a run opening 27 June 1961. Both productions were directed by John Dexter and designed by Jocelyn Herbert.

Substantial changes were made after the author directed the play while 'Distinguished Artist in Residence' at the University of Wisconsin at Madison September/October 1990. It is this version which was revived at The Royal Court in February 1994 by Stephen Daldry.

The first film version was made in 1961.

Further cuts and changes were made after a second film script was written by the author for an Italian film company in 2004/2005. The various versions have since been performed in the following cities – either as theatre or TV or both.

Amsterdam
Antwerp
Athens
BBC TV
Barcelona
Bergen
Bruxelles
    (in French, twice, and Flemish)
Budapest
Buenos Aires
Caracas
Copenhagen
Dijon
Dusseldorf
Essen
Frankfurt am Main
French TV3
Gothenberg (twice)
Hamburg
Helsinki
Hungary – Szeged
    National Theatre
Lausanne
Liege
Lisbon

London – Royal Court (twice)
London – National Youth Theatre
Los Angeles
Lyon – National Theatre of France and tour.
Madison – University of Wisconsin – author's production.
Madrid (twice, awarded 'Critics'and public' Gold Medal')
Magdeburg
Manneheim
Mineapolis
Montevideo
Montreal
Moscow
Moscow TV
Munich
New York

Norkopping – Linkoping
Paris (twice)
Perth, Scotland
Prague
Puerto Rico
Quebec
Resita, Romania
Rio de Janeiro
Rome
Sao Paulo
Seoul, Korea
Sofia
Stockholm
Tatabánya, Hungary
Tel Aviv
Tokyo (seven productions)
Toulouse
Toulouse (toured France)
USA tour
Warsaw
Wrocslav
Zurich

Part One

There is no curtain. The kitchen is always there. In semi-darkness.

The night porter, MAGI, enters, stretches, looks at his watch, registers with distaste where he is. It is seven in the morning.

He 'lights' a taper, 'fires' the first of the seven ovens. Each oven explodes into a burn. With each burn comes more light.

Light and sound accumulate. The kitchen's hum builds to a small roar – a battle with dialogue to the end.[1]

MAGI lights the fourth oven – MAX enters.

MAGI Morning, Max.

> *MAX grunts, goes directly to the cold-cupboard, collects a bottle of beer, opens and drinks.*
>
> *MAGI lights the last oven – BERTHA enters.*

BERTHA Good morning, Magi.

MAGI Morning, Bertha.

BERTHA Good morning, Max.

> *MAX belches.*
>
> *Enter HETTIE and VIOLET from street, en route to changing room.*

HETTIE What bloody agency found you this job?

VIOLET A very respectable agency, I thought.

HETTIE Well you thought wrong, didn't you!

> *BERTHA needs help with a full pot.*

BERTHA Hey, Magi, give us a hand with this.

MAGI OK, love.

> *BETTY and WINNIE enter en route to changing room, pausing to glance at the day's menu chalked on a board.*

BETTY I can't help it, weather affects me.

---

1   Balanced so that neither audience nor actors are strained.

WINNIE I never let anything affect me…

BETTY Everything affects me…

WINNIE Life's too short.

BETTY …music affects me, neighbours affect me…

WINNIE Problem is, I don't get very angry with anything.

BETTY …this bloody kitchen affects me with its bloody boring menu.

WINNIE But I don't get very happy at anything either, know what I mean?

> *They've gone.*
>
> *During next moments MANGOLIS comes on and off depositing dustbins in various positions.*

MAGI Bertha –

BERTHA Yes?

MAGI I've got a confession –

BERTHA So early?

MAGI – that ten shillings…

BERTHA You haven't got it? So you haven't got it! You emigrating?

MAGI No.

BERTHA Then I'll wait.

MAGI You're a good girl, Bertha.

BERTHA Good – I am, but a girl?

MAGI Go on, *I* could fancy you.

BERTHA Fancy? Boy, I'd crack you in a crunch. Crrrrrunch!

MAGI Bertha, you worry me.

BERTHA I *worry* him.

> *PAUL and RAYMOND from the changing room make for their corner, tools in hand.*

PAUL (*To the world.*) Good morning, good morning. (*To BERTHA.*) Morning, me old darling.

BERTHA Morning.

PAUL (*To MAX.*) And to you, Max.

MAX   (*Soul not yet returned.*) Mornin'.

RAYMOND   Max, it's escallop of veal on today?

MAX   How many?

RAYMOND   Three. I'll take them now and put them in my box, before the others get here.

> *GASTON followed by DIMITRI enter en route for changing-room.*
>
> *RAYMOND, noticing GASTON's black eye, whistles.*
>
> *GASTON glares.*
>
> *DIMITRI gestures RAYMOND to desist.*

MAX   (*Handing RAYMOND the escallops.*) And don't forget my puff pastry tomorrow.

RAYMOND   Usual?

MAX   A little extra. My wife's family is coming for Sunday lunch. Magi, give us a hand.

> *MAGI helps MAX carry tray of beef to ALFREDO's station.*
>
> *KEVIN enters, lost.*

New cook?

KEVIN   New cook.

MAX   Changing room's there.

> *KEVIN moves to changing rooms.*

PAUL   (*To RAYMOND.*) Don't forget it's Religieuse today.

RAYMOND   (*Saluting.*) Aye, aye, Commandant! But please let me make them? All week I've been making fruit bands, fruit bands! All week.

PAUL   Alright, alright – Christ! you're a nag.

> *HETTIE and VIOLET en route to the dining-room.*
>
> *VIOLET is new, and aghast at what she's walking through.*

HETTIE   Follow me to the dining-room.

VIOLET   I'm not used to working in places like this, I used to be at the old Carlton Tower.

MAX   (*To BERTHA.*) The where?

BERTHA The old Carlton Tower, don't you know.

PAUL (*To RAYMOND.*) If I make you dinner tonight will you come and fix my motorbike?

RAYMOND Be my pleasure.

PAUL How do you know about motorbikes?

RAYMOND In the war I was a dispatch rider, *mea culpa*! I *had* to know.

PAUL Your wife won't mind?

RAYMOND Sometimes it's a good thing to miss a wife.

PAUL (*Ruefully.*) You think so?

RAYMOND Shit! I forgot.

PAUL Forget it. She was a fool.

RAYMOND So it doesn't hurt she left you?

PAUL What hurts is that one day she's going to have children and those kids are going to have a fool for a mother.

Enter ANNE to her station.

PAUL Good morning, Anne. (*She doesn't hear.*) Good morning, Anne.

RAYMOND (*Louder.*) Good morning, sweetheart.

ANNE Good morning, boys, good morning.

PAUL That's better.

ANNE Hello, Max.

MAX (*His soul returned.*) Top of the mornin' to you Anne.

ANNE (*Putting coffee in metal jug to warm on oven.*) An' the rest o' the day to yersel', dear. (*Stretching herself.*) Ah, me bed was lovely.

RAYMOND (*Lasciviously.*) I bet it was.

She points a cautionary finger at him.

ANNE Paul, tell me, what happened to Peter in the end, you know, last night?

RAYMOND Big mouth! He's got a big mouth. I don't even know what it was all about. You know, Paul?

PAUL All I know is he had a fight with Gaston. Why? I don't know. Over a ladle I think or maybe a…

MAX He's a bloody German, a fool, that's what he is. He's always quarrelling, always. There's no one he hasn't quarrelled with, am I right? No one! That's some scheme that is, exchanging cooks! What do we want to exchange cooks for? Three years he's been here, three years!

But he's more interested in getting another beer.

ANNE Ah, the boy's in love.

RAYMOND What love!

ANNE He's no parents you know.

RAYMOND You see him? When Monique does a turn as hostess by the stairs he watches her through that mirror there.

ANNE Exaggeration!

RAYMOND And he walks round the kitchen looking to see if she's talking or flirting with any of the customers.

ANNE I've never seen it.

RAYMOND You've never looked?

PAUL And they quarrel in front of everybody as well. Shout at each other. Shout! Sometimes she doesn't even look at him, and waits for orders with her back turned.

ANNE But what happened last night? I want to know.

MAGI re-enters.

MAX Ask Magi.

MAGI Any coffee, Anne?

ANNE Help yourself, dear.

RAYMOND Hey Magi, what happened with Peter last night?

MAGI (*Unconcerned.*) They nearly killed him.

ANNE Oh God.

RAYMOND But what was it all about, tell me?

MAGI Well *you* should know that – I wasn't here.

PAUL   All we know is that they suddenly started shouting at each other. And you know Peter, always shouts more than the others, you can always hear Peter – well, so then it stopped, and then a few seconds later they were fighting, and I saw Gaston raise a boning knife and Peter knock it out of his hand, and then…

RAYMOND   And then he lifted him and nearly sat him on the stove and ..

PAUL   And the chef came along and…

ANNE   And I heard the chef separate them and I heard Gaston say 'I haven't finished yet, it's not over yet' but I still don't know what it was all about.

PAUL   Who cares? I say good morning to Peter but never good night.

RAYMOND   Magi?

MAGI   Well I came in at nine last night. The boys were changing and suddenly Peter comes and Gaston follows him. Gaston says Peter called him a lousy Cypro and the boys make circle round him and want to murder him! All of them…but Peter says 'No, everyone for me is the same – it makes no difference race, you misunderstand…' They all wanted to hit him! And he was scared! I've never seen him so white.

ANNE   But what was it about to begin with?

MAX   A ladle, I tell you.

PAUL   Who knows? There's always fights, who knows how they begin?

MAGI   Well, I've had enough of this ol' kitchen. I'm going before the smells get in my hair.

PAUL   Have a good kip old son.

ANNE   And I must get started too. (*Looks round barely populated kitchen.*) You wouldn't think this place will become a mad-house in two hours, would you now?

> *Hold. Only the sound of work.*
>
> *DAPHNE to ANNE for a coffee.*

GWEN and CYNTHIA en route to the dining-room.

DAPHNE So if he doesn't come home tonight I'm going to leave.

CYNTHIA Well he does have to work in the afternoon.

GWEN She's right you know.

DAPHNE You always think everyone's right.

GWEN That's life, deary, everyone usually is right.

MAX Any luck on the pools, Ray?

RAYMOND (*Contemptuously.*) Huh!

MAX Norwich and Leyton let me down. Twenty points. Twenty points.

HETTIE from dining-room to ANNE for a coffee.

HETTIE Morning, Annie love.

PAUL (*To MAX.*) Read about the man in the mental home who won thirty-five thousand pounds…?

RAYMOND …and his wife turned up after eighteen years!

PAUL Eighteen years!

MOLLY and JACKIE en route to the dining-room.

MOLLY Who the hell can afford a lawyer? I sent my brothers after him.

JACKIE They beat him up?

MOLLY The kids need his money not his blood.

JACKIE And did you get it?

MOLLY Not yet.

JACKIE Beat him up!

DIMITRI enters. A Cypriot kitchen porter, young, good-looking and intelligent. He's happily carrying a home-made radio to PAUL. Speaks with an accent.

DIMITRI I make it, Paul, I make it. There! She does not look handsome. I'm sorry for that.

PAUL Clever boy, Dimitri, clever boy. Can we play it?

They look around to check authority is not in sight.

DAPHNE and HETTIE approach.

HETTIE What is it, Paul?

PAUL   Is Marango around yet?

DAPHNE   Not yet. Whose is it?

PAUL   It's mine. Dimitri here made it.

RAYMOND   All those little wires and plugs? Tell me, why you waste your time with dishes in this place. You can't get a job in a factory?

DIMITRI   A factory? You think I find happiness in a factory? What I make there? This little wire, you see it? This I would make, or that…what you call it?

PAUL   Knob.

DIMITRI   Knob. That perhaps I could put in. All day. I would fix knobs. I tell you, in a factory a man makes a little piece till he becomes a little piece, you know what I mean?

> *DIMITRI turns knobs looking for…a station. Crackles, hisses, foreign voices.*
>
> *DAPHNE fiddles with another knob. He slaps her wrist.*

Don't touch!

DAPHNE   Owee! That hurt.

DIMITRI   I'm looking for a station, dummy.

RAYMOND   Hey, Dimitri, *you* know what happened to Peter last night?

DIMITRI   They nearly kill him.

DAPHNE   Oh my gawd!

DIMITRI   But you think it was Peter's fault? They all wanted to fight. You put a man in a plate room all day – dishes to clean, stinking bins to take away, floors to sweep – what else is for him to do? He want to fight. He got to show he is a man some way. So – blame him!

> *DIMITRI has found a station playing loud rock and roll.*
>
> *PAUL grabs a reluctant DAPHNE to dance.*
>
> *HETTIE attempts to involve DIMITRI.*

HANS enters, grabs HETTIE.

At the height of the dance MONIQUE enters with tray of dirty glasses en route to plate-room.

MONIQUE Marango's in the dining-room!

ALL What! What!

MONIQUE Marango's in the dining-room.

Scatter and scramble. Work resumes. DIMITRI vanishes with radio to plate-room. HANS continues to changing-room. Atmosphere of innocence.

ALFREDO enters, surprised at the scene.

ALFREDO It's only me, ladies and gentlemen, the mouse not the cat, and good morning to you all.

MAX (*Indicating ALFREDO's station.*) Your beef's there.

ALFREDO (*Studying menu on the board.*) Thank you, thank you.

MAX You'll find the new cook in the changing-room.

ALFREDO (*Dryly.*) I can't wait.

MONIQUE en route to dining-room.

PAUL I thought you said Marango's coming.

MONIQUE I said he's in the dining-room and he's probably still there.

RAYMOND Monique, perhaps you can tell us what happened last night?

MONIQUE Gaston has a black eye and I'm as angry as hell and I don't want to talk about it.

PAUL A right morning we're going to have this morning then.

RAYMOND And Peter – nothing?

MONIQUE He was lucky.

RAYMOND You mean he was with you so they couldn't touch him.

MONIQUE I mean he was lucky. They waited for him outside.

RAYMOND And?

MONIQUE   He teased them. 'You want to play gangsters?' he says to them, 'Go bring me Marlon Brando and I'll play gangsters.'

RAYMOND   A time like that and he teases.

MONIQUE   And then he shakes hands with them and says 'Good night, bonne nuit, gute nacht and kalinka' one by one. And he leaves them all standing. (*Smiles despite herself.*) What could they do? (*Smile fades.*) The bully!

> *HEAD WAITER from dining-room to menu-board, copying it out on his pad.*

HEAD WAITER   Monique…

MONIQUE   Morning, Harry.

HEAD WAITER   Janey is sick.

MONIQUE   Not again. That girl's anaemic, I swear she's anaemic.

HEAD WAITER   Take over for the day, please.

MONIQUE   But I'm not dressed for hostess.

HEAD WAITER   That dress looks alright to me.

MONIQUE   This one?

HEAD WAITER   Just take off the apron.

MONIQUE   But it's not ironed.

HEAD WAITER   You only have to show the customers to their table not dance with them. (*Exits.*)

MONIQUE   (*Calling to him.*) That's three times this week I've been hostess. (*But he's gone.*) Here, Bertha, look after this apron for me.

BERTHA   I'll sit on it and keep it pressed.

> *DAPHNE, GWEN and HETTIE en route depositing dirty glasses, plates, cutlery, collecting fresh ones.*

MONIQUE   Hettie, Janey's sick again, take over my station will you love? Daphne, give her a hand will you?

DAPHNE   I'm on glasses don't forget.

MONIQUE   True… I forgot. Who's left then? Winnie's on ten. Gwen's on… Gwen, what station you on today?

GWEN   Seven.

MONIQUE Seven…that's your hands full.

HETTIE What about the new woman?

The thought mischievously delights everyone.

MONIQUE Mmmmm. Good idea, she claims to be an old hand. She can help you, and you can keep an eye on her – come on, let's move.

PAUL And may God bless you all.

MONIQUE At least it means I won't have to stand in front of that bully all day.

They've gone.

PAUL Fancy that sort of relationship?

RAYMOND Peter and Monique? It's not so bad for them – it's her husband I wouldn't like to be.

PAUL (*Ruefully.*) No, you wouldn't.

RAYMOND There – I've done it again. Big feet! I'm sorry, Paul.

PAUL That's alright, I don't mind being cuckolded – better men than me…

MICHAEL en route from street to changing-room.

MICHAEL (*To BERTHA.*) Morning, fatty. How are you?

BERTHA And you can shut up for a start, little boy. I can wring your napkins out any day. With you tucked in them any day.

MICHAEL passes GASTON coming from changing room.

MICHAEL Your eye's black.

GASTON YOU TELLING ME SOMETHING?

MICHAEL Alright, alright…phew…he looked as though he wanted to kill me.

PAUL Who'd want to kill you, Michael?

MICHAEL Quite right…who'd want to kill me? Young man in his teens, all the world in front of him. Look at it… (*Takes in the stage.*) …a lovely sight, isn't it? Isn't she beautiful? A bloody great mass of iron and we work it. Praise be to God for man's endeavour – what's on the menu today? (*Looking.*) I don't know

why I bother – it's always the same: vegetable
soup, minestrone, omolletteeeee au jambon – ah
well! One day I'll work in a place where I can
create masterpieces, master bloody pieces. Beef
Stroganoff, Chicken Kiev, and that king of the Greek
dishes – Moussaka.

GASTON Never. You'll never create a Moussaka. Chips you
can make – chips with everything!

MICHAEL There was a time when the English knew how to eat.

GASTON There *was* a time.

MICHAEL Aye – well – yes – there was a time.

> *HANS escorts KEVIN into the kitchen. NICHOLAS not
> far behind.*

HANS I not know where you work. On fish perhaps. Paul!
new cook!

PAUL We've met.

> *ALL continue to work while KEVIN watches.*

KEVIN Is there much doing here?

PAUL Everything's relative – is two thousand customers a
day 'much'?

> *While KEVIN shares PAUL's humour an incident
> explodes elsewhere.*
>
> *BERTHA has been to the cold cupboard and emerged
> with a tray of sliced, cold potatoes.*
>
> *Following behind, about to start his work, is
> NICHOLAS, a beer in his hand.*

NICHOLAS (*To BERTHA.*) Where you go with that?

BERTHA I need it for sauté.

NICHOLAS (*Attempting to snatch tray.*) Oh no, no, no, that's for
me. Me. I prepare that yesterday for my salad.

BERTHA (*Holding on to tray.*) You get your salad from the
veg-room.

NICHOLAS No, bloody hell! You get *yours* from the veg-room.

BERTHA You don't bloody hell me, my son. You bloody hell
in your own country.

NICHOLAS   This is my country.

BERTHA   The lavatory is your country.

NICHOLAS   The lavatory is *your* country. And the sewers, you
know that? The sewers.

> *Finally snatches tray from her.*
>
> *She moves to take out another.*

BERTHA   I'll pay you, sonny. You cross me once, that's all, just
once. Lousy little foreigner you!

NICHOLAS   *She* calls *me* a foreigner! Listen to her…

ALFREDO   (*Approaching cupboard for his own stock.*) Excuse me
friends, you can carry on in a minute.

> *But the quarrel has died away. NICHOLAS approaches
> pastry section.*

NICHOLAS   D'you hear her? The cow! Paul, you got some tart or
cake, anything? I need something sweet!

> *PAUL hands him a tart. NICHOLAS turns to KEVIN
> who has been watching with amusement.*

You the new cook?

KEVIN   Yes.

NICHOLAS   Good luck to you, you'll need it. You know where
your station is?

KEVIN   I don't even know what stations there are.

NICHOLAS   Here I'll show you. Right, for a start there's the
menu for the day, chef writes it out each night. Over
here, this is where I work on the cold buffet. This is
Max the butcher. And there, you see that fat bitch
down there? Well she works, or says she works, as
the veg cook. And here is my Aunty Anne who's on
teas and coffee. Next, Paul and Raymond are the
pastry cooks – they have an easy life, make pastries
in their own time which they give sweet Annie here
to serve. And here – here is the front line. A lot
of blood gets lost here. Alfredo on the roast, very
efficient. Michael on soups and omelettes, very
cheeky. Coco works here on fried fish but he's very
absent so perhaps you take his place. Hans here on

deep fry. And over there is second chef, Frank, on poultry. And here, here is the best chef in the house and my best friend, Monsignor Gaston, who will grill steaks and chops, which puts him next to Peter on boiled fish. Peter very mad very bad. Gaston hates Peter…

> *At which moment PETER enters in a great hurry, he is late, as always. He laughs his laugh.*

PETER   H'ya, h'ya, h'ya! Auf geht's! Auf geht's!

NICHOLAS   Peter, the new cook, I give him to you.

PETER   So what shall I do with him? (*To KEVIN.*) You know where it is you work?

KEVIN   Not yet I don't.

PETER   Where do you come from?

KEVIN   Ireland.

PETER   No, I mean what restaurant you work in before?

KEVIN   Parisito, Shaftesbury Avenue.

PETER   (*Rubbing his thumb and finger together.*) Good pay?

KEVIN   (*Shaking his head.*) That's why I came here.

PETER   Oh, you get good money here – but you work! Oh yes, you work! Now, you help me. Can you make a sauce Hollandaise! You know, eggs and… (*Makes motion of whisking.*)

KEVIN   I can. I can. Yes, yes, I can.

PETER   (*Briskly.*) The eggs are already in a tin in the cold cupboard. There is a pot, the whisk is in the drawer and I melt margarine for you.

> *By now EVERYBODY is hard at work. Each CHEF has entered at some moment or other.*
>
> *The ovens hum. The sounds of clash, rattle, and chopping on boards are an orchestrated kitchen symphony.*
>
> *The movement of CHEFS and waitresses are the slow part of a choreography that will grow into a dazzling 'ballet' by the end of the first act.*

MOLLY hands out the printed menu of the day. CYNTHIA parcels out fresh 'baguettes' for kitchen staff lunch. HANS shyly attempts to flirt with her.

HANS   Oh baby, wait a moment. I… I… I… Du gefällst mir, du hast mir schon vom ersten Tag an gefallen! Könnten wir nicht mal was zusammen arrangieren?

She listens to him amused but uncomprehending before just walking away.

MAX   (*To FRANK.*) We got no lamb cutlets.

FRANK   Three carcasses came in yesterday.

MAX   So?

FRANK   So!

MAX   So you come and help me cut them up. I'm on my own today.

FRANK   What you got?

MAX   Veal cutlets.

FRANK   OK, so veal cutlets then. (*To KEVIN.*) New cook?

KEVIN   (*Sweating, still beating his sauce.*) Yes, chef.

FRANK   Right, you work on fried fish this morning.

PETER   Thank you. Thank you, but I got six dishes to prepare.

GASTON passes by. PETER catches sight of the black eye. He's surprised. GASTON glares.

FRANK   Coco is off today. Someone must do the fry.

PETER   Bloody house this is. Middle of summer and we got no staff. I got six dishes.

The CHEF enters carrying his day's roses which he hands to ANNE whose job it is to replace them for yesterday's roses.

HANS   Morning, Chef.

PETER   Morning, Chef.

FRANK   Morning, Leo.

MICHAEL   Morning, Chef.

ALFREDO   Morning, Chef.

CHEF (*Handing roses.*) Anne!

FRANK (*To KEVIN.*) Here, you, get your fish out of the cold cupboard and come here, I want to show you something.

HANS (*To PETER.*) Du, gestern Abend hat's dich aber beinah' erwischt!

PETER Sie sind nur mutig, wenn sie zusammen sind!

HANS Haben sie draussen auf dich gewartet?

PETER Ja, da waren auch welche. Leider war ich mit Monika zusammen und jetzt spricht sie nicht mehr mit mir.

HANS Sie wird auch wieder mit dir reden!

PETER Ach egal! Auf geht's.

> *He and HANS boisterously sing their 'Hi lee, hi lo, hi la!' song. Ending in laughter.*

GASTON (*Passing at that moment.*) Madmen, lunatics!

PETER Hey, Gaston, I'm sorry – your black eye, I'm sorry about it.

> *MONIQUE enters, watching.*

GASTON DON'T TALK TO ME.

PETER I say I'm sorry that's all.

GASTON You sorry because half a dozen Cypriot boys make you feel sorry. But we not finished yet.

PAUL Gaston! What's the matter with you? A man is saying sorry – so accept.

GASTON Accept? He gives me this (*Pointing to black eye.*) and I must accept? (*To PETER.*) We not finished yet, I'm telling you.

PETER What you not finished with? Tell me.

> *MONIQUE moves appealingly to PAUL.*

You want to give me a black eye? That makes you feel happier? Alright! Here, give me one and then we'll be finished, eh?

> *He opens his arms and thrusts forward his face.*

GASTON   (*Moving away.*) Don't laugh, Peter, I'm telling you, it gets worse, don't laugh.

> *PETER mockingly drops to his knees, his arms still out.*
>
> *GASTON turns and bears down on him, fists raised.*
>
> *PAUL rushes to intervene and keep them apart.*

PAUL   (*To PETER.*) So why are you tantalising him? Lunatic! Nobody knows when to stop. One of them is prepared to apologise, the other doesn't know how to accept – and when someone knows how to accept so the other...

> *PETER sings his mocking song.*

...ach! Lunatics!

> *Throws up hands in despair. Retreats to his corner.*
>
> *PETER singing goes off to collect something from the cold-room.*
>
> *MONIQUE calls GASTON aside to look more closely at his eye.*

MONIQUE   Show me the eye.

GASTON   Listen to him –

MONIQUE   Beautiful! First prize! (*Kisses it.*)

GASTON   – your boyfriend!

MONIQUE   He makes a lot of noise but he's not really dangerous.

GASTON   Now Monique, don't protect him.

MONIQUE   You know he wouldn't hurt anyone intentionally.

GASTON   This eye –

MONIQUE   It was an accident, you know it was, between us you know it was, don't you? Why don't you just let me try and handle him?

GASTON   You? You're like a bit of paper – the wind blows you about.

MONIQUE   I manage.

GASTON   Manage? What sort of a life is 'manage'? Manage! He needs a big scare, a big fright.

MONIQUE   Fright? (*Turning to PETER who blows her a kiss.*) Nothing frightens that boy.

GASTON   Boy? Baby! You just threaten to leave him and you'll see how frightened he'll get.

MONIQUE   I've threatened but it doesn't scare it only angers him. Angers him confuses me, frustrates us both. I could run this place with my eyes closed – but our relationship…? A weak, indecisive thing, me. Made for comfort, not crisis.

GASTON   Listen to him – baby!

   HEAD WAITER to CHEF's desk.

HEAD WAITER   (*Handing CHEF a letter.*) Read it.

CHEF   What's this one about?

HEAD WAITER   Read it. Read it.

CHEF   (*Reading.*) Sour soup? What sour soup?

HEAD WAITER   Yesterday's sour soup.

CHEF   I was off yesterday, see Frank.

HEAD WAITER   (*Mumbling, en route to FRANK.*) He was off yesterday… a kitchen he runs.

FRANK   What do you want? (*Meanwhile calling.*) Nicholas! Twelve chickens!

NICHOLAS   There's only six.

FRANK   Well phone for some more then! (*To HEAD WAITER.*) What sour soup? When sour soup?

   NICHOLAS en route to phone, followed by HANS who gooses him from behind.

HANS   Auf geht's, Nicholas! Twelve chickens please, Nicholas. Move yourself Nicholas. Bonjour Raymondo, comment ça va?

RAYMOND   Ça va, toujours au boulot, etcetera.

HANS   Vive le frigue!

MAX   (*Suddenly and violently to HANS.*) You're in England now. Speak bloody English. Everybody speaking in a different language – French, Italian, German.

You come here to learn English didn't you? Well
bloody-well speak it then!

PETER   What's the matter Max? You frightened of
something? Have another beer.

MAX   I'm not frightened of you, I tell you that straight, so
you can keep quiet.

PETER   (*Approaching close to MAX and talking in his ear.*) You
know your trouble Max? You been here too long.

MAX   (*Trying to move away from him.*) Yes, yes, yes, Peter,
alright.

PETER   (*Following him.*) How long have you been here?
Twenty-one years? You need a change.

MAX   (*Trying to move away again.*) Yes, yes.

PETER   (*Following him.*) Why don't you go work a season in
Germany?

MAX   Sure to.

PETER   Visit other kitchens! Learn more.

MAX   Yes, yes. Get on with your work.

PETER   Don't you worry about my work!

HANS   Genug, Peter.

PETER   You can't bear a change? A new face upsets you?

MAX   Let's drop it? Kapiret, yes?

PETER   Oh, oh, oh, oh, oh! He speaks German!

HANS   Stop it, Peter.

CHEF   Alright, Peter – let's have some work!

> *MR MARANGO appears.*

HANS   Marango!

> *PETER returns to his work, as does everyone else – with
> excessive energy.*
>
> *MARANGO walks slowly round his kitchen inspecting
> everything – placing his hand on the hot plate to see
> if it's warm enough, a mechanical movement – it's a
> mechanical tour.*

KEVIN   (*To PETER.*) Is it like this everyday? Look at me, I've never sweated so much since me glorious honeymoon.

PETER   It is nothing, this. This is only the preparation. Wait till we start serving – then! (*Raises his hands.*) You in place?

KEVIN   More or less. I've got me salmon cut.

PETER   Good, we eat soon.

> *By which time MARANGO has arrived at KEVIN's station.*

MARANGO   (*Gently.*) New cook?

KEVIN   Yes, sir.

MARANGO   (*Consolingly.*) It's hot eh, son?

KEVIN   Sure, an' a bit more.

MARANGO   Never mind, I pay well. Just work hard, I pay well. (*Continues tour.*)

KEVIN   (*To PETER.*) He seems a kind old man.

PETER   You think he is kind? He is a bastard! He talks like that because it is summer now. Not enough staff to serve all his customers, that is why he is kind. Wait till winter. Fewer customers. Then you'll see. The fish is burnt! Too much mise-en-place. The soup is sour! A man? A restaurant! I tell you – he goes to market at five-thirty in the morning, returns, reads the mail, goes to the office and then comes down here to watch the service. Here he stands, sometimes he walks round touching the hot-plate, closing the hot-plate doors, looking inside this thing then that thing. Till the last customer he stays, then he has a sleep upstairs in his office. Half an hour after we come back, he is here again – till nine-thirty, maybe ten at night. Everyday, morning to night. What kind of a life is that, in a kitchen! Is that a life I ask you? Me, I don't care, soon I'm going to get married and then whisht! (*Movement to signify 'I'm off'.*)

HANS   (*En route with large tray to cold-cupboard.*) Auf geht's, Irishman! I must not speak German to you. I'm in

England and have to speak bloody English. Hi lee, hi lo, hi la!

MONIQUE passes in front of PETER.

MONIQUE Bully!

PETER Go to hell. (*To KEVIN, proudly.*) That's my wife, or she will be soon. Look. (*Takes postcard from wallet.*) This card she sent me when she was on holiday. (*Reading aloud.*) 'I am not happy till you come. I love you very much.' And look, her lipstick marks. She is very lovely, yes?

KEVIN She looks like a girl I knew, all bosom and bouncing. You know?

PETER (*Not really understanding.*) We eat soon, eh? (*To HANS.*) Hans, hilf mir.

They take a large, heavy pot off from the oven, and pass the contents through a strainer into a small pot which PETER has prepared on the ground.

KEVIN has been comparing his printed menu with that on the board.

KEVIN Look here, it says on the printed menu 'fried plaice' and on the board it says 'fried sole'.

PETER See the chef.

KEVIN Good morning, Chef. Look, it says here fried plaice and on the board it's got fried sole.

CHEF I don't know anything about it. It was my day off yesterday, see the second chef.

KEVIN Have we got any plaice?

CHEF (*Sarcastically looking inside his apron.*) It's not here.

KEVIN (*To RAYMOND.*) Doesn't he care about anything?

RAYMOND Only when it's gone wrong.

MONIQUE passes in front of PETER again carrying a tray of glasses.

MONIQUE Bully!

PETER is angry. Tries to make his quarrels with her secret, but it's never possible in the kitchen.

PETER   Why do you keep calling me bully? All day you call me bully.

MONIQUE   (*En route still.*) Bully!

PETER follows talking, as is his habit, in her ear.

PETER   You think to make me angry? What is it you wanted me to do? Let him fight me?

MONIQUE   (*Turning on him.*) He's got a black eye now you see?

PETER   I see. I see. But he raised a knife to me.

MONIQUE   (*Continuing on her way.*) Bully!

PETER   (*Following, the pathetic, jealous lover.*) And remember you're hostess today, I can see you through the glass, no flirting, do you hear? No flirting.

MONIQUE   I shall talk to who I like.

PETER   All the restaurant can see you. (*To himself.*) Cow! Disgusting cow!

MICHAEL   (*Shouting.*) Who has the strainer? Gaston? Peter?

PETER   I got it here. You'll have to clean it. (*To MANGOLIS, passing.*) Hey, Mangolis, you clean this for Michael, please.

MANGOLIS offers a rude sign. MICHAEL must heave strainer to clean himself.

HETTIE   (*Attempting confidentiality with PETER.*) Hey, Peter, tell me exactly what happened last night, did they…

PETER   (*Dismissively.*) No, no, cowards, all of them. It was nothing.

PAUL   (*Rescuing her.*) Hey, Hettie, did you go last night?

HETTIE   (*Relieved. Ecstatic.*) Mmmm.

PAUL   He's a good actor?

HETTIE   What a man! One night, just one night with him, and I'd wash dishes the rest of my life. (*Moves off.*)

RAYMOND   (*To PAUL.*) You wonder my wife doesn't make love like she used to?

PAUL   And that's why I'm not going to marry again. I buy picture books and I'm happy.

At which point the long procession of WAITRESSES bear down upon the CHEFS who have laid trays of staff food on the serving counters. The WAITRESSES help themselves.

GWEN Alright boys, staff meal coming up – what have you got for us this morning?

ALFREDO Curried cats and dogs.

BETTY We ate curried cats and dogs yesterday.

ALFREDO Some people never eat curried cats and dogs.

GWEN Some people prefer never to eat curried cats and dogs.

JACKIE Is this cabbage from yesterday?

HANS It's still good, eat it, eat it!

VIOLET What on earth are these?

HANS Very good, very good. Cauliflower and white sauce.

VIOLET White sauce, it smells.

HETTIE Got anything *really* good, Hans?

MOLLY Like *fresh* boiled potatoes?

BETTY Or *fresh* boiled carrots?

MOLLY Or fresh boiled *anything*?

HANS Not cooked yet, not ready yet, always complaining. You don't like? Go to Chef!

CYNTHIA Does anyone know how to cook in this kitchen?

Another conflict explodes in between DAPHNE and her husband NICHOLAS who is making their quarrel too public for her liking. He is a little drunk.

DAPHNE Liar!

NICHOLAS Me? Me? Me a liar?

DAPHNE Yes, you.

NICHOLAS Oh! So I lied when I say I pass the catering exams, eh? I lie when I say I got a rise, eh? I lie when I say I got us a flat, eh? I always *do* and you always say I *don't*. That's a good marriage is it?

DAPHNE You're not satisfied? Move!

NICHOLAS Listen to that woman's twisting! Come and ask him then, come on. You don't believe me, believe him then. (*Calling.*) Frank!

DAPHNE No, Nicky, no…now stop.

NICHOLAS Well if I tell you I got to work the afternoon, why don't you believe me? Frank! Frank! Where is he now.

Wanders off in search of FRANK while DAPHNE waits deeply embarrassed.

RAYMOND (*To DAPHNE.*) Hit him! Go on, you're big enough.

FRANK (*Dragged into the scene by NICHOLAS.*) What the hell is it now?

DAPHNE Nicky, don't be a fool. (*To RAYMOND and PAUL.*) Oh for Christ's sake, what do you think of this man!

NICHOLAS No, ask him, go on. You don't believe me.

FRANK Ask him what, for hell's sake?

NICHOLAS Have I got to work in the afternoon or haven't I?

FRANK (*Incredulous.*) You called me for *that*? You mad or something? Do me a favour and leave me out of your quarrels, will you? (*To OTHERS.*) Asks me to solve his marriage problems. (*To NICHOLAS.*) I'll tell you how to do it as well.

Crashing in on their laughter is a loud scream from the steam-room.

HANS runs out, his hands covering his face.

HANS My face! My face! I've burnt my face.

PEOPLE crowd round him.

FRANK What happened?

HANS Who bloody fool put a pot of hot water on steamer?

PETER It fell on you?

HANS Bastard house! I never worked before so bad. Never, never…

PETER takes him off to first aid.

FRANK He'll live.

MOLLY   (*Calling after them.*) Put some of that yellow stuff on him.

FRANK   You're not paid to advise. (*To CROWD.*) Alright! Break it up! The drama's over. (*Moves to CHEF.*) No matter how many times you tell them they still rush around.

CHEF   (*Not really interested.*) Since when did youth listen to age? The new chap alright?

FRANK   Seems to be. (*MARANGO approaches.*) Look out.

MARANGO   How did it happen?

CHEF   I don't know. I wasn't there. Frank, how did it happen?

FRANK   (*Wearily.*) Someone left a pot of hot water on one of the steamers and he tipped it over his face.

MARANGO   He's burnt his face. It's not serious but – it might have been. (*Moves away shaking his head sadly.*)

CHEF   What can I do, Mr Marango? They rush about like mad, I tell them but they don't listen.

     But MARANGO has gone.

     (*To FRANK.*) Much he cares. It interrupts the kitchen so he worries. Three more years, Frank, three, that's all and then – whisht! Retire, finish! Then you can take over.

FRANK   Oh no! Not this boy. I'm in charge one day a week – enough! They can find another madman.

CHEF   Do you think I'm mad?

FRANK   Do you enjoy your work?

CHEF   Who does?

FRANK   So on top of not enjoying your work you take on responsibility – that isn't mad?

CHEF   I've got a standard of living to keep up – idiot!

FRANK   (*Moving away.*) So go mad!

CHEF   Idiot!

     During this exchange trestle tables must be set up and laid out with cutlery, glasses, bread – for the CHEFS' lunch-break. Whether it's the kitchen porters or the CHEFS themselves who set up the tables is a choreographic decision for the director.

NICHOLAS, FRANK and MAX eat at one table.

KEVIN, MICHAEL, PETER and HANS at another.

GASTON sulks on his own.

ALFREDO, the loner, eats at his own station.

CHEF (*To MICHAEL.*) Michael!

MICHAEL Chef?

CHEF The soup was sour yesterday.

MICHAEL Sour?

CHEF Sour!

MICHAEL But it was only a day old.

CHEF I've had letters from customers.

MICHAEL (*Contemptuously.*) Customers!

CHEF And Michael – don't take chickens home with you.

MICHAEL (*Innocently.*) Chickens?

CHEF Take cutlets, take cold meats, take an apple or two but not chickens. Chickens are bulky. Wait till you're my age before trying chickens.

MICHAEL Ah! I must graduate to it like.

CHEF That's right, you must graduate to it like. You can have your lunch now.

PETER and HANS return.

KEVIN You alright?

HANS throws his hands, fed-up.

PAUL Let's see. You look beautiful.

KEVIN A Red Indian.

PETER Come on, let's eat.

ALL move to their tables to eat.

There is less activity in the kitchen now – a calm before the storm.

A few WAITRESSES wander around. MANGOLIS sweeps, DIMITRI scatters sawdust.

KEVIN (*To PETER.*) How long have you been here?

PETER Three years.

KEVIN How did you stick it?

MICHAEL Sick already?

KEVIN I don't think I'll last the day.

PETER People are always coming and going.

HANS I think me I'll go soon.

MICHAEL (*To KEVIN.*) The worst is to come. (*To OTHERS.*) Am I right? You wait till the service – ha! But you'll get used to it after a while.

PETER We all said we wouldn't last the day, but tell me – what is there a man can't get used to? Nothing! You just forget where you are and you say 'it's a job'.

MICHAEL He should work on the eggs. Five dishes I've got, five! Hey, Paul, got any Religeuse left?

PAUL Sorry, Annie's got them all – some tart left from yesterday…?

MICHAEL (*Whispered to KEVIN.*) Liar!

PAUL Sorry!

KEVIN I thought you could eat what you liked here.

MICHAEL You can, but you have to swipe it. Even the food for cooking. If I want to make an onion soup that's any good, I go to the cold-room and I take some chickens' wings to make my stock. No questions, just in and out – whisht!

PAUL (*Guilty to RAYMOND.*) Why do we say there isn't fresh cake when there is?

RAYMOND Don't worry yourself they eat plenty.

PAUL So do we! Have you ever caught yourself saying something you don't mean to say? Why did I refuse Michael a cake? Doesn't hurt me to give him a cake, most times we do but there's always that one time when it irritates to be asked. Irrational, really. First thing in the morning I joke with him, then half way through the day I lie to him. Defending the

governor's property! As though it was me own! I
don't know *what* to be bloody loyal to half the time.

PETER Hey, where's Gaston? Why is he not with us, eating
here? I black his eye not his arse.

PAUL Leave off, Peter – the row's over. Patch it up.

MICHAEL (*To KEVIN but loud enough for PAUL.*) When husbands
and wives can't patch up their rows who are we to
succeed?

PAUL My wife was a mean-minded woman, Michael, so
don't talk about what you don't know. She came
from a well run and comfortable home but she was
mean-minded. Every time someone asked 'how are
you?' she'd snap at them – 'busy-body!' (*MICHAEL
laughs.*) Oh yes you can laugh, cocker, but I used
to have to spend hours listening to her bitch about
other women. For hours on end – bitching! I even
tried…

　　　Suddenly realises his explanations are pathetic.

Ah! What the hell do I bother to explain to you for,
here – take your bloody bit of cake!

　　　*Over their embarrassment – another exchange – between
　　　ANNE and BERTHA who spoon food for their lunch
　　　out of various CHEFS' pots and pans.*

ANNE I'm not a pub person myself…

BERTHA Nor me – but I've got to confess, I like my little
tipple…

ANNE Drunk men! They embarrass me…

BERTHA Not excessive, mind…

ANNE Sentimental, violent, and repetitive…

BERTHA Just enough to face the truth, but not act on it…

ANNE Wise, Bertha, wise…

BERTHA Otherwise I'd murder someone, see?

ANNE …wise, wise, wise!

　　　Back to the OTHERS.

HANS I think I go to America.

KEVIN   (*Impressed.*) America?

HANS   (*Building, to impress more.*) I already been twice. (*Beat.*)
Worked on a ship. (*Beat.*) On a ship you waste more
than you eat. (*Beat.*) You throw everything into the
sea before you come into land. Imagine! Whole
chickens! To the gulls – they fly behind, and wait.

KEVIN   (*Eagerly.*) Tell us about New York.

HANS   (*Kissing his fingers.*) Mmmm. New York! New York,
das ist die schönste Stadt der Welt!

> *PETER pokes.*

PETER   (*Warning.*) English!

HANS   – when you arrive – the skyline! The Empire State
Building! Coney Island! The Statue of Liberty
and Broadway, a beautiful city. Open three in the
morning, bars, night-clubs, rush here, rush there…
And Kevin – women!

> *The OTHERS cheer him on good-naturedly.*

I think this house not very good.

KEVIN   It's not, eh?

PETER   (*Moving to get a glass of water.*) You got to turn out food
hot and quickly. Quality – pooh! No time!

MICHAEL   (*Lighting a cigarette.*) It's this that counts. (*Rubs thumb
and fingers together.*)

PETER   Money, money, money!

KEVIN   I don't believe it. It must be possible to run a small
restaurant that offers good food and also makes
money.

PETER   Of course it's possible, my friend – but you pay to
eat in it. It's money. It's all money. The world chase
money so you chase money too. (*Frantically snapping
his fingers.*) Money! Money! Money!

> *PETER is near FRANK. A prank occurs to him.*
> *Shushing the OTHERS he places glass of water into the*
> *cavity of FRANK's tall white hat, and creeps away.*

Frank!

> *FRANK turns abruptly and of course the water spills over him.*

FRANK (*Jumping up.*) One day you'll lay an egg too many and it'll crack under you. Yes – you laugh…

PETER Frank is also unhappy.

> *GWEN approaches and lays a friendly hand on MICHAEL's shoulder who can't resist raising his hand to her buttocks.*

GWEN Who's on fish today?

MICHAEL Do you love me?

> *GWEN takes his hand from her behind and thumps it very hard between his legs.*

GWEN I think you're irresistible. Who's on fish?

KEVIN Me.

GWEN (*Moving off.*) Right, I order four plaice.

> *KEVIN immediately rises to serve. PETER pulls him back into his seat.*

PETER You got time. You not finished your lunch yet. The customer can wait. Be like Mr Alfredo. Nothing disturbs Mr Alfredo. Mr Alfredo is a worker and he hates his boss. He knows his job but he does no more, no less and at the right time. Mr Alfredo is an Englishman. (*Looks at his watch.*). Time to pilfer.

> *He points to ALFREDO who is by a store-cupboard from which, after looking around, he takes something and tucks it in his apron.*

VIOLET (*To FRANK.*) Mr Marango would like a leg of chicken and some sauté, please.

FRANK Mr Marango can go to hell, I'm eating.

VIOLET (*Moving off.*) I'll call for it in five minutes.

FRANK If he thinks I'm going to eat half a lunch for him…!

MAX You heard they nearly killed Peter last night?

FRANK I wouldn't have missed him – madman. I've had three years of him. Enough already!

NICHOLAS They should kill 'em off! Boche! Kill 'em off! The lot! I hate them, you know? I don't hate no one like I hate Boche. And they want to *abolish* hanging now – you read about it?

MAX (*To FRANK.*) Do you think that bill'll go through?

NICHOLAS Me, I think if a man kills then he should be killed too.

MAX (*Approvingly.*) An eye for an eye...

NICHOLAS And we should use the electric chair. It's no good this hanging.

MAX (*Insensitive delight.*) Remember those two they put on the chair in America for spying? The bloody thing didn't connect. They had to do it again. Ha! I bet the duty electrician got a bollocking.

FRANK What do you want them to use – gas ovens?

> *Which at once kills their laughter.*

> *MONIQUE saunters front of stage, cup of tea in hand, waiting for PETER to join her – their lunch-time ritual.*

PETER You forgive me?

MONIQUE I can't keep up a row, I laugh after a while.

PETER I'm a good boy, really. When's your day off?

MONIQUE Tomorrow.

PETER Then I won't see you.

MONIQUE No.

PETER How you spend your day off?

MONIQUE Er...let's see... In the morning – shopping. In the afternoon – the hairdressers. And in the evening – I'm going dancing at the Astra.

PETER Why do you have to go there? Prostitutes go there.

MONIQUE I am going with Monty.

PETER Then tell him. Tell Monty tonight.

MONIQUE I can't tell him yet.

PETER We can't go on like thieves. We do damage to ourselves.

MONIQUE Peter, not here, please.

PETER Here – inside here (*Knocks his head with hand.*) damage! We insult ourselves. I'm not going to wait much longer, you'll see. You think I like this Tivoli.

MONIQUE Now stop it! Why do you always choose a public place to talk about it? You go on and on, and I keep telling you to give me time. I've promised I will, and I will, so be patient.

PETER Patient! Me, patient! You don't believe me I won't wait, do you?

MONIQUE (*Coldly.*) Please yourself!

PETER (*Despairingly.*) What do you want me to do? Do you want to make me something to laugh at? Three years I'm here now, three…

MONIQUE (*Leaving him.*) Oh, ye Gods!

PETER turns his fury on KEVIN.

PETER Auf geht's, Irishman. Finish now. Auf geht's.

KEVIN ignores him. PETER repeats it louder, pulling his chair from under him.

Auf geht's. Irishman, auf geht's.

KEVIN Alright, alright.

CHEF (*Calling.*) OK, Frank.

FRANK (*To EVERYONE.*) Alright, let's get some work done.

CHEF Clients are waiting, Michael. Mangolis! Dimitri! Clear!

MANGOLIS Sir.

DIMITRI and MANGOLIS clear away the lunch tables.

ALL return to their stations.

CHEF to KEVIN.

CHEF You alright?

KEVIN Yes, Chef.

CHEF Let me see.

Watches KEVIN demonstrate the actions of dipping fish into egg into crumbs into fryer.

(Moving away.) Good. But quicker quicker quicker!

PETER Quicker quicker quicker, Irishman!

HANS Quicker quicker!

PETER Watch him now, the Irishman, soon he won't know
what's happening…hya hya hya!

He and HANS sing their lunatic song.

KEVIN Does your mother know you're out?

*Freeze. The entire kitchen of CHEFS,
KITCHEN-PORTERS, some WAITRESSES freeze
in mid-action, mid-movement – a tableau of a
machine about to go into action.*

The freeze breaks after MOLLY's first order.

*WAITRESSES shout their orders at the appropriate
station, not necessarily in front of them, en route to
somewhere else.*

*Dishes are handed out in varying forms: depending on
the size of the order a CHEF will give a small, medium
or large silver tray which the WAITRESS will place
on top of a pile of plates. Sometimes single orders are
served straight onto the plates, and WAITRESSES often
cradle three or four at a time.*

*Service begins very slowly and builds, gaining
momentum in five stages of increasing speed.*

*Important note. The following sequence of orders is
based on a specific layout of the kitchen which enables
the stage to be constantly peopled with movement.*

*A different layout may necessitate a different sequence of
orders so that the kitchen is never entirely denuded.*

*The first stage begins with a count of eight beats
between each order.*

MOLLY *(To HANS.)* Two veal cutlets.

HANS Two veal cutlets.

GWEN *(To PETER.)* Four cod… Do we order cod or is it
ready?

PETER It's Friday, you order cod.

WINNIE *(To MICHAEL.)* Two omelettes.

MICHAEL   Two omelettes.

CYNTHIA   (*To HANS.*) Four veal cutlets.

HANS   Four veal cutlets. Oh baby, wait a moment. I… I…
I… Hast du dir's überlegt? Gehen wir zusammen
aus? Ich lade dich ein! Wir gehen ins kino und
nachher tanzen. Willst du?

CYNTHIA   (*Loud, as though to someone deaf.*) No,
I – have – to – go – and – get – my – plaice.

> *HANS, away from his station, gazes at her as she moves
> around the kitchen.*

DAPHNE   (*To FRANK.*) Three legs of chicken.

FRANK   Three legs of chicken.

HETTIE   (*To NICHOLAS.*) Two chicken salad.

NICHOLAS   Two chicken salad.

GASTON   (*Shouting.*) Hans! Comen sie!

HANS   Oh, my Gott! my cutlets are burning.

CYNTHIA   (*To KEVIN.*) Party of eight plaice to begin with.

KEVIN   Eight plaice. *She's* a worker.

PETER   It's nothing, this, Irishman.

JACKIE   (*To GASTON.*) Five grilled chops.

GASTON   Five grilled chops.

DAPHNE   (*To NICHOLAS.*) Three french salad, darling.

HETTIE   I was first.

DAPHNE   Special!

HETTIE   Special nepotism.

NICHOLAS   Three french salad.

DAPHNE   (*To FRANK.*) What's nepotism?

MOLLY   (*To GASTON.*) Six steaks.

GASTON   Six steaks.

MOLLY   (*Calling to MICHAEL.*) Four minestrone.

MICHAEL   Four minestrone.

GWEN   (*To FRANK.*) Two roast chicken and sauté.

FRANK   Two roast chicken and sauté.

CYNTHIA (*To HANS.*) These my veal cutlets?

HANS These are your cutlets. Four kalbskotletts only for you, baby.

CYNTHIA Oh really.

HANS (*To PETER.*) Wunderbar! Peter look! Wie die geht! Wie die aussieht, die ist genau meine Kragenweit!

PETER (*Singing.*) 'Falling in love again...'

KEVIN Hey Peter, any more plaice?

PETER In the cold-cupboard.

KEVIN en route bumps into DAPHNE.

DAPHNE Watch it, Irishman.

MONIQUE enters with a plate of soup, calling –

MONIQUE Chef, soup's sour again.

PETER (*Continuing to tease HANS.*) 'Falling in love again...'

HANS Oh Peter, stop it! Ich weiss nicht, was ich anstellen soll! I speak quite good English already, but –

VIOLET (*To PETER.*) Four cod.

PETER Shut up!

HANS (*To PETER.*) But with her I forget every word.

VIOLET I said four cod.

They ignore her.

HANS Cynthia, she is smashing, yes?

VIOLET (*Giving up.*) Prima donnas!

CHEF and MONIQUE have moved down to MICHAEL's station.

MONIQUE, arms folded, stands waiting with her back to PETER.

CHEF (*Returning plate of soup.*) Michael, the soup is still sour.

PETER (*To MONIQUE.*) Now remember, don't forget to remember.

MONIQUE Remember what?

PETER You ask me 'what'? You don't know what you are doing?

MONIQUE No, I don't.

PETER Flirting! Flirting!

MONIQUE That's my job and there (*Pointing.*) is yours.

> *While engaged with PETER, MICHAEL tipped the soup from one bowl into another and now hands the plate to her which she takes into the dining-room.*

BETTY (*To ALFREDO.*) Two roast beef.

ALFREDO Hold it, hold it!

BETTY Oh, is it ready?

ALFREDO 'Course it's ready.

BETTY Surprise, surprise!

PETER Mangolis, plates!

MANGOLIS Plates coming up.

GWEN (*To PETER.*) Are my four cod ready?

PETER Ja, ja, all ready just for you.

> *Second stage from here on with a count of six beats between each order.*

DAPHNE (*To NICHOLAS.*) One salad.

NICHOLAS One salad.

WINNIE (*To FRANK.*) Two roast pheasant, darling.

FRANK Oh charming. I love you. You'll have chicken and like it!

HETTIE (*To HANS.*) Two sausages.

HANS Two sausages.

JACKIE (*To ALFREDO.*) One roast pork.

ALFREDO One roast pork.

DAPHNE (*At KEVIN's station.*) Two plaice. Oh, where the hell is he?

HETTIE (*At KEVIN's station.*) Three grilled turbot.

JACKIE (*To PETER.*) Two cod.

PETER Two cod.

> *KEVIN rushes into view.*

DAPHNE (*To KEVIN.*) Two plaice. Come on, come on, Irishman.

KEVIN Oh Jesus, Mother of God!

GASTON Exo!

MOLLY (*To HANS.*) My veal cutlets ready?

HANS What do *you* think!

HETTIE (*To KEVIN.*) Three grilled turbot.

KEVIN Three grilled turbot.

> *Third stage from here on with a count of four beats between each order.*

MOLLY (*To NICHOLAS.*) One lobster, one ham salad.

NICHOLAS One lobster, one ham.

CYNTHIA (*To MICHAEL.*) Three omelettes au jambon.

MICHAEL Three jambons.

BETTY (*To GASTON.*) Three entrecote steaks.

GASTON Three entrecote steaks.

ANNE (*To PAUL.*) I need fruit flans, Paul.

PAUL Fruit flans coming up, old darling.

ANNE Less of the 'old'!

GWEN (*To NICHOLAS.*) Two ham salads, Nicholas.

NICHOLAS Two ham salads, Gwen.

GWEN Annie, love, I need two coffees, please.

ANNE Two coffees for Gwen.

WINNIE (*To HANS.*) Two veal cutlets.

HANS Two veal cutlets…oh God! (*Calling.*) Max! More veal cutlets and sausages!

MAX Alright, alright.

GASTON (*Almost hysterical.*) Max! Send up steaks and mutton chops quick.

MAX Wait a bloody minute will you!

GASTON (*In panic.*) I got six steaks ordered already.

MAX So what am I supposed to do?

GASTON (*To nobody in particular.*) Everybody the same in this bloody house. Slow! Slow!

Fourth stage from here on with a count of two beats between each order.

WINNIE (*To* KEVIN.) One plaice, please.

KEVIN One plaice – right!

BETTY (*To* FRANK.) One roast chicken.

FRANK One roast chicken.

HANS Come on, Max, my cutlets and sausages.

HETTIE (*To* KEVIN.) Two grilled salmon, do we order it?

KEVIN Yes, five minutes. Go on, hop it!

JACKIE (*To* KEVIN.) One grilled trout, please.

KEVIN (*Rushing.*) One grilled trout right away!

MOLLY (*To* KEVIN.) Two plaice, please.

KEVIN Alright! Alright!

PETER (*Shouting while he serves.*) Ha – ha! He – he! Ho – ho! They're here! They come!

HETTIE (*To* NICHOLAS.) One chicken, one ham salad.

NICHOLAS One chicken, one ham.

CYNTHIA (*To* PETER.) One cod.

PETER One cod.

WINNIE (*To* MICHAEL.) One hamburger.

MICHAEL One hamburger.

VIOLET Are my four cod ready?

GWEN (*To* HANS.) One veal cutlet.

PETER (*To* VIOLET.) When did you order them?

HANS One veal cutlet.

VIOLET Five minutes ago. I came past and you were talking to Hans, remember?

PETER I remember nothing. Come back in five minutes. Next?

VIOLET You weren't listening, that's what it was.

PETER You ordered nothing, I say, now come back in five minutes – next!

MOLLY (*To* MICHAEL.) Two minestrone.

MICHAEL   Two minestrone.

PETER   – Five minutes!... Next?

VIOLET   Prima donnas!

GWEN   (*To PETER.*) One steamed turbot.

PETER   One steamed turbot.

BETTY   (*To HANS.*) Three veal cutlets, please.

HANS   (Mimicking.) Three veal cutlets, please.

> *HEAD WAITER appears looking for VIOLET. He calls her and they pull aside while she complains about PETER, after which they move up to the CHEF.*

JACKIE   (*To NICHOLAS.*) Two ham, one lobster salad.

NICHOLAS   Two ham, one lobster.

DAPHNE   (*To ANNE.*) Three fruit flan.

ANNE   Three fruit flan.

HANS   (*To BETTY who has been waiting.*) What you waiting for, you can't see the cutlets cook?

BETTY   Well, last time I waited.

HANS   (*Mocking.*) Well, last time I waited.

BETTY   Oh get lost!

WINNIE   (*To GASTON.*) Three steaks.

GASTON   Three steaks.

HEAD WAITER   (*To CHEF.*) Ten minutes ago Violet ordered four cod. They're not ready yet.

> *TRIO move down to PETER while –*

KEVIN   Plates!

GASTON   Plates!

MICHAEL   Plates!

CHEF   Peter...the cod not ready yet?

PETER   She's a liar that one, she ordered nothing.

CHEF   Come on, come on!

PETER   (*Dishing out.*) One cod...two cod...

DAPHNE   (*To ANNE.*) Two coffees, Annie.

ANNE   Two coffees.

PETER   …three cod…four cod…

As VIOLET turns with her plates of cod MANGOLIS, passing, collides with her. Plates crash to the ground. She follows to her knees.

VIOLET   Oh God, God, God! I can't, I can't!

JACKIE   (*To ANNE.*) Three coffees.

ANNE   Three coffees.

CHEF   Frank! Broken plates!

FRANK   Mangolis! Broken plates!

MANGOLIS   Broken plates! I can see! I can see!

VIOLET   Look at it all –

GWEN   (*Bending to help.*) Don't upset yourself, love.

VIOLET   – I can't work like this. I'm not used to this way of working.

BETTY   (*To MICHAEL.*) One minestrone.

MICHAEL   One minestrone.

VIOLET   I've never worked like this before, never, never!

PETER   Too old, too old my sweetheart. Go home old woman – for the young this work – go home!

HANS   Leave her alone, Peter. Look! your cod she smokes.

PETER rushes back to his station. His movements are vast and theatrical. He always wants to play the fool.

PETER   (*To KEVIN.*) Oh God! She burns! The cod! Hya, hya, hya! She burns, Irishman. No good, no good!

He rushes the frying pan with burnt fish to the dustbin.

HANS   That is not too good work, Peter, not good work, mein lieber. Pigs work.

Final stage. From here on no gaps between orders.

GWEN   (*To HANS.*) One veal cutlet.

HANS   One veal cutlet.

PETER laughs to KEVIN who has large queue at his station.

PETER   We have busy time, Irishman, yes?

KEVIN   Bloody comedian!

HETTIE   (*To KEVIN.*) My salmon ready yet?

KEVIN   Your what?

HETTIE   Me grilled salmon, love, me grilled salmon.

KEVIN   How many do you want?

HETTIE   Two.

CYNTHIA   (*To MICHAEL.*) My three omelettes.

MICHAEL   Your three omelettes.

DAPHNE   (*To KEVIN.*) Two salmon.

KEVIN   Two salmon.

JACKIE   (*To KEVIN.*) Three sardines.

KEVIN   Three sardines.

WINNIE   (*To KEVIN.*) Three plaice.

KEVIN   Three plaice.

>   *KEVIN has repeated their orders but hasn't served them*
>   *because he's overwhelmed and behind.*

KEVIN   Peter, for God's sake will you give me a hand?

HETTIE   (*To MICHAEL.*) Two veg soups.

MICHAEL   Two veg soups.

PETER   (*Helping KEVIN.*) Let's go Irishman, let's go. The next?

DAPHNE   Two salmon.

PETER   Two salmon.

BETTY   (*To HANS.*) My veal cutlets.

HANS   Your veal cutlets.

PETER   And the next?

JACKIE   Three sardines.

PETER   Three sardines.

BETTY   (*To HANS.*) Oh come on, lobster face.

HANS   What does it mean, lobster face?

PETER   And the next?

WINNIE   Three plaice.

PETER   Three plaice.

HANS   (*To BETTY.*) Ein, zwei, drei!

PETER   (*To WINNIE.*) One, two, three! The next?

BETTY   Two plaice.

PETER   Two plaice.

> *While PETER has been helping KEVIN, the following three orders pile up on his unattended station.*

MOLLY   One turbot.

GWEN   One steamed halibut.

CYNTHIA   Two cod.

MOLLY   Oh come on, Peter.

> *PETER rushes to his station, laughing, a merry fool going into battle, enjoying it all.*

PETER   Look at this – hya, hya! Good morning, ladies, and the next?

MOLLY   One turbot.

PETER   One turbot. Next?

GWEN   One steamed halibut.

PETER   One steamed halibut.

CYNTHIA   Two cod.

PETER   Two cod.

JACKIE   (*To FRANK.*) Three legs of chicken.

FRANK   Three chicken.

KEVIN   (*To PETER.*) I've run out of lemons.

PETER   (*With rude indifference.*) Well cut some more then.

KEVIN   Let me borrow your cutting-board then, please.

> *KEVIN moves to take it from PETER's bench.*
>
> *PETER stops serving, leaps at KEVIN to grab board back – it's every man for himself now.*

PETER   Oh no, no, no, no, my friend. The plate-room, the plate-room, in the plate-room you'll find one. This is mine, I have need of it.

KEVIN   But I'll give it back in a few seconds.

PETER (*Pointing.*) The plate-room! (*Slams hand down hard on his cutting board. To CYNTHIA.*) What do you want?

KEVIN (*Going to plate-room.*) Well speak a little human-like, will yer, please?

PETER No time, no time! Next?

CYNTHIA (*To PETER.*) Two cod, for Christ's sake.

PETER Two cod, for Christ's sake.

JACKIE (*To NICHOLAS.*) One cheese salad.

NICHOLAS One cheese salad.

VIOLET (*To NICHOLAS, tearfully.*) One ham salad.

NICHOLAS (*Tearfully.*) One ham salad.

BETTY (*To GASTON.*) My steaks ready yet?

GASTON About time!

BETTY I had other orders didn't I.

VIOLET (*To ANNIE.*) One fruit flan, two coffees.

ANNE One fruit flan, two coffees.

DAPHNE (*To FRANK.*) Two roast chicken.

FRANK Two roast chicken.

WINNIE (*To ALFREDO.*) Two roast veal and spaghetti.

ALFREDO Two roast veal and spaghetti.

JACKIE (*To MICHAEL.*) One prawn omelette.

MICHAEL One prawn.

GWEN (*To ALFREDO.*) Two roast beef.

ALFREDO Two roast beef.

MOLLY (*At KEVIN's station.*) Two sole.

CYNTHIA (*At KEVIN's station.*) Three plaice.

DAPHNE (*To GASTON.*) Two lamb chops.

GASTON Two lamb chops.

HETTIE (*To MICHAEL.*) Two minestrones.

MICHAEL Two minestrones.

MONIQUE (*To PETER.*) Four cod,

PETER What?

MONIQUE Violet's four cod.

MOLLY (*About KEVIN.*) Where is he? He's never here this one.

PETER (*To MONIQUE.*) You wait for me afterwards?

MONIQUE I'll wait for you.

CYNTHIA (*Calling.*) Come on Irishman, my plaice.

PETER (*To MONIQUE.*) We go for a stroll.

MONIQUE Yes, we go for a stroll.

BETTY (*To MICHAEL.*) One minestrone.

MICHAEL One minestrone.

MOLLY (*To CYNTHIA.*) We'll lose all those tips.

GWEN (*To HANS.*) Four veal cutlets.

HANS Four veal cutlets.

KEVIN rushes to his station.

MOLLY (*To KEVIN.*) Me sole, lovey, where's me sole?

KEVIN Wait a bloody minute, can't you?

MOLLY (*To KEVIN.*) Two of them.

GWEN (*To PETER.*) Two halibut.

PETER Two halibut.

BETTY (*To MICHAEL.*) Three hamburgers.

MICHAEL Three hamburgers.

CYNTHIA (*To KEVIN.*) Three plaice.

KEVIN Let me breathe will you?

CYNTHIA No time for breathing, Irishman.

KEVIN Is this a bloody madhouse?

NICHOLAS Plates!

MANGOLIS Plates!

KEVIN Have you all gone fucking, raving, bloody mad?

The final frenzy can be stylized:

On KEVIN's last line all the WAITRESSES move in a circle round the CHEFS shouting out the same sequence of orders which began from the freeze. At the same time the hum of the ovens builds and the lights hanging over the ovens burn with increasing intensity to a white light until –

– the HEAD WAITER rushes in and shouts across to the CHEF –

HEAD WAITER The bloody soup is still bloody sour.

At which –

FREEZE. BLACK OUT.

END PART ONE.

INTERVAL.

(It is of course possible to perform the play without an interval, just as it's possible to choreograph the final frenzy naturalistically rather than stylistically. The decision is the director's.)

Interlude

Lights FADE UP on the sound of a guitar.

It is afternoon break. The sounds of the oven are low.

PAUL and RAYMOND work in their corner – the only two who work through the afternoon. KEVIN is flat out on his back on a wooden bench, exhausted. DIMITRI slowly sweeps the morning's debris. PETER squats waiting for MONIQUE. HANS in another corner, with guitar, singing 'Ah Sinner Man'.

KEVIN Finished! I'm done! You can serve me up for supper.

PAUL (*Ordering.*) Boiled Irishman, please!

RAYMOND (*Continuing.*) Fried tomatoes on his ears, potatoes round his head, and stuff his mouth with parsley and peas.

KEVIN I'll produce me own gravy! Did you see it? Did-you-see-that? Fifteen hundred customers, an' half of them eating fish. (*Beat.*) *I* had to start work on a Friday!

RAYMOND It's every day the same, my friend.

KEVIN I'm soaking. This jacket, I can wring it out. That's not sweat, no man carries that much water. Kevin, you'll drop dead if you stay. Get out! This is no place for a human being. You've got your youth, Kevin, keep it!

DIMITRI Hey, Irishman, what you grumbling about this place for? Is different anywhere else? People come and people go, big excitement, big noise. (*Makes noise, gesticulates.*) What for? In the end who do you know? You make a friend, you going to be all your life his friend, but when you go from here – pshtt! You forget! Why you grumble about this one kitchen?

PETER You're a very intelligent boy, Dimitri.

DIMITRI And you're a bloody fool. I'm not sure I want to talk with you.

KEVIN   Oh, not the Gaston row again. It's the break, no
        rows, peace, silence. Can you hear it? Silence.
        Nothing. It's lovely – ahhhhh! (*Moves.*) Ooooh – I'm
        drowning – in me own sweat! Christ! What a way to
        die!

DIMITRI   (*To PETER.*) A bloody fool, you!

> *PETER reaches for an empty cardboard box which he*
> *playfully dumps over DIMITRI's head. Returns to his*
> *chair, dejected again.*
>
> *DIMITRI angrily flings it off and is about to throw*
> *it back but sees PETER with his head in his hands.*
> *Instead, he takes out a cigarette box and rolls one for*
> *PETER, giving PETER the paper to lick before folding*
> *it and sticking it in PETER's mouth.*

PETER   Hey, Irishman, I thought you didn't like this place?
        Why don't you go home and sleep?

KEVIN   Me home is a room and a bed and a painting of the
        Holy Virgin. It will always be there.

PETER   Like this place, this house – this too, it'll always be
        here. That's a thought for you, Irishman: when you
        go, when I go, when Dimitri go – this kitchen stays.
        When we die, it stays, think about that. We work
        here – eight hours a day, and yet – we take nothing.
        Here – the kitchen, here – you. You and the kitchen.
        And the kitchen don't mean nothing to you and you
        don't mean to the kitchen nothing. Dimitri is right,
        why do you grumble about this kitchen? What about
        the offices and the factories? What about them?

KEVIN   You want to come in one morning and find it gone?

PETER   Why not? Great idea. One morning. Imagine it – all
        this – gone!

KEVIN   You'd be out of work!

PETER   So? I'd die?

HANS   Du träumst schon wieder.

KEVIN   What's he say?

PETER   He say – I'm dreaming.

> *PETER stands, idly strolls round the kitchen, picks up
> a dustbin lid, a long ladle – shield and sword – clangs
> them inviting RAYMOND to a duel. RAYMOND picks
> up a whisk and a tiny saucepan lid. Comic duel ensues
> till PETER raises his arms in surrender.*

PETER   Yah! War! (*To KEVIN.*) Did you use to play like this,
Irishman? War, with dustbin lids and things? Yah!
Not very good, eh, Irishman? War? Kids playing
at war grow up peaceful they say. I think not so
simple. Me, I never liked war games. I had my
own group – boys, we'd build things – castles, huts,
camps. Romantic! Youth! The world was young.
Everything was possible.

> *During this PETER has taken two dustbins, one on
> either end of the serving counters, their lids reversed
> so that he can put a container on top of each and a
> saucepan on top of the containers. From DIMITRI he
> takes a broom to lay across the top, and over it hangs
> a dishcloth. What else? He notices the CHEF's roses,
> grabs them, selects the largest and finds a prominent
> place for it on his structure, giving the remainder to
> PAUL.*

> *Back to the audience he faces his creation at which all
> the OTHERS stare.*

PAUL   Beautiful! What is it?

PETER   It's my arch, and I was…and I was… (*Grabs long
ladle to use as saluting sword.*) … I was ein grosser
Deutscher Ritter!

HANS   Hey, Peter – weisst du noch?

> *HANS strums the Horst Wessel song. PETER goose-steps
> through his arch mocking the Nazi past.*

> *PAUL showers him with roses.*

KEVIN   (*Muttering to himself.*) Fucking Nazis!

> *He can't comprehend that PETER and HANS are
> being irreverent. Feels he must counter with an Irish
> revolutionary song.*

KEVIN (*Singing over them.*) 'Oh Paddy dear and did you hear the news that's going round...the shamrock is by law forbid to grow on Irish ground.'

PETER You think we were serious?

KEVIN Well if you weren't it was a bloody tasteless game

PETER In games you can dream. My arch was a dream.

KEVIN Yeah! Of fucking world domination.

PETER That was a dream of the past. Over! Finished with. Now my arch is a bridge. A new dream. When a man dreams he grows.

HANS Du bist zu alt, Peter!

PETER I'm *not* too old! Never too old. When you're dead you're too old. Hey Irishman, do you dream? Tell us what you dream.

KEVIN You play your own games, Peter, leave me out of it, I'm past it.

PETER Why are you ashamed of being a child, Irishman? We all friends here, why you ashamed to dream? I give you a chance.

KEVIN I'm obliged!

PETER Hey, Paul, Raymondo, Dimitri, stop work a minute. You got time. Here, come here. We are all given a chance to dream. No one is going to laugh, we love each other, we protect each other – someone tell us a dream, just to us, no one else. The ovens are low, the customers – gone, Marango – gone, it's all quiet. God has given us a chance now. We never have the opportunity again, so dream – someone – who? Dimitri – you, you dream first.

DIMITRI In this place? With iron around me? And dustbins? And black walls?

PETER (*Coaxing, inspiring.*) Pretend! There's no dustbins. That's a big beautiful arch there – pretend! The walls are skies, yes? The iron – it's rock on a coast. The tables – they're rose bushes. And the ovens are the noise of the winds. Look at the lights – stars, Dimitri.

HANS   Peter, du verschwendest deine Zeit!

PETER   So what! So what if I waste my time? I got another sixty years to live, I can afford it. Dimitri – dream – a little dream – what you see?

DIMITRI   A small, a small, er – what you call it – a small house, a sort of…

PAUL   A hut?

DIMITRI   No –

KEVIN   A shed?

DIMITRI   That's right, a shed. With instruments, and tools, and I make lots of radios and television sets maybe, and…

PETER   Ach no, silly boy. That's a hobby, that's not what you really want. You want more, more, Dimitri –

DIMITRI   More?

PETER   More! More!

DIMITRI   (*Ironically.*) More, more, more, more…!

PETER   Poor Dimitri! Hey, Irishman, you – dream!

KEVIN   I told you, leave me out of your games.

PETER   Come, a dream, a little sweet dream. You can do it. For us. Your friends.

KEVIN   Sleep! I dream of sleep. Most people sleep and dream, me – I dream of sleep, sweet sleep.

PETER   What is it with you all? Hans – you, what are your dreams?

HANS   Money! Geld, Peter. Geld! With money I'm a good man, I'm generous, I love all the world! Money, Peter, money, money, money, money! (*Continues singing.*)

PETER   How can you talk of money, Hans, when you make music?

HANS   Dreaming, mein lieber, dreaming, dreaming!

PETER   Raymondo?

RAYMOND   Me? Women!

PETER   Which women? Large, small? Happy? Black? Yellow? What kind?

RAYMOND   There is more than one kind?

PETER   Raymond, you make me very sad. Paul – you!

PAUL   Do me a favour.

PETER   Please!

PAUL   No.

PETER   Please, please.

PAUL   No, no, no! I – listen, Peter, I'm going to be honest with you. You don't mind if I'm honest? Right, I'm going to be honest with you. I don't like you. Now wait a minute – let me finish. I don't like you. I think you're a pig. You bully, you're jealous, you go mad with your work, you always quarrel. Alright! But now it's quiet, the ovens are low, the work has stopped for a little and now I'm getting to know you. I still think you're a pig, only now – not so much of a pig. So that's what I dream. I dream about friendship. You give me a rest, you give me silence, you take away this mad kitchen – so I make friends. So I think – maybe all the people I thought were pigs are not so much pigs.

PETER   You think people are pigs?

PAUL   Listen, I'll tell you a story. Next door to me, next door where I live in Hackney is a bus driver. Comes from Hoxton. He's my age, married, got two kids. He says good morning to me, I ask him how he is, I give his children sweets. That's our relationship. Somehow he seems frightened to say too much, you know? God forbid I might ask him for something. So we make no demands on each other.

          Then one day the busman go on strike. He's out for five weeks. Every morning I say to him 'Keep going, mate, you'll win!' Every morning I give him words of encouragement, I say I understand his cause. I've got to get up earlier to get to work but I don't mind

– we're neighbours – we're workers together – he's pleased.

Then one Sunday there's a peace march. I don't believe they do much good but I go, because in this world a man's got to show he can have his say. The next morning he comes up to me and he says, now listen to this, he says 'Did you go on that peace march yesterday?' So I says, yes, I did go on that peace march yesterday. So then he turns round to me and he says, 'You know what? A bomb should have been dropped on the lot of them! It's a pity,' he says, 'that they had children with them cos a bomb should have been dropped on the lot!' And you know what was upsetting him? The march was holding up the traffic, the buses couldn't move so fast!

Now, I don't want him to say I'm right. I don't want him to agree with what I did – but what terrifies me is that he didn't stop to think that this man helped me in my cause so maybe, only *maybe*, there's something in *his* cause – I'll talk about it. No! The buses were held up so drop a bomb, he says, on the lot! And you should have seen the hate in his eyes, as if I'd murdered his child.

And the horror is this – that there's a wall, a big wall between me and millions of people like him. And I think – where will it end? What do you do about it? And I look around me, at the kitchen, at the factories, at the enormous bloody buildings going up with all those offices and all those people in them, and I think – Christ! I think, Christ, Christ, Christ!

I agree with you, Peter – maybe one morning we should wake up and find them all gone. But then I think: I should *stop* making pastries? The factory worker should stop making trains and cars? The miner should leave the coal where it is? (*Pause.*) *You* give *me* an answer. You give me *your* dream.

KEVIN   Hush, Patissier! Hush! It's quiet now. Gently now.

Long silence.

PETER I ask for dreams – he gives me nightmares.

PAUL So – I've dreamt. Is it my fault if it's a nightmare?

HANS throws one of the red roses to PAUL, who sticks it into his lapel, returns to his station.

The ovens hum on.

HANS continues playing.

Everyone is subdued.

KEVIN We're waiting for your dream now, Peter boy.

DIMITRI (*Energetically attempting to break the atmosphere.*) This is the United Nations! A big conference. Every country is here. And they got on a competition. Is finished the wars, is finished the rows. Everybody gone home. We got time on our hands. A prize of one millions dollars for the best dream. Raymondo he want a new woman every night. I want a workshop. Paul he wants a friend. Irishman he wants a bed, and Hans he just want the million dollars. Big opportunity! Come on, Peter, a big dream.

PETER appears excited, as though a dream is growing inside him.

PETER All this gone?

DIMITRI You said so. One morning you come here, to this street here, and the kitchen is gone. And you look around for more kitchens and is none anywhere. What you want to do? The United Nations wants to know.

ALL wait expectantly.

PAUL Come on, come on!

PETER Shush, shush!

They wait on.

But – confronted with his own idea – PETER is embarrassed, coy, hoisted by his own petard. He laughs like a mischievous child caught out.

I can't, I can't.

MONIQUE arrives and PETER forgets everything, the all-consumed lover, the excited child. Is 'love' his dream?

MONIQUE Ready?

PETER Ready, ready. I come, I come. Hey, Irishman, it's soon time to come back. Go home. Change. You'll catch pneumonia. Auf geht's, auf geht's!

The mad PETER rushes out with his MONIQUE.

DIMITRI (*Shouting after PETER.*) Bloody fool! We wait for a dream.

But he has abandoned them. HANS strums, the ovens hum.

PAUL He hasn't got a dream.

KEVIN It's all mad talk if you ask me. I see no point in it. I don't see no point in that Peter bloke either. He talks about peace and dreams and when I ask him if I could use his cutting-board to cut me lemons this morning he told me – get your own. Dreams? See yous!

KEVIN leaves. HANS plays on. DIMITRI returns to his sweeping.

PAUL (*To DIMITRI.*) So *you* tell me that point to all that. I don't even know what I was saying myself.

DIMITRI Why should I know? (*Sweeping as he talks – to take the edge off his 'message'.*) Sometimes things happen and no one sees the point – and then suddenly, something else happen and you see the point. Peter not a fool. You not a fool. People's brain moves all the time. *All* the time. I'm telling you.

DIMITRI sweeps on.

HANS finishes his song, rises, bows, exits.

The next moments happen very, very slowly to denote the passing of time.

PAUL wanders idly to a position upstage, RAYMOND to another position. The triangular relationship of the three men embraces the kitchen.

PAUL Best part of the day.

      Silence.

RAYMOND When they're gone I slow down.

      Silence.

PAUL Longest part of the day, though, isn't it?

      Silence.

RAYMOND Yes, the longest part.

      MANGOLIS enters humming the melody of a Greek dance.

      DIMITRI strikes part of the arch.

      The afternoon is over.

      GASTON enters and joins in with the melody, DIMITRI follows. The three men begin a dance. NICHOLAS enters, joins the dance…

Part Two

… At the end of the Greek dance DIMITRI kicks a cardboard box – a football game!

MICHAEL enters, intercepts box at his feet.

MICHAEL And that great little inside left, Michael Dawson, has the ball again. Will he miss this golden opportunity? Can he hold his own against the great Arsenal backs? He does! Yes! Past Wills, past MacCullough, past Young – and he's going to shoot. He shoots! And it's a goal! A goal – yes! His fifth goal making the score Leyton Orient eighteen, Arsenal nil. What a game! What a boy! (*Beat.*) Look at this place, like a battlefield, grrr – it smells of the dead.

MONIQUE stamps through the kitchen, furious. All watch.

PAUL Well, *they* started the afternoon happy. Did you have a good afternoon, Michael?

MICHAEL Too bloody good. St. James Park…lying in the sun… dozing…the girls…mmmm! (*Beat.*) Saw Nick and Daphne there.

PAUL There's nice for you.

MICHAEL Rowing on the lake.

RAYMOND Ahhhhhh – touching!

MICHAEL Guess who was doing the rowing… (*Beat.*) You're the lucky ones, though – not having to break in the afternoon, come back to work…

PAUL I thought you liked the place.

MICHAEL I don't mind the coming in, it's the coming back.

ALFREDO has returned, straight to his station.

Not old Alfred, though. Look at him – in, out, cook, serve – he doesn't mind.

PETER has followed him in, but hung back, morose.

ALFREDO Well come on, Peter boy, work! It won't hurt you. Stock up! Replenish! Life goes on!

PETER My arch! Who took down my arch away? I want Marango see it.

> *GASTON is tauntingly emptying waste into one of the bins.*

You leave it! Leave it!

> *PETER sits on a stool, aside.*
>
> *OTHERS slowly return.*
>
> *CYNTHIA and HETTIE en route from street to changing room.*

CYNTHIA There's a lot goes on in the restaurant I could tell you about.

HETTIE Well tell me, tell me, tell me!

> *ALFREDO approaches to pacify PETER.*

ALFREDO You're not ill are you?

PETER Who knows.

ALFREDO No pain nor nothing?

PETER No. Alfre–

ALFREDO Good! You have all your teeth?

PETER Yes, look –

ALFREDO Good! You have good lodgings?

PETER Yes, look Alfre–

ALFREDO So tell me what you're unhappy for?

PETER (*Rolling himself a cigarette.*) Alfredo, you're a good cook, yes? You come in the morning, you go straight to work, you ask nobody anything, you tell nobody anything. You are ready to start work before we are, you never panic. Tell me, is this a good house?

ALFREDO (*Drily.*) Depends. It's not bad for Mr Marango!

MICHAEL (*Approaching PETER.*) Peter, got one of those for me?

> *PETER hands him the one he's just rolled and begins to roll another. MICHAEL lingers.*

ALFREDO I'm an old man. It's finished for me. Mind you I've worked in places where I could do good cooking. But it doesn't matter now. Now I work only for the money.

MICHAEL Quite right! Light?

PETER (*To MICHAEL as he looks for match.*) You like it here, don't you?

MICHAEL The ovens –

PETER I got no matches.

MICHAEL I love the sound of the ovens. (*Calling.*) Raymondo, got a light?

RAYMOND throws him matches.

PETER Idiot! He 'loves' the sound of the ovens! You stand before them all day! They're red hot! Someone orders an onion soup and you put soup and bread and cheese in a tin to grill – jump! Then someone orders ham-and-egg, in another tin – jump! Then someone orders an omelette and you jump to mish that; then someone throws you a hamburger and you jump to fry that. You go up you go down, you jump here you jump there, you sweat till steam comes off your back –

MICHAEL – I love it –

PETER – good luck to you!

MONIQUE strolls up.

ALFREDO (*To MONIQUE.*) Here, you talk to him – he's your generation.

PAUL (*To RAYMOND.*) Come on Lightning, let's get some work done.

MONIQUE (*To PETER.*) Still sulking? You started the row, not me. You're just like a little boy.

PETER Would you like me old and fat, like your husband?

MONIQUE Stop hating him so much.

PETER I don't hate him. I try but I can't. It would be easier if I could but I can't. A good man, kind and no vices – who can hate such persons.

VIOLET and BETTY on route to the dining room.

VIOLET I'm bruised all over, bruised!

BETTY You'll get used to it.

VIOLET   Never!

BETTY   You get used to anything if you have to.

MONIQUE   I'm sorry I left you standing in the street.

PETER   You're always sorry afterwards. Like a dog she leaves me.

MONIQUE   Where did you go?

PETER   Never mind – I went! Go on, go! Go wipe your glasses, it's nearly time. (*Pushing her roughly.*) Go, leave me!

MONIQUE   Look at you. Look at you…is it any wonder I'm confused when you behave like this? I come to apologize, to be reasonable, to say I'm sorry, but you…you…you…

> *She leaves him.*

> *DAPHNE and HETTIE giving out new menus.*

KEVIN   I'll be taking my leave tonight by Christ.

GASTON   You'll get used to it, stay! It's good money.

KEVIN   To hell with the money an' all. I like me money but this isn't work, it's hell and high pressure. An' the food! No one cares, that's what gets me, no one cares.

VIOLET   Nor about the waitresses, either. They don't even care about themselves, letting themselves be pushed around, get this get that, faster, faster.

HEAD WAITER   Won't be so bad this evening, Violet. If you survived lunch you'll last out. It'll just be hot – hot and close. For everyone!

VIOLET   I can remember working in places where you had to move like a ballet dancer, weave in and out of tables with grace. There was room, it was civilized.

KEVIN   Starch and clean finger-nails – I heard about it.

> *HETTIE pirouettes off –*

VIOLET   (*After her.*) And we didn't mind, either – we had to queue up and be inspected, all of us, chefs too – it was civilized. I once served the Prince of Wales. Look at me, bruises!

KEVIN　Look at me! Three stone lighter!

HANS　(*To KEVIN.*) Marango will try to make you stay.

KEVIN　Now there's a man. Have you watched him? One of the girls dropped some cups by there this morning and he cried, 'me wages' he cried. 'All me wages down there!' And do take notice of the way he strolls among us all? I thought he'd a kind face, but when he's done talking with you his kindness evaporates. In thin air it goes, sudden, and his face gets worried as though today were the last day and he had to be closing for good and he were taking a last sad glance at everything going on. This mornin' he watched me a while, and then walked away shaking his head as though I were dying and there was not a drop of hope for me left an' all.

HANS　(*To PETER.*) What he has said?

PETER　Marango spielt den lieben Gott!

> *RAYMOND en route across kitchen with tray of tarts.*
> *DAPHNE swipes one as he passes.*

RAYMOND　Bon appetit!

GASTON　Paul, you got some cake?

PAUL　(*Calling to RAYMOND.*) Give the boy some cake.

> *Which he does from his tray.*

(*To HANS.*) You got over this morning yet?

HANS　This morning, ach! He's a big fool, that Max. He's like a dustbin – full of what other people throw away!

RAYMOND　So why you take notice. Listen to them.

> *He refers to MAX and NICHOLAS who are just then entering from the changing-room in the middle of a quarrel.*

NICHOLAS　No, no, no! I'm never going to listen to you again, never!

MAX　Good! Very good! I'm fed up with you hanging around me anyway. 'Max should I do this, Max should I do that?' Well, Max isn't your father.

NICHOLAS You're damn right he's not my father. My father was
          a man with kindness, my father never betray what I
          tell him.

MAX   Well *I* didn't betray what you told me either, I keep
          telling you, I –

NICHOLAS My father brought up nine children and all of them
          good people. My –

MAX   I didn't tell anyone, I keep telling you –

NICHOLAS My father –

MAX   Your father nothing! He's been dead since you was
          three years old so don't give me 'my father' bullshit.

          *BERTHA enters from the street en route to changing-room
          and catches RAYMOND's words.*

RAYMOND   The first thing in the morning they come in and
          drink a bottle of beer – then they're happy. All day
          they drink.

BERTHA   And their breaths smell, and their words slur, and
          they become stupid in a way that only men can
          become stupid.

PAUL   So Hans, what are you going to do about Max the
          bigot?

HANS   He doesn't like I talk in German, what can I do!
          (*Tragically.*) You know, Paul, you – you are a Jew, and
          me – I am a German. We suffer together.

          *PAUL snorts, cynically, unsure if HANS comprehends
          what he's uttered. Gives him the benefit of the doubt,
          takes the rose from his lapel and hands it to him.
          Reconciliation!*

KEVIN   Is that a Jew, then?

HANS   (*Sentimentally.*) A very good boy.

KEVIN   Well who'd have thought that now?

          *He regards the remains of PETER's arch which is in
          his way.*

          Is he ever going to take his arch down?

BERTHA   Take it down.

KEVIN   Not me, I value my life.

BERTHA   Well look at that for a sight!

A TRAMP wanders into the kitchen and becomes the centre of attraction.

MAX   (*Shouting to BERTHA.*) Bertha, your old man has come to take you home.

BERTHA   I'll come after you – then see who'll laugh.

TRAMP   (*To KEVIN.*) 'Scuse me. The Chef please, which'n is he?

KEVIN   Napoleon there.

By which time the CHEF has reached him.

TRAMP   'Scuse me, Chef, (*Tapping his knee.*) war disabled, I don't usually ask for food but I lost me pensions book, see, I don't like to ask but...

CHEF   Michael, clean a tin and give him some soup.

TRAMP   (*To KEVIN.*) Don't usually do this. Can't do anything till they trace me book. (*To HANS, tapping his knee again.*) Got it in the desert, 'gainst Rommel.

HANS   (*Wryly.*) Rommel! Ah ha!

TRAMP   Got papers to prove it, too. Here, look, papers! Always carry these around with me. Everyone got to have his papers and I always carry mine. Be daft for the likes of me to leave them anywhere, wouldn't it? Who'd believe me otherwise, see? Papers! (*Beat.*) Watcha making? Spaghetti Bolonaizeeee? That's good – Italian food. Do you put bay leaves in? Good with bay leaves, not the same without. Bay leaves, red peppers, all that stuff. (*Catches sight of ruins of arch.*) What's this? A dream castle?

PETER regards the TRAMP appreciatively.

MICHAEL hands him a tin of soup.

MICHAEL   Here you are.

TRAMP   Got a cigarette?

MICHAEL   Yes, and I'm smoking it.

MAX   (*Who's passing.*) Go on, 'op it, be quick, we got work.

PETER approaches TRAMP, takes tin of soup out of his hand, offers it to MAX.

PETER   You drink it?

MAX   Go to hell, you and your high and bloody mighty gestures. *I* work for my living, fool!

>   *PETER tosses tin of soup into dustbin. From HANS' station he hurriedly snatches two meat cutlets which he thrusts into the TRAMP's hands gently pushing him on his way.*

PETER   Take these cutlets and go, quick, whisht!

>   *But he's not quick enough. The CHEF has observed.*

CHEF   (*Quiet and menacing.*) What's that?

PETER   I gave him some cutlets.

CHEF   Mr Marango told you to give him?

PETER   No, but…

CHEF   You heard *me* say, perhaps?

PETER   No, I…

CHEF   You have *authority* suddenly?

PETER   (*Impatiently.*) So what's a couple of cutlets – we going bankrupt or something?

CHEF   It's money, that's what, and it's me who's Chef that's what, and…

>   *PETER moves away muttering dismissively 'ach!' The CHEF follows him, furious.*

Don't think we're too busy I can't sack you. Three years is nothing you know, you don't buy the place in three years, you hear me? Don't go thinking I won't sack you.

>   *MARANGO has arrived on his rounds.*

MARANGO   Yes?

CHEF   The tramp – Peter gave him a cutlet, it was his own supper.

>   *CHEF returns to his station leaving MARANGO to nod sadly at PETER, as though PETER had just insulted him. He continues on his rounds nodding all the time, muttering –*

MARANGO Sabotage… It's sabotage you do to me… It's my fortune here and you give it away…

PETER But it…

MARANGO (*Not bothering to look round.*) Yes, yes, yes! I'm always wrong, of course, yes, yes, yes…

> PETER *attempts a final explanation as* MARANGO *disappears into the dining-room.*

DIMITRI Don't tantalize the boss, Peter. Listen to this friend.

PETER Dimitri, I need a cup of very black coffee.

DIMITRI (*Going to get it.*) You need friends and a good kick up the arse, that's what you need.

HANS Oh, pass auf, der ist wirklich hinter dir her!

PETER Ach, er erwartet, dass die ganze Welt auf seine Küche aufpasst!

KEVIN I seem to remember being told not to grumble by someone.

PETER A bastard man! A bastard house!

KEVIN And he also said you could get used to anything.

PETER But this house is like – is like –

PAUL Yes? What is it like?

PETER God in heaven, I don't know what it's like. If only it – if only it –

KEVIN Yes, yes – if only it would go.

PETER Just one morning – to find it gone.

PAUL And then what? We couldn't depend on you for a dream, could we?

PETER A dream?

PAUL Yes, a dream, a dream. The United Nations is waiting for Peter's dream.

PETER I can't, I can't.

JACKIE Annie, I've got a late tea party. A dozen mixed desserts, please.

PETER (*Violently pulls down half his arch.*) I can't dream in a kitchen!

HANS Aha! Und jetzt spielst du wieder den wilden Mann!

BERTHA and MONIQUE have been watching this from different corners. BERTHA sets aright a dustbin which brings her close to MONIQUE.

BERTHA Why don't you hop it out of here, girl like you –

MONIQUE Girl like me *what*?

BERTHA Pack it in, Monique. Peter I mean – dissolve it.

MONIQUE Just like that?

BERTHA Just like that.

MONIQUE If only it was so simple. Twice he's given me a baby, twice I've disappointed him. He wanted them both. Dissolve that.

BERTHA (*Leaving her.*) Ah, why don't we all hop it?

MONIQUE Good question, Aunty Bertha.

PETER sidles up to MONIQUE from behind, arms round her waist, talking close to her ear.

PETER I'm sorry.

MONIQUE remains stiff, her arms folded.

MONIQUE Not an attractive future, is it? Apologising – first you, then me...

PETER Did you see that tramp?

MONIQUE What tramp?

PETER You didn't hear?

MONIQUE Hear what?

PETER (*Proudly, laughing, trying to recapture her.*) I had a row about him. Mr Marango and the Chef there, they wanted to give him a dirty tin full of soup so I threw it away and gave him some cutlets.

MONIQUE And Marango caught you?

PETER (*Imitating.*) 'Sabotage' the old man said, 'sabotage! All my fortune you take away.'

MONIQUE Oh, Peter!

GWEN (*To MICHAEL.*) Two sour minestrone.

MICHAEL I'll sue you for defamation of character.

PETER (*Tenderly.*) You want to know where I went this
       afternoon?

MONIQUE Where?

PETER To buy you a birthday present.

MONIQUE But it's not my birthday.

*PETER takes out a necklace, places it round her
neck.*

PETER I will make every day your birthday.

*She's delighted and now turns to pull him to her,
biting his neck.*

HETTIE (*To HANS.*) One veal cutlet.

HANS One veal cutlet.

WINNIE (*To NICHOLAS.*) Two ham salads.

NICHOLAS Two ham salads.

CYNTHIA (*To HANS.*) One veal cutlet.

HANS One veal cutlet.

*By now HANS and CYNTHIA have a relationship. She
lingers to chat with him.*

GWEN (*To MICHAEL.*) Minestrone.

MICHAEL Minestrone.

PETER Ah, you want to eat me. How do you want me?
       Grilled? Fried? Underdone? Well done?

*While PETER and MONIQUE are locked in embrace
a cry comes up from the back of the kitchen. WINNIE
has doubled up in pain and passed out.*

*A crowd rushes to her. It all happens very quickly,
hardly noticed. PETER and MONIQUE do not even
hear.*

*FRANK lifts her in his arms and takes her into the
changing-room.*

ALFREDO Alright! Don't crowd! Give her air.

PAUL (*To MOLLY.*) Who was it? What's happened?

MOLLY It's Winnie, she's passed out.

KEVIN (*To GASTON.*) Well what was all that about now?

GASTON   (*Guessing.*) The heat. Always affecting someone.
          Terrible.

PETER   (*To MONIQUE.*) Did you – have you – are you still
          going to do it? I mean I…

MONIQUE   Don't worry, Peter, I've told you I shall see to it. It's
          not the first time, after all.

PETER   You don't think we should go through with it?

MONIQUE   I had a dream last night –

          *A strange quiet descends on the kitchen. Huddles of
          PEOPLE around the stage.*

          *It is as though everyone is exchanging something private
          with someone else.*

          – about blood.

PETER   I don't mind being responsible.

MONIQUE   I was in a slaughter house…

PETER   After all it is my baby.

MONIQUE   …walking through it, like a roving camera's eye.
          There were men *and* women, all working on
          carcasses. The odd thing about the women was that
          they were all made up, beautifully groomed hair,
          carefully lipsticked and rouged and powdered. But
          splashed with blood. Blood. It was everywhere.
          The most horrifying moment was when I came
          across a group of slaughterers standing around a
          cow, and although the cow was skinned and had
          its eyes gouged out yet it was still alive and on its
          feet. Somehow I seemed to know that doing it this
          way improved the quality of the meat. And there
          was one man in particular, with a long stick at the
          end of which was a curved, very sharp knife, and
          he was slicing off the right-hand cheek of the cow's
          face. And the animal just stood, shuddering, blind,
          passive.

          *The moment ends. The groups disperse. Work
          continues.*

PETER   The dream warns. You should have the b–

MONIQUE   Enough! I'm not going to talk about it any more.

She seems a changed personality.

PETER   You mean you've told Monty about us then?

MONIQUE draws lipstick and a powder puff from her pocket, attends to her make-up.

MONIQUE   You really must stop rowing with Marango, darling.

PETER   Did you speak to Monty as we agreed?

MONIQUE   You'll lose your job, you'll see.

PETER   Did you speak to Monty?

MONIQUE   He won't stand your cheek forever.

PETER   You haven't have you!

MONIQUE   I keep warning and warning –

HETTIE   (*To FRANK.*) Two chicken.

PETER   Monique, I love you.

MONIQUE   Not this again, please.

FRANK   Two chicken.

PETER   Please listen to me that I love you.

MONIQUE   I know you do.

PETER   And I know you love me.

MONIQUE   Peter, please.

PETER   But you don't say to your husband this thing.

She doesn't answer.

You're not going to leave him are you?

MONIQUE   I can't live under this pressure.

PETER   What d'you want I should do?

MOLLY   One minestrone.

PETER   Tell me what I should do, I'll do it.

MICHAEL   One minestrone.

PETER   Tell me.

MOLLY   (*To MICHAEL.*) You sober enough to make an omelette?

PETER   We could leave any day.

MICHAEL   One OM-EL-ETTE. Witch!

PETER   I have money. We could go for a long holiday first. Skiing in Switzerland, perhaps.

HETTIE   Two coffees, Annie.

PETER   Let's leave tomorrow. Tomorrow, Monique. Imagine – fly from all this to somewhere beautiful. Think about it.

MONIQUE I'm going to the hair-dresser tomorrow.

PETER   Monique, we row this morning, we row this afternoon, this evening we are in love again... Answer me.

GWEN   (*To ALFRED.*) Two roast beef.

PETER   Monique – answer me!

MONIQUE Did I tell you Monty is buying us a new house?

PETER   (*Screaming.*) Monique!

> *She glances around, embarrassed. Mutters 'you fool!' Stalks off.*

> *VIOLET approaches PETER.*

VIOLET   You serving yet, Peter? I want three turbot. Special for Marango.

PETER   It's half-past six yet?

VIOLET   It's nearly...

PETER   Half past six is service.

VIOLET   But it's special...

PETER   Half-past six!

DAPHNE   (*To HANS.*) Two sausages.

HANS   Two sausages.

> *Service is starting up again, not so hectic, and taking longer to get into stride.*

> *WAITRESSES appear. Most people are by now at their station, except for a knot of KEVIN and HANS around GASTON's station.*

BETTY   (*To KEVIN.*) Two plaice.

KEVIN   Two plaice, I'm coming, I'm coming. (*To HANS as he moves to his station.*) Me, I'd have a Jaguar. It's got a luxury I could live with.

GASTON Have you seen the new French Citroen? Just like a mechanical frog it looks.

HANS And the Volkswagen? It's not a good car?

KEVIN Now there's a good little car for little money.

HANS No country makes like the Volkswagen.

KEVIN You've gotta hand it to the Germans.

Service is gentle, and orders ring out in comfort.

CYNTHIA, an order in her arms, pauses by the CHEF's station to gossip. MAX and NICHOLAS stand by, listening.

CYNTHIA Heard what happened to Winnie? She's been rushed to hospital. Pregnant.

CHEF Miscarried?

CYNTHIA And no accident neither.

MAX Silly woman, silly woman.

CHEF She's got seven children already. Why do they do it?

CYNTHIA Affection. Women don't crave sex, they crave love.

CHEF Who doesn't?

CYNTHIA Marango's hopping mad. She got her first pains in the dining room and spilt wine over a customer.

NICHOLAS Why she get pains?

CYNTHIA She took pills, that's why. And I'll tell you something else – there are four other girls here took the same pills. There! Four of them!

BETTY (*To HANS.*) Two veal cutlets.

HANS Two veal cutlets.

CYNTHIA And you know who one of the four is?

She inclines her head in PETER's direction.

MAX Monique?

CYNTHIA (*Nodding with unctuous delight.*) Now don't you tell anyone I told you, mind. But you ask Hettie, ask her, she bought the stuff. Two plaice, please.

KEVIN Two plaice.

GWEN (*To HANS.*) Two hamburgers.

HANS Two hamburgers.

MAX (*Know-all.*) Knew this would happen…

HETTIE (*To PETER still on stool, dejected.*) Two halibut.

MAX … Knew it! Can't be done, though. What makes them think that by taking a tablet through the mouth it will affect the womb?

HETTIE Oh come on, Peter, two halibut.

PETER slowly rises to serve her.

MAX There's only one way, the way it went in. What happens with a tablet? Nothing! Nothing can –

PETER serves only one halibut.

HETTIE I said two.

MAX The stomach is irritated, that's all, squeezed see? Forces the womb. Presses it.

NICHOLAS What the hell do you know about this? A doctor now?

MAX Oh I know about this all right.

HETTIE Two flans, Annie.

ANNIE Two flans.

MAX Only one drug is effective through the mouth. (*Secretively.*) And you know what that is? Ergot? Heard of it? Only thing to do it. And that's rare. Oh yes, I studied this in the forces when I had nothing else to do. Very interesting, this psychology. Complicated! I knew Winnie was in pod as soon as she came here.

NICHOLAS (*Leaving him contemptuously.*) Barrack-room lawyer!

The PASTRYCOOKS, having cleared up their station, leave with goodbyes thrown to their colleagues.

PAUL/RAYMOND 'Night!… 'Bye… Arrivederci…

MAX Some people have it easy!

MOLLY (*To HANS.*) Two sausages.

HANS Two sausages.

GWEN (*To PETER.*) One turbot.

DAPHNE (*To PETER.*) Three cod.

PETER It's not ready yet.

DAPHNE Oh come on, Peter, three cod.

PETER It's not ready yet, come back five minutes' time.

> *GASTON leads other CHEFS in a mocking chorus of 'Hi-li, hi-lo, ha-ha'. The waitresses try to shush them, they can see PETER is in a state.*

MOLLY (*To HANS.*) Four veal cutlets.

GWEN (*To PETER who's dished out more.*) Only *one* turbot for Christ's sake.

JACKIE (*To PETER.*) Two halibut.

VIOLET (*To PETER.*) My three turbot.

> *The queue has grown. PETER is not in control.*
>
> *VIOLET becomes impatient.*

Can't bloody wait for him.

> *She picks up plate and moves behind the serving counter to the oven attempting to help herself from a tray.*
>
> *PETER takes it from her and pushes her back.*

PETER You wait for me, yes? *I* serve you. You ask *me.*

VIOLET But you were busy and this is special.

PETER I don't care. This is my place and there (*Points to other side of serving counter.*) *there* is for you!

VIOLET Now you wait a bloody minute will you? Who the hell do you think you are, you?

PETER You don't worry who I am. I'm the cook, yes? And you're the waitress, and in the kitchen I do what I like, yes? And in the dining-room you do what you like.

> *PETER turns his back on her imagining his word will be taken as final.*
>
> *Not for VIOLET who takes another plate and again pushes past him attempting to serve herself.*

VIOLET I won't take orders from you, you know, I…

> *PETER screams and smashes the plate from her hand.*

PETER   Leave it! Leave it there! I'll serve you. Me! Me! Is *my* kingdom here. This is the side where *I* live. This!

VIOLET   (*Very quietly.*) You Boche, you. You bloody German bastard!

> *She turns to report to, presumably, MARANGO in the dining-room.*

> *PETER is about to snap. Follows her.*

PETER   What you call me? What was it? Say it again! SAY IT AGAIN!

> *His scream halts her, petrified.*

> *It also turns everyone's attention on him, as on a frightened animal. He wheels around, in a frenzy, looking for something violent to do.*

> *He sweeps plates off his counter. Other CHEFS run to grab and control him. He heaves them off, sees a meat-axe, reaches for it, raises it, everyone backs away, he seems about to chase VIOLET with it.*

> *Freeze.*

> *PETER turns to the gas-lead at which he hacks with an 'auf geht's'!*

> *There is a slow hiss. All the fires in the ovens die down.*

> *There is a second of complete silence before anyone comprehends what has happened. Then all happens at once.*

> *PETER storms into the dining-room, VIOLET imagines he's after her and flees.*

> *CHEFS rush after him.*

> *Everyone holds a cloth to their mouth.*

> *There is a sound of crashing crockery.*

> *Orders are hurled around.*

FRANK   Hold him, grab hold of him!

MICHAEL   He's broken the gas lead! Someone turn off the main.

CHEF   Mangolis!

MANGOLIS (*Rushing off.*) Yes, chef!

KEVIN Holy Mother 'o Mary, he's gone berserk.

GASTON The lunatic! He's swept all the plates off the table in there.

MICHAEL He's ripped his hands!

KEVIN I knew something like this would happen, I just knew it.

> *The mains have been turned off. The hiss dies to silence.*
>
> *Everyone faces dining-room entrance, waiting.*
>
> *MONIQUE rushes in en route to get first-aid.*
>
> *The crowd by the entrance to the dining-room make way as ALFREDO and HANS bring PETER back.*

CHEF Phone an ambulance.

JACKIE Monique is doing that now.

> *We can imagine his hands are dripping with blood, they droop. He looks spent.*
>
> *MICHAEL finds a stool.*
>
> *MONIQUE rushes in with first-aid box. Tries to dab his hands with iodine. Pain. He pushes her away. Distressed, she flees.*
>
> *PETER regrets his action.*

PETER (*To DIMITRI.*) Go to her.

> *DIMITRI obeys. ALFREDO takes over binding PETER's hands.*

It hurts!

ALFREDO Shut up!

> *CHEF has been watching, horrified, from a distance, somewhat helpless.*

CHEF (*Calling out.*) Fool! Fool! So? What? The whole kitchen is stopped. Fool!

PETER (*To ALFREDO.*) Now he cares!

> *This is too much for the CHEF who, incredulous and furious, bears down on PETER.*

CHEF   What do you mean, 'now he cares'?

ALFREDO   Leave him, chef. Leave him now.

CHEF   What do you mean, 'now he cares'? You have to
        make me care? Forty years and suddenly you have
        to make me care?

        *The crowd breaks to allow MARANGO in. He surveys
        the damage, and to begin with seems amazed and hurt
        rather than furious.*

MARANGO   (*With terrible calm.*) You have stopped my whole
        world. Did you get permission from God? Did you?
        There – is – no – one – else! You know that? *No* one!

FRANK   All right, Mr Marango, the boy's going, he's going.
        He's ill, don't upset yourself.

MARANGO   (*To FRANK, gently appealing.*) Why does everybody
        sabotage me, Frank? I give work, I pay well, yes?
        They eat what they want, don't they? I don't know
        what more to give a man. He works, he eats, I give
        him money. This is life, isn't it? I haven't made a
        mistake, have I? I live in the right world, don't I?
        (*To PETER.*) And you've stopped this world. A shnip!
        A boy! You've stopped it. Why? Maybe you can
        tell me something I don't know. Just tell me. I want
        to learn something. (*To all in the kitchen.*) Is there
        something I don't know?

        *PETER rises and in pain moves off. MARANGO cries
        after him.*

BLOODY FOOL!

        *This arrests PETER who stops. MARANGO bears down
        on him and wheels him round.*

What more do you want? Tell me, what is there
more?

        PETER again tries to leave.

What is there more?

        *PETER seems about to attempt an answer – looks
        around at the OTHERS, shrugs, shakes his head at
        MARANGO as if to say 'if you don't know, I cannot
        explain'. And leaves.*

MARANGO is left facing his staff who stand around, almost accusingly, looking at him. He asks again.

Tell me, what is there more?

There is no work can be done. They turn to leave him, embarrassed by his pleading. He calls again.

What is there more?

They stop, backs to him.

What, what is there more?

One by one they turn to face him, accusingly, as –

SLOW BLACKOUT

End

VOICES ON THE WIND

A play for young people (9 – 12 years old) in three acts with incidental music, electronic sounds, laser sets and the inventiveness of the performers enacting a story within a story within a story

Characters

Six adults and nine child actors perform: ten youngsters, eleven adults and the Islanders of Tamak

Act One

The adults
FATLIPS
  an old man of sixty
MISTER AMERSHAM
MRS AMERSHAM
SUSAN AMERSHAM
  their daughter aged
  sixteen
MR HARDY
MRS HARDY
A STRUGGLING OLD MAN

The youngsters
JOEL AMERSHAM
MAISY HARDY
MERVYN HARDY
SEBASTIAN
GINGER
HECTOR
BLAKEY
RUSTY
MAVE

Act Two

AMULA
AMULA'S HUSBAND
ALUMA
  an old woman of sixty
LEOJ
ISLANDERS OF TAMAK
and
CALIMAN
LYDICA
THE VOICE OF AMULA
  Fatlips' wife-to-be
THE VOICE OF YOUNG
AMULA

DOUBLING

SUSAN *doubles with* AMULA

MRS AMERSHAM *doubles with* ALUMA

MR AMERSHAM *doubles with* CALIMAN

JOEL *doubles with* LEOJ

MR HARDY *doubles with* A STRUGGLING OLD MAN, *and* AMULA'S HUSBAND

MRS HARDY *doubles with* LYDICA

MAISY *doubles with* YOUNG AMULA'S VOICE.

ISLANDERS *made up with everyone from Act One except* FATLIPS, AMULA, *and anyone else not doubling.*

Voices On The Wind is carefully structured to use as many theatrical devices as possible:

Street Games

Strange and Ethereal Moments

A Storm at Sea

Ghostly Voices

Simple Story-telling (Against a Visual Background of Action)

Flying

Quick-change Sets

Construction on Site

A Birth

Masks

Electronic Sounds

Specially Composed Music

No play that I've yet seen has used the extraordinary devices worked out by LIGHT FANTASTIC which demonstrated its effects at The Royal Academy in 1977, or the techniques of the Czech LATERNA MAGICA.

This play for young people is written in the hope that the designer supported by his theatre will risk breaking new ground and exploit those effects.

Voices on the Wind *is a textural framework open to improvisation and, more important, to theatrical invention at indicated key points.*

NOTE: I am aware this play calls for more than the advisable number of performers but as it also calls for sophisticated technology I've thrown caution to the wind in the hope that it may be sufficiently admired to encourage theatres to seek special sponsorship for its production.

Settings

ACT ONE

Scene 1   Prow of the upper deck

Scene 2   Another part of upper deck

Scene 3   Crossroads below deck

Scene 4   Prow of the upper deck

Scene 5   Section of AMERSHAM cabin below deck

Scene 6   Section of HARDY cabin below deck

Scene 7   Prow of the upper deck

Scene 8   Section of AMERSHAM cabin below deck

ACT TWO

Scene 1   Verandah and part of a kitchen in the
                 Philippines

Scene 2   Moving panorama of scenes

Scene 3   The island of Tamak

ACT THREE

Scene 1   Section of AMERSHAM cabin below deck

Scene 2   Upper deck

*Note: It would be preferable to construct the set so that acts two
and three merge into a single act with five scenes.*

Act One

Sound of a ship heaving through sea. Gentle, rocking, evocative.

Spotlight on face of an OLD MAN.

Sad face, bulbous nose, hair flying out from the side of a bald head, thick lips.

As the spot widens and the lights build we see the OLD MAN is leaning over the rail at the prow of the upper deck of a moving ship. He is utterly still, statuesque. His name is FATLIPS.

Slowly, one by one or in couples, NINE YOUNGSTERS appear, shuffling, as if drawn by him.

They keep their distance, playing their own games: hop-scotch, skipping, ball against the wall, wrestling…always at least one of them holding him in their gaze.

Soon they cease playing and huddle in corners whispering, giggling, pushing each other towards him.

The stillness of the OLD MAN, the long silence is almost unbearable. Finally –

RUSTY I bet by the time I count ten he'll move. One, two, three, four, five, six, seven, eight, nine –

> *She holds, hopefully. He doesn't move.*

– nine and two eighths, nine and three eighths…

MAVE He's not human he's a statue.

MERVYN Poke him you'll break your finger.

BLAKEY I saw him blink.

MAVE It was the wind!

BLAKEY I saw him breathe.

MAVE The ship's heaving!

RUSTY Nine and nine sixteenths, nine and ten sixteenths, nine and eleven sixteenths…

SEBASTIAN   He's been there right from when we left this
                 morning. Nearly a whole day, without moving,
                 without moving a muscle, not a muscle.

GINGER   He went for a meal.

SEBASTIAN   He didn't move I tell you.

GINGER   I seen him go.

SEBASTIAN   And I seen him stay.

GINGER   Don't tell me, the bloke was eating not more'n two
              tables away.

SEBASTIAN   You sure?

GINGER   Certain! He went to his cabin first thing, came
              straight out, stayed all morning, went in for lunch,
              went to his cabin, came straight out, stayed still like
              he is now, broke for a cup of tea and came back out
              here.

SEBASTIAN   Oh well, then.

GINGER   I watched him.

SEBASTIAN   You know then.

GINGER   I'm a studier of human nature.

SEBASTIAN   You must be right, then.

MERVYN   Makes you sick.

SEBASTIAN   Makes me nervous.

MERVYN   Stupid old git.

HECTOR   He'll hear you.

MERVYN   What do I care? Standing there all day. What's he
              doing standing there all day?

SEBASTIAN   Who is he, that's what I'd like to know. Can't bear
                 not knowing who somebody is. Makes me nervous.

RUSTY   Nine and twenty-one thirty seconds, nine and
            twenty-two thirty seconds, nine and twenty-three
            thirty seconds…

HECTOR   Let's have guesses.

MAVE   About what?

HECTOR   Who he is, what he does.

MAVE He doesn't have to do anything.

HECTOR Yes he does. This is a ship of emigrants, right? We're all leaving the old country and going to a new one. It's newly developing and it needs new people to work. Right? Well that's why we're going anyway. My father's a printer, they need printers. (*To MAVE.*) What's your father do?

MAVE Electrical engineer.

HECTOR Right! They need electrical engineers. (*To SEBASTIAN.*) What's your father do?

SEBASTIAN Welder. Steel girders for tall buildings. Makes me nervous.

HECTOR Right! They need spidermen. (*To MERVYN.*) What's your father?

MERVYN Plumber.

HECTOR The new country needs plumbers? Along comes plumbers.

MERVYN Pinches more than he joins up, though. Ha, ha!

MAVE The new country needs thieves? Along comes thieves.

MERVYN Stupid git!

HECTOR (*To MAISY who's been silent and fretful.*) Yours?

MERVYN She's my sister.

HECTOR (*To JOEL.*) Yours?

JOEL (*More assured than the rest.*) Foreman in a car factory.

HECTOR There you go. They're building cars, need a foreman. (*To RUSTY.*) Yours?

RUSTY Nine and forty-five sixty fourths, nine and forty-six sixty fourths – mechanic – nine and forty-seven sixty fourths…

HECTOR Where? In agriculture? Train engines? Power stations?

RUSTY Nine and fifty sixty fourths – agricultural equipment – nine and fifty-one sixty fourths…

GINGER And my mum and dad are farmers.

HECTOR   So there you are! Everyone's got to have a profession or else they wouldn't be allowed into the new country. Can't carry duds can they?

BLAKEY   You haven't asked me what my mum and dad do.

HECTOR   Alright, what do your mum and dad do?

BLAKEY   I'm glad you asked me what my mum and dad do. Because I don't know.

HECTOR   You don't know what your parents work at?

BLAKEY   Oh, I know that. They're chemists. Work for a huge chemical factory. But I'm stupid in science and I've never understood what they tried to explain. Give up on me, didn't they! 'You're thick as mud' they tell me. And they're right. That's me. Thick. Put me in a laboratory and I'd make cheese!

MAVE   You'd be very clever if you made cheese.

BLAKEY   Not the cheese I'd make.

HECTOR   We've gone away from the point. Fatlips. He must be something. Now what?

BLAKEY   Well he's not a labourer.

MAVE   A doctor?

HECTOR   Too sloppy.

MAVE   A sloppy doctor, then!

GINGER   A professor?

MAVE   A sloppy professor!

HECTOR   Looks like one, but a professor would say something.

BLAKEY   Maybe he's a thinking professor and not a talking one.

MAVE   A sloppy thinking professor!

HECTOR   But even a thinking professor moves. He hasn't moved.

MAVE   An unmoving sloppy thinking professor.

RUSTY   He'll move before I finish to ten. Nine and seventy-five hundred and eighths, nine and seventy-six hundred and eighths, nine and seventy-seven hundred and eighths…

MAVE   He's an artist.

BLAKEY   Where's his paints and easel then?

MAVE   Maybe he's still deciding what to paint.

HECTOR   No, no. Look at his hands. No paint on them. All painters have bits and pieces of paint left on their fingers.

MAVE   You'll never get on in this world, you're too logical. Maybe he's a thorough-cleaner-of-paint-from-off-his-fingers. (*Pause.*) A sloppy thorough-cleaner-of-paint-from-off-his-fingers!

SEBASTIAN   Why doesn't he move? I'll go barmy if he doesn't move or say something.

MERVYN   Anybody quiet like that must have something to hide.

BLAKEY   That's stupid. Maybe he's shy or frightened or upset. I think we should leave him alone.

> *Meanwhile the girl called MAISY who, like her brother, is an unhappy child, has been creeping up on FATLIPS.*
>
> *The others watch her, mesmerised.*
>
> *She's terrified but determined. Suddenly she blows a raspberry.*
>
> *Good God! What'll happen? The air is tense with silent expectation.*
>
> *FATLIPS turns and beams an incredibly sweet and gentle smile on her.*
>
> *Its special quality seems to invoke sounds in the air.*
>
> *Everyone is held, spellbound, except MAISY.*
>
> *At first wide-eyed, then panic-struck, she bursts into tears and flees.*
>
> *The moment passes.*

RUSTY   Nine and ninety-nine two hundred and sixteenths! There! I told you he'd move before I counted ten!

MAVE   (*Marvelling.*) Did you see that smile?

SEBASTIAN   Sent a shiver up my spine.

HECTOR Made me go all warm inside.

BLAKEY Maybe he's the ship's mascot.

GINGER Or a guard of some sort.

RUSTY He's an angel in disguise.

MAVE I just felt this urge to go up and stroke him.

MERVYN He's a trouble maker, I can tell you. A spy sent to sneak on us.

RUSTY A spy from where? To sneak on us doing what? You don't make sense.

MAVE Stop being logical. Spiteful people never make sense.

BLAKEY (*To MERVYN.*) You're the trouble maker.

MERVYN Who says?

BLAKEY I says. Ever since you and your family boarded this boat you've been complaining. A family of moaners and complainers that's what you are.

MERVYN You say that again I'll –

BLAKEY – what? You'll what?

MERVYN Don't push me.

HECTOR Gentlemen! We're supposed to be taking love and neighbourliness to the new country, no scrapping here, please!

BLAKEY Watch out! Here she comes! Moaning Mervyn's moaning mother and moaning sister Maisy.

MRS HARDY enters dragging a whining daughter.

MRS HARDY (*To FATLIPS.*) You're still there standing then! I'm surprised after what you just did to my little girl. Standing there frightening everyone. What do you think you're doing standing there frightening everyone? You damn well just plain mad?

No response.

BLAKEY Fatlips isn't m–

MRS HARDY No one's talking to you so you shut up for a start. (*Back to FATLIPS.*) Well don't answer then, see where that'll get you. Everyone's talking about you, standing there frightening all the children. You're not natural standing there, saying nothing, frightening all the children. You've spoken to nobody! No one don't know anything about you!

MAVE Not true, he's a sloppy-thorough-cleaner-of-paint-from-off-his-fingers type artist, isn't he?

MRS HARDY gives her a look to kill.

Well *I* thought he was a thorough-cleaner-of…etc (*She mumbles on.*)

MRS HARDY (*Over MAVE.*) Well they can put up with it but I won't, you'll see, I'll complain to the captain that you've lured all the youngsters and you're up to no good. We all knew you were up to no good. My gal says you yelled to her. She says you yelled obscenities at her. A little girl like that and she says you yelled dirty things at her.

This is too much for some of the other children who pipe up.

TOGETHER He didn't! He didn't! It was Maisy's fault! Your Maisy's fault!

MRS HARDY (*Threateningly.*) My Maisy's fault? My Maisy's fault?

The YOUNGSTERS retreat in fear before her screaming.

JOEL, a small quiet boy who's said little, steps forward.

JOEL Excuse me, Mrs Hardy, but she poked her tongue out at him I'm afraid. (*To MAISY.*) Didn't you?

At which MAISY bursts into tears again.

MRS HARDY (*Scolding her daughter.*) You? You started with him? You dragged me here with lies? I'll thrash you good and hard for this my girl. Bring me up here to make a fool of myself. Come on back with me I'll show you.

She pulls her daughter away with her, calling back as she goes.

But it won't go well for you either, old man, standing there saying nothing. You must be up to something

rotten standing there like a goblin. Something
not right's brewing in you that's for sure standing
there…

> *She's gone. MERVYN follows glowering at JOEL.*
> *The atmosphere settles.*

SEBASTIAN   (*Who's eating an apple.*) Well you must admit, it is
unnerving. I mean you can't settle, can you? You've
got to know who a person is.

MAVE   Why?

SEBASTIAN   You just have to. One way or another you've got to
know if someone's good or bad, if they're friendly or
dangerous, if you like them or you don't.

> *He's obviously worked up and not going to let matters*
> *rest.*

I'm going to do something.

MAVE   Like what?

SEBASTIAN   Don't know. Something to provoke him, get a
response.

MAVE   (*Calling to others.*) Here! Sebastian's plotting a hatch.

BLAKEY   Did she say plotting a hatch?

MAVE   Did I say plotting a hatch? I never did say plotting a
hatch. Did I say plotting a hatch?

> *Everyone, except JOEL, gathers round SEBASTIAN.*
> *They wait.*

HECTOR   Well?

> *SEBASTIAN is standing, uncertain, challenged, tossing*
> *his apple-core up and down in his hand as if to appear*
> *nonchalant.*

EVERYONE   Weeeeeeeelll?

> *Suddenly determined, SEBASTIAN pulls back his arm*
> *and throws the core at FATLIPS.*
>
> *As he does so the others gasp.*
>
> *FATLIPS, hit, whips round and stares furiously at*
> *SEBASTIAN who, isolated by the others, seems to freeze*
> *as if receiving some message from FATLIPS' eyes.*

The moment is held, electronic sounds, lights signifying its strangeness.

As it dies away, FATLIPS' look becomes a friendly caution. He turns to his gazing.

SEBASTIAN relaxes.

SEBASTIAN   That's better. Now I can get on with my life. Who's for a game of scrabble?

RUSTY   What's better?

SEBASTIAN   We know, don't we?

BLAKEY   Know what?

SEBASTIAN   A good man!

BLAKEY   But he looked furious enough to murder you.

RUSTY   I thought he was going to murder you.

SEBASTIAN   Well, he didn't murder me.

MAVE   Here, did I really say 'plotting a hatch'?

HECTOR   Well, even if he didn't murder you how did you know he was a good man?

SEBASTIAN   Well, he could've done.

HECTOR   And friendly?

SEBASTIAN   'Cos he could have gone off and complained about me.

BLAKEY   And he didn't.

SEBASTIAN   And he didn't.

HECTOR   So you like him.

MAVE   God! He's so logical. Here, I can't believe I said 'plotting a hatch'.

SEBASTIAN   Those eyes! They spoke! Told me there was nothing to worry about. He understood I needed to know. Now, that game of scrabble.

They all disperse to play their separate games.

MAVE   I'm sure I didn't say 'plotting a hatch'. You're all having me on, trying to make me think I'm going mad, like Joan Crawford in that film where Bette Davis is her sister, what's the name of it? Here, did you see that film where Bette Davis…

Peace.

Calm and pleasantness return.

Out of it JOEL approaches FATLIPS.

JOEL   My name is Joel, Joel Amersham. Do you mind if I stand with you, please?

FATLIPS merely nods. After a pause –

FATLIPS   Joel. Joel. That's Leoj backwards isn't it?

JOEL   That's right.

JOEL behaves as though he knows why FATLIPS has said this, and in fact from now on acts as though there's an unspoken affinity and understanding between them.

Music.

The sigh of a ship lifting in and out of waters.

YOUNGSTERS playing.

FATLIPS   Joel, you'd better go in now, there's a storm coming up.

JOEL   Alright. (*To the others.*) Fatlips says there's a storm coming up. We'd better go in.

The games cease. They unquestioningly go in.

JOEL moves to his family.

SCENE 2

Another part of the deck.

The FAMILY AMERSHAM are lounging – MR and MRS and daughter, SUSAN.

JOEL   Better come in now, there's a storm coming up.

MR AMERSHAM   Storm?

MR AMERSHAM looks around.

No sign of any clouds. Can't feel any heaving.

JOEL   Even so, it's coming.

MR AMERSHAM   And what makes you think that, skipper?

JOEL   Fatlips said so.

MRS AMERSHAM Fatlips?

JOEL The old man by the ship's prow.

MRS AMERSHAM You call him 'Fatlips'?

JOEL Everyone does.

SUSAN Does he know you call him Fatlips?

JOEL Of course.

SUSAN But he hasn't spoken to anybody.

MR AMERSHAM Except Captain Joel, here, and told him there's a storm coming up. Right?

JOEL Right! Come on, you lot. Let's get somewhere safe.

SUSAN But there's absolutely no sign of a storm.

MRS AMERSHAM That's because you've no sea-sense, Susan, you've no sea-legs like your young mariner brother.

JOEL (*With weary, adult-like patience.*) Oh well, patronize me if you like, don't believe me if you like, but if Fatlips –

MRS AMERSHAM Fatlips! Do you think he'd like to know you call him that?

JOEL I've told you, he does know.

SUSAN How do you know he knows if no ones spoken to him?

JOEL Because some people know things about each other without speaking.

MR AMERSHAM (*Suddenly pointing.*) Look!

Shadow of a dark cloud approaches.

The boat heaves.

Sounds of wind and hissing sea.

Good God! But how could the old man know?

SUSAN Perhaps he used to be a sailor, perhaps he can tell such things. Come on! Below deck!

The crackling of a huge storm is heard as people rush to and fro to safety.

Thunder and lightening. Glorious noise. A mixture of exhilarating fun and menace.

SCENE 3

Some days later.

A cross roads below deck.

MERVYN stands menacingly blocking the path of JOEL.

JOEL smiles, MERVYN glowers.

JOEL That was a thrilling storm the other night.

MERVYN Get lost!

JOEL I only said that was a pretty thrilling storm the other night.

MERVYN And I said 'get lost'.

JOEL Alright, I will.

> *He tries to get past. MERVYN blocks him. Leers.*

MERVYN Seems you didn't hear me. I said get lost.

JOEL (*In control.*) Seems you didn't hear me. I said 'alright, I will'. Now, may I get past, please?

> *JOEL's self-confidence irritates MERVYN even more.*

MERVYN Oh I know your sort. Your sort…your sort use words all the time, your sort just use words and words and words and words.

JOEL I'm really quite happy not to use words. Just let me pass and…

MERVYN Don't use words as me!

JOEL I'm not, I just…

MERVYN Don't, I said.

JOEL But…

MERVYN TAKE YOUR WORDS OFF ME I SAID. I KNOW YOUR SORT!

> *Unable to find his own words MERVYN uses a fist.*
>
> *Wham! A clenched, ringed fist straight in JOEL's left eye.*

JOEL Good God!

> *JOEL staggers but is more surprised than angry.*
>
> *MERVYN flees.*

SCENE 4

Prow of the upper deck.

FATLIPS is startled.

He moves to where the AMERSHAMS are lounging.

FATLIPS   I'm sorry, but your son's just been hit by the Hardy boy. He's alright, bleeding a little but I think you'd better go to him.

MR AMERSHAM   Did you see it happen?

FATLIPS   Er…no. I wasn't exactly…er…on the spot.

MR AMERSHAM   Then how do you know?

FATLIPS   Because some people know things about each other without speaking.

SUSAN   That's just what Joel said.

MRS AMERSHAM   (*Believing him at once, rises.*) We'll ask questions later. Come.

SCENE 5

Section of the AMERSHAM cabin below deck.

JOEL has made his way to the cabin and is sponging his cut.

The family arrive. They gasp. He grins.

JOEL   My first black eye, folks. Where's the champagne?

MRS AMERSHAM takes over sponging and ointmenting and laying on of Band-Aid.

SUSAN   Did you hit him back?

JOEL   Hit who back?

SUSAN   Mervyn Hardy.

JOEL is amazed. Looks at each of his family.

JOEL   But how did you know it was Mervyn Hardy who hit me? I've only just this minute come in. Straight from the bashing. I haven't told anyone. Not anyone.

A creepy moment. Cold shivers.

SUSAN (*Carefully.*) Because some people know things about each other without speaking.

JOEL Oh, Fatlips. Of course. That's alright then.

MR AMERSHAM I want a word with that man.

MRS AMERSHAM Don't be foolish, it's the Hardy family you must talk to first.

MR AMERSHAM But this Fatlips fellow is odd. I mean more than odd, he's strange.

SUSAN You mean more than 'strange', he's – sinister.

JOEL Fatlips isn't sinister, he just – connects.

MR AMERSHAM What does that mean? 'Connects'! 'Know things without speaking'! What rubbish is he putting into our children's heads?

MRS AMERSHAM The Hardys!

SCENE 6

Section of the HARDYS' cabin below deck.

Despite only a few days at sea it's already a slum.

AMERSHAMS knock. MERVYN answers, his cocky posture slumps to contrition as soon as he sees them – eyes to the ground, the air of a victim.

MR AMERSHAM Are you the boy?

MERVYN What you talking about?

MR AMERSHAM We want to speak to your parents.

MR HARDY What's all this about? Can't a family get privacy on this boat?

They are a family of victims.

MR AMERSHAM It seems your son hit our son for absolutely no reason at all, and your son's older and bigger than ours and we want to know what you're going to do about it.

MR HARDY Two lads scrapping? Who can do anything about that? What I say is if two lads scrap – leave them to it. No point everyone scrapping is there?

MRS AMERSHAM If that's what happened we might agree but it
didn't and we don't. Joel here did nothing.

> *MR HARDY attempts to close the door and be done
> with it.*

MR HARDY I'll sort it out, don't worry.

MR AMERSHAM (*Holding door open.*) That's not good enough. If
you don't do something about it now your son will
bully his way the rest of his life. (*To MERVYN.*) What
the hell made you hit him? He did nothing to you.
Nothing for God's sake.

> *MERVYN shuffles uncomfortably.*
>
> *Everyone waits for his answer.*

MR HARDY Well? Come on. What did you hit this lad for? He's
smaller'n you. Look at 'im. You must have 'it 'im
'ard. Look at that eye. And with that ring on. 'Ow
many times 'ave I told you to throw that bloody
old ring away? Well? Tell us. What did you 'it the
lad for?

MRS AMERSHAM Well?

SUSAN Well?

MRS HARDY Well?

MERVYN For fun!

SUSAN Fun? You give someone pain for fun? (*Pinches his
arm.*) Did you find that funny?

MRS HARDY No need for little revenges.

MR HARDY (*Weakly.*) He was honest at least.

MRS AMERSHAM Honest! To be honest about what should shame
him doesn't mitigate the guilt.

> *Too subtle for the HARDYS.*
>
> *FATLIPS' VOICE reaches out to the AMERSHAMS.*
>
> *As we hear it the light comes up on FATLIPS gazing
> out to sea.*

FATLIPS' VOICE Go. Leave them. They understand nothing. Go, go.
Leave them. A family of victims. They'll complain
about everything. It's never their fault. Leave
them. Go.

The AMERSHAMS leave, and climb to –

SCENE 7

– the prow of upper deck.

FATLIPS gazing out to sea.

FATLIPS (*To JOEL.*) It'll hurt for a bit. Sorry I couldn't prevent it.

JOEL That's alright. It's all experience, isn't it, Fatlips?

MRS AMERSHAM Joel! You mustn't call him that.

FATLIPS That's what I'm always called.

He smiles at them, his beautiful, haunting smile which creates lovely sound waves and bathes the AMERSHAM FAMILY in what seems like a revelatory light.

Each discovers something which they utter to themselves.

MR AMERSHAM I'm certain, now, making this move was the wisest decision I've ever made. (*Pause.*) What made me say that?

MRS AMERSHAM I want a third child. And it'll be a girl. I know it. (*Pause.*) What made me say that?

SUSAN I know – I know what I'm going to do with my life – become a doctor. (*Pause.*) What made me say that?

The moment passes.

MR AMERSHAM What a strange man you are Mr…er…can we have a talk together? Will you join us for a drink in our cabin? We're rather curious about you knowing how Joel had been struck the very moment he was struck.

Ominous music.

Lights fade.

SCENE 8

Lights up on section of AMERSHAM cabin.

Everyone seated around FATLIPS.

Storytime.

FATLIPS (*Taking out snuff box.*) Knew I'd have to explain
things on this trip. Worried in case there wouldn't
be anyone I liked. Snuff, anybody? (*No one accepts.*)
Mind you (*Sniffs.*) should have known…but then…
well… (*Sniffs.*) that's my problem.

> *Pauses to reflect on that problem. Sniffs again.*

Magic's going see. Fading. Can't do the things I used
to do. Sad.

> *Allows it to sink in, unaware he's saying anything
> unusual. So are the AMERSHAMS. He could be talking
> about his charm – which would just be odd.*
>
> *They exchange bemused looks.*
>
> *He continues.*

Sad, sad, sad! You ask me why I look so sad? Well,
that's it. Magic's leaving me. Evaporating. Oh dear!

> *It dawns on them he really does mean 'magic'.*

Yes, born with it. Powerful stuff. Want to know how I
first discovered it? Well, it was like this.

Dad was a miner in Wales, a place called Ystrad-
y-fadwg, and when I was seven there was a mining
disaster. They brought out one hundred and fifty-one
dead and sixty-seven injured. Gassed! And my father
was among the injured. I can remember my mother
weeping: 'They won't live, none of them, I've seen it
before.' And they shouldn't have lived, but they did,
and everyone thought it was a miracle, but it wasn't.
It was me.

> *He lets this sink in, too.*

You see, when my mother said 'They won't live', I
cried out 'I want them to! I want them.' Very natural,
a little boy crying over his dad. And when they did
live, I knew – it was me! No one else believed it but
I knew. I *knew*!

> *Takes a pinch of snuff.*

Well, from them on I just began making things
happen. Every disaster in the world that I got to
know about I saved people from. Not the dead ones,

of course, but soon ever I heard of a disaster – 'save the living!' I cried, and saved they were, even if they only had an ounce of life in them. Course, those I didn't get to hear about I couldn't save, but you name it I bet I saved someone from it.

JOEL   The Swiss avalanche disaster?

FATLIPS   Yes.

JOEL   The Indian famines?

FATLIPS   Those.

SUSAN   (*Despite feeling foolish for asking.*) The Mississippi floods?

FATLIPS   Missed those.

JOEL   (*Becoming more excited.*) The Titanic?

FATLIPS   Before my time.

MR AMERSHAM   (*With bitter, disbelieving sarcasm.*) And the last war? How did you fail to prevent that?

FATLIPS   (*An admonishing mixture of sadness and anger.*) I can't prevent men's madness I can only pick up the ruins.

> *Uncomfortable silence.*
>
> *All seem embarrassed except JOEL which worries MR AMERSHAM more.*
>
> *FATLIPS continues oblivious to their doubts. Sniffing his snuff.*

Of course, soon ever I discovered I had the power I was very worried. Everything happened as I wanted it to happen, look. Frightened me quite a bit I can tell you. When something had to be moved I just looked at it and it flew from one place to another. Once saw an old man struggling up a hill...

> *Light up on a corner of stage.*
>
> *An old man puffs his way up a hill. Stops. Breathes heavily, wheezing asthmatically, sits to rest, takes out cigarette, lights up, coughs, outs it, starts up hill again.*

Suddenly he feels a force lifting him. At first he's frightened, bewildered, resisting – until he finally begins to enjoy himself.

He's flying up the hill! His delight is comical.

When he lands he cries out:

OLD MAN I can fly! I can fly!

He walks around telling 'everyone' – the imagined villagers –

I can fly, I really can, honest, watch me.

He tries but can't.

His protestations become desperate.

I did fly! I did!

Desperation turns into urgency, and then into mumbling madness.

I did fly! I did! I flew! I was a bird, up there with the birds, flying, talking to them, flying, talking, flying…

It has moved from a comic moment into a chilling one.

FATLIPS That taught me. Not everyone can take help, you see. You need grace. Accepting help is a grace.

So I had to learn how to use my magic in a way that no one knew, in a way that didn't confuse them or put them under obligation. Dangerous thing, magic. Gave me many a sleepless night, I can tell you.

Sniffs snuff.

And then I began to get lonely. Surely, I thought, there must be others like me in this world? I can't be the only one who's blessed with this power. What's so special about me? I mean I'm not what you call an intellect. You should have seen the stupid things I did with it – picked piles of sweets off apple trees then couldn't eat them. And when I tried to give them away they accused me of stealing. Yes! Sounds easy, magic, but it isn't, believe me.

Sniffs.

Lonely. So I began to look. Now, how does one magic person look for another person of magic?

The AMERSHAMS are too absorbed either to reply or express incredulity.

I'll tell you.

From a distance, cooing, lovingly, a woman's voice calls:

AMULA'S VOICE Fatlips… Fatlips… Fatlips…

Music, sounds, ethereal light.

FATLIPS You know how a safe works, don't you? A dial, you have to turn, until each gap is filled by the right tooth. Right? Well, people of magic are like that.

Absent-minded pause, then –

You look confused? (*Pause.*) It's like – you go into a crowded room, someone comes up to you, starts talking. You wait to see what they're like, right? The sound of a voice, what they say, the look in their eyes. So-called vibrations. And if they fit, you reach for them – as a friend or a partner or a wife. Am I right? The same with us, only more complicated. Our vibrations must reach all over the world. Difficult. Never much good at it, me. Kept getting tangled with the radio waves. If your radio blew raspberries it was probably my vibrations crossing the lines.

JOEL giggles.

So it's taken me a long, long time to connect. In fact… (*He becomes dreamy.*)… it's taken me a lifetime. (*Beat.*) Till now. Till a month before this journey. (*Beat.*) On the very day I became sixty years of age – miracle! My vibrations connected. But also on that day something else happened.

Long, long pause.

He seems to forget the others are present.

Contact! Everything went click! After sixty years – a voice came through.

AMULA'S VOICE Fatlips, Fatlips. Can you hear me, Fatlips?

FATLIPS I can't describe how gentle and sweet that voice was. My name doesn't make a lovely sound but she could make it sound like the only name worth having in the entire wide world.

AMULA'S VOICE Fatlips, Fatlips! I've been trying to make connections with you for fifty years. You're the slowest magi-man ever. Your senses are blunt, your responses are dull, and you don't answer letters.

FATLIPS What was she talking about? What letters?

AMULA'S VOICE The others are fast, you're slow as mountains.

FATLIPS 'Slow as mountains'… It was love at first sound!

FATLIPS smiles, forcing the FAMILY to smile with him.

JOEL Tell us about Amula and why you didn't answer her letter.

MRS AMERSHAM Now, Joel, that's rude.

FATLIPS Not at all, not at all! To my mind a very reasonable request. Very reasonable indeed…yes…very…

He's rummaging around in his pockets for something.

Indeed, indeed… reasonable… very. Sort of question I'd have asked myself. Now where is it?

He draws from his pockets: money, orange peel, screwed-up paper, handkerchiefs, documents frayed and curled at the edges, a wallet with photographs, chewed pencils, jewellery – presents of rings, bracelets, necklaces, etc – some dead wild flowers, keys, seashells, a feather fan, empty snuff tins, a tie, a pack of cards, a penknife, postcards, and a tiny music box which plays.

All the time – talking.

'You don't answer my letters'. What letters? I'd not received any letters. None. And I asked her 'what letters you on about? I never had letters from a woman named Amula!'

All the FAMILY except JOEL are shocked. They look at him.

He and FATLIPS are oblivious to the FAMILY's horror.

SUSAN Joel knew. He knew her name. Joel knew her name was Amula. How? How? Mummy I'm frightened. How could he know?

JOEL Don't be frightened, Sue, I told you: some people know things about each other without speaking.

They calm her down. FATLIPS, besides, can't be stopped.

FATLIPS Letters! Letters! Letters! I hadn't received any let – and then! I remembered! Amula! When I was ten. A mad note. From a mere child. Thought it was one of my school-friends playing pranks. Now where is it?

Eccentric that he is, he's not really looking but instead is distracted into breathing upon and polishing bracelets, listening into the sea-shells, unscrewing pieces of paper.

Thought it was the girl next door, actually, a pink and cheeky thing she was – ah! Here it is.

He smooths out the most rumpled of his screwed-up sheets. It's a sheet from a school exercise book, torn and brown on the sides.

At the same time on a screen is projected the sheet, blank, waiting to be written upon. And indeed, the letter which YOUNG AMULA, now reads aloud is slowly writing itself out on the screen, we can even hear the sound of the pen scratching on paper.

AMULA's letter.

YOUNG AMULA'S VOICE I'm the best runna in my school. Win all the time. My mum says I mustn't do it becus it's not nachrul. But my dad says that's just what it is. Nachrul. And I must train becus one day I may be in big races. Mum says women musent run races. But I don't run races. I make words and music. When I

run the wind talks in voices and instaments. That's
how I met you. In the wind. Will you please rite to
me. I'm Amula and live at 27 shops road in gatehigh
which is nere the river spindel and my granee.

FATLIPS   There! What would you make of a letter like that? I
couldn't make nor head nor tail of it. Mystery! Who
wrote it? I asked around but everyone disowned
it. So I forgot it. Until about ten years later, when I
received this, this, this (*Looking.*) now, where's the
second letter, ah, no, yes, this!

> *Takes from his wallet a sheet of India paper folded
> four times.*

This. Very faded now of course, came from an island
in the Philippines. This. Just as mysterious. Just as
nutty! Totally, totally incomprehensible. I mean,
read it for yourself. You'll see. Read it, read it!

> *SUSAN takes it.*

> *In a corner of the stage is lit a young woman. She's
> on a bench. Between her legs is propped a cello. She's
> playing.*

> *Against the background of a beautiful piece of music
> for unaccompanied cello, her melodious, slightly sad,
> voice is heard reading the letter.*

AMULA'S VOICE   Well, now, aren't you the most difficult person
ever? Why didn't you answer that note ten years
ago? Whenever I ran races, I heard you on the
wind and tried talking back to you on the wind, but
nohow could I make you hear me. My parents have
moved out here now so I don't run many races,
except sometimes on the hard sands with the locals.
They're very fast, almost as fast as I am. My dad's
a government engineer and he's building a dam, so
we're here for five years at least.

Who can I marry here, I say to mum and dad,
here's the end of world for me. Maybe you'd
come, I thought. Oh, I do like your voice so. Do you
know they call me eccentric here, which I suppose
I am. Want to know why? Just because I sit on the

sands almost every evening and play the cello. By a special rock. It must look strange, when I think about it. But there's an old lady loves my playing. Lives about 2000 miles away. Lady called granny Lombe, with a thousand creases in her face. It was she persuaded me to learn an instrument in the first place. So I sit on the sands and play to her. Must go. Mother's coming. If she catches me she'll ask who am I writing to, she thinks she knows all the people I know, but of course she can't, can she? They don't do they? I'll write soon if I can't catch you on the wind.

The AMERSHAMS are spell-bound.

SUSAN (*Softly, sheepishly.*) There's no signature.

FATLIPS Right! No signature! No address! And I was supposed to know who it was from. Racked my head till it nearly burst. And then – I remembered. The first note! I'd kept it! Amula! It was her. But who was she? And why didn't she write to me again, as she'd said she would? Mystery! And as time passed, I forgot her. Forgot all about her. Until that day when everything went 'click' and that voice came through, that buzzing, that lullaby.

Sounds. Music.

And from then on we talked and talked and I heard all that had happened to her. You want to hear? I'll tell you then. I'll tell you…

Sounds and music grow.

Fade lights.

END OF ACT ONE.

Act Two

SCENE 1

Before curtain up – music.

FATLIPS' VOICE Amula! It was her! But who was she? And why
didn't she write to me again as she said she would?
Mystery! And as time passed, I forgot her. Forgot
all about her. Until that day when everything went
'click' and that voice came through, that buzzing,
that lullaby…

AMULA'S VOICE I'm old now, Fatlips. Old and tired. It's been a hard
life, magic or no magic. Only your voice kept me
going, even made me laugh sometimes. Shall I tell
you how I've spent these years? I know how you've
spent yours cos I've heard you plotting and cursing
and laughing your way through yours. But try all I
could, I could never make my vibrations connect.
Well now…

> *Curtain up on the veranda and part of a kitchen in a
> house in the Philippines.*
>
> *A MAN is just returning from work. His wife, tired
> and weary of him, is bringing him food, attending his
> needs. He's ill-tempered. She is AMULA.*

…you last heard from me when I wrote to you from
the islands. I was twenty then. Full of hope that
you'd hear me. But you didn't, so I married a man
who worked as assistant to my father. Kind to begin
with but he guessed there was no love, and without
love kindness turns sour.

The first years were a disaster. And to make them
worse and almost unbearable, my parents died of a
tropical fever for which there was no vaccine. My
poor, beloved parents… Once I was so miserable
that I made time move fast, and in an hour a year
was gone!

*Extraordinary things happen on the stage – probably
with the air of strobe lighting – to show a year passing
in a moment.*

*Furniture, crockery, ornaments are exchanged or move
position. It makes the man ill and he must take to
his bed.*

AMULA'S VOICE Only I'd forgotten to change the time perceptions
of my husband so he felt the year go quickly. Made
him ill for six weeks, and then my real problems
started…

HUSBAND What's happened? Why do I feel so ill? Why do
I feel the earth's spun round the sun so fast it's
made me giddy and sick and all churned up. Did
the rains come? And where has the summer gone?
And (*Looking at certain objects in the room.*) was that
there a minute ago? Or that? And didn't I shave this
morning? And wasn't I thinking different things?
And why do I feel I know a lot more but can't work
out what? And why am I agitated while you're still
calm as if you know something I don't? Eh? Why,
why, WHY?

No answer.

Witch! You're a witch. That's what you are a witch!

AMULA It'll never get better, will it?

*At which she goes 'through' the door and immediately
flies up, hovering out of his sight.*

*Her HUSBAND comes out of the door looking for her.
He can see no one and looks utterly astonished.*

HUSBAND Witch! Witch! Witch!

SCENE 2

AMULA is flying. Landscapes pass by.

As we hear her voice recounting, so it is enacted.

*We will need all our resources of 'stage-magic' to match her
magic!*

AMULA'S VOICE For once he was right. I'd rarely used my magic, but this time I had to. And there I was, a witch in space, too miserable to care where I was going, but staying up there, with clouds and stars and winds, for weeks, drawing my food to me: fruits and nuts off the trees, the fresh corn from the fields, and even warm milk, straight from poor old startled cows who knew they were being milked but couldn't see the milker.

And I cared for nothing in the world. Until one day, after seven weeks of drifting from country to country, I realised – I had a baby in me. Now that was a serious business. I couldn't be floating around in space in that condition, could I? But what was I to do? Where was I to go? Oh well, I thought, what does it matter, I'll just drop here, where I am. Which I did. And I landed on a strange island called Tamak.

SCENE 3

The island and its inhabitants came into view.
It is, and they are, as she describes.

AMULA'S VOICE At least, that's what the islanders called it, I don't know what the map-makers called it. And weren't they a very strange people indeed: primitive, innocent, with terra-cotta coloured skin. Of course my appearance, so sudden coming among them, made them think I was God. Foolish, but understandable. We have some powers but none of us are God-like? Though I bet you've met some magi-men who because they can disappear now and then or heal a boil or two imagine they can do anything.

> *The ISLANDERS gather round her. Touch her, seem in awe of her.*
>
> *An old woman, ALUMA, appears from among them. She seems to be bullying, goading them into simply staying alive.*

ALUMA   Alright! Enough staring and touching and prodding, you'll bruise her to death. She's nothing special, just a visitor, though to compare your faces to her's you'd think she was special. Look at you all! You've got faces like worn-out leather and you walk around like used-up cart horses! (*To a WOMAN.*) You there, Lydica, your child's wandering by the sea-shore, look after her.

LYDICA   Why? Just tell me why?

ALUMA   She'll drown, that's why.

LYDICA   There's others there.

ALUMA   She's your responsibility.

LYDICA   She'll be alright.

ALUMA   Do as I say or I'll report you to the council.

> *LYDICA goes off reluctantly.*
>
> *ALUMA turns to another.*

You, are you Caliman?

CALIMAN   Can't you tell? I'm the only one's got blue eyes.

ALUMA   Your eyes are closed so much of the time I can't tell who's who.

CALIMAN   Well? And now that I've told you?

ALUMA   Your hut, it's falling down. Aren't you ashamed?

CALIMAN   Why? Everything's falling down.

ALUMA   All the more reason to repair it.

CALIMAN   What's the use!

ALUMA   Your family needs shelter, that's the use.

CALIMAN   Family? Have I got a family? I don't remember having a family.

ALUMA   You're as dozy as a donkey! Go home and repair your house or old as I am I'll beat you with this stick.

> *CALIMAN goes off.*
>
> *ALUMA descends on a GROUP OF THREE.*

And you lot, why aren't you helping to bring in the crops?

1ST ISLANDER   What crops?

ALUMA   The maize and the rice I forced you to plant like I have to force you to do everything.

1ST ISLANDER   You call them crops?

2ND ISLANDER   They're not worth gathering.

1ST ISLANDER   We'll use up more energy than they can replace.

ALUMA   You'll all end up rooted to the ground. You never move.

2ND ISLANDER   Yes we do.

ALUMA   Like glue!

3RD ISLANDER   I moved yesterday. From here to there!

4TH ISLANDER   And I move my arms. Look! (*A small movement.*)

ALUMA   Slothmongers! You'll become crops yourselves, for the crows! And then corpses for the vultures. Move I tell you, to the fields, move and gather the paltry harvest that's left to this miserable community, move! or I'll see your rations of food are halved. All of you! Everyone of you! Sow your seeds, look to your cattle, tend to your children, repair your houses! Your joints will rust – every damn one of you! Move! Move! Move!

> *They do so.*
>
> *She notices AMULA.*
>
> *The old and the young confront each other. It's a strange, moving moment, as always when the 'same ones' meet.*

ALUMA   Amula, at last! I've got you here, and just in time. Welcome!

> *They embrace.*

AMULA   I feel sadness in the air? Why have you brought me here?

ALUMA   There's a great despair on this island. Everyone wants to die.

AMULA   Why is everything happening in slow motion?

AMULA   It struck. One day. Like a curse.

ALUMA What struck?

ALUMA The disease of Tamak – lethargy!

AMULA Lethargy?

ALUMA That's why everyone looks ugly.

AMULA How, when, who brought it, from where?

ALUMA All in good time. You'll understand everything in good time. But just now I must show an example. Every day I select a task that's normally too much for an old woman, trying to shame them. And now, there's that roof.

> *At that moment a young boy, LEOJ, unlike the others in that he's got an energy they've lost, comes running on with a ladder. He places it by a hut. The old woman climbs up and begins to thatch a roof.*

LEOJ (*To AMULA.*) Hello, you're Amula and my name's Leoj.

AMULA Leoj? That's Joel backwards isn't it?

> *It's another strange confrontation as the 'same ones' meet.*
>
> *When the moment passes AMULA sits watching as the boy stands by the ladder…*
>
> *Music…*
>
> *Time passes. A day, we feel.*
>
> *The old lady, very tired, descends and the boy climbs up to take over.*
>
> *The old lady is ill from over-strain. She directs AMULA to take her to her hut where AMULA cares for her – cushioning her, covering her with blankets, mopping her brow, offering her drink, humming – while LEOJ thatches and more time passes.*
>
> *She is recovering.*

ALUMA Lethargy is an illness of the soul. Not physical. The soul. Anything can bring it on – fear, ignorance, heartache, frustration, or all of them!

AMULA Don't upset yourself.

ALUMA Terrible disease.

AMULA   Rest, rest.

ALUMA   If I rest, this island comes to a standstill.

AMULA   If you don't rest you'll come to a standstill.

ALUMA   I'm rested, rested! I'm so rested I'm like a plum pudding.

AMULA   You don't look ready to eat to me.

> *They exchange smiles.*

> Now tell me – what's caused the lethargy?

ALUMA   I'll tell you in time. Patience.

AMULA   I can't help if I don't know the cause.

ALUMA   Patience. I must attend to things.

AMULA   But you're ill.

ALUMA   I'm ill and shrill, feverish and liverish, anxious and bumptious…

LEOJ   (*From the roof.*) …and urging and scourging, and ailing and wailing, and cadaverous and sulphurous…

ALUMA   There's someone who's enjoying himself at least. My prop and cop, my friend and mend…

LEOJ   Your eyes and ears, your smiles and tears…

AMULA   …while I doubt and shout and seem left out!

ALUMA   Patience! Everything will make sense in time. See – I'm better now. Thank you for your care.

> *She rises, helped by AMULA, and leaves.*

> *AMULA moves outside the hut. She's very heavy with pregnancy. She sits down to sleep.*

> *Time passes.*

> *She's woken by the activity of LEOJ who is erecting what seems to be a wind shield.*

AMULA   Is a heavy wind expected?

LEOJ   It's not a wind shield, Amula, it's a sun shield.

AMULA   A sun shield? But there's no need for one, I can go in doors, or sit in the shade somewhere. Besides, it's not such a hot sun, I've lived in worse.

LEOJ   You'll see.

He leaves her.

Slowly we are aware of a light growing, one that seems to rock with heat as it swells and fills the stage.

AMULA realises that her shield is not simply a cover but a deflector. It's constructed on a pole, like a sail, and she can turn it round as the sun moves.

This she does, her anxiety growing as now a low moan of many people is added to the scene. The sound is one of helpless effort accompanied by defeat, as if the work being done is known to be doomed.

The stage is filled with activity. In the centre are ALUMA and LEOJ, urging everyone to a certain activity.

ALUMA   No idlers! Everyone to the dam! Any child who can lift a stone – to the dam! Close all schools, all shops, leave beds unmade, the floors unswept…

LEOJ   … Everyone move…

ALUMA   … The sun's never been so hot…

LEOJ   … Everyone move! Move!

ALUMA   You want water to drink?

LEOJ   Move!

ALUMA   You want water for crops?

LEOJ   Move! You want water to keep clean?

ALUMA   Move!

> *ALUMA approaches a bewildered AMULA.*

Now is the time for you to help us.

AMULA   But I still don't understand.

ALUMA   Look!

> *She draws her to a high point from which they look down, back of stage.*

AMULA   The river. Where we all bathe.

ALUMA   Look at the water. Look how quickly it's drying up.

AMULA   My God! I've never seen a river sink so swiftly. But what is everyone doing?

ALUMA   They're building a dam.

AMULA   But that's not the way to build a dam. The water
         will seep through. I've watched my father build
         them. And besides – that's not what they should be
         doing at all! Oh! This is terrible! Now I understand.
         Drought!

ALUMA   Every summer.

LEOJ   And each summer gets worse.

ALUMA   And they try to prevent the river from running away.

LEOJ   But they can't, and each year they save less and less.

ALUMA   And each year more crops wither, cattle and people
         die.

LEOJ   And they can't think what to do.

ALUMA   Their confidence runs away with the river.

AMULA   But with your powers?

ALUMA   Too old! The magic goes when you're old.

AMULA   But Leoj? He's one of us.

LEOJ   I wanted to use my magic but Aluma explained
         – magic will bring water but not self-confidence.
         Something must happen which they've done by
         themselves.

AMULA   Well a dam is not what they should be building.
         They haven't the resources, it's too late, and it's the
         wrong structure, besides. In fact anything's too late
         for this year.

ALUMA   But next year? Can the slothmongers do something
         for next year?

         AMULA hesitates.

         All wait on her words.

AMULA   A reservoir.

ALUMA   Of course.

LEOJ   Digging a hole is easier!

AMULA   Easier than building a water-tight wall.

ALUMA   (*Delightedly chanting.*)

         Digging a hole is easier, easier, easier

         Than building a water-tight wall

Both shout down to the ISLANDERS.

LEOJ A hole!

ALUMA A hole!

LEOJ A hole, hole, hooooole.

The groaning from below stops. Silence.

Everything, except the heat, seems to stop. The new idea sinks into them slowly.

1ST ISLANDER A hole!

2ND ISLANDER A hole!

3RD ISLANDER A hole!

Soon everyone is shouting and chanting.

OTHERS A hole! A reservoir! Of course!

Digging a hole is easier, easier, easier

Than building a water-tight wall!

Digging a hole is easier, easier, easier

Than building a water-tight wall!

Digging a hole is easier, easier, easier

Than building a water-tight wall!

Once more the stage is a flurry of activity, but with a new kind of energy.

ALUMA (*To AMULA.*) Will you go down and direct them?

AMULA I'm very pregnant you know.

But nothing will stop the old lady.

She beckons to some TAMAKIANS who joyfully lift AMULA and, to cheers, take her down to the river, chanting:

ISLANDERS Digging a hole is easier, easier, easier

Than building a water-tight wall!

Digging a hole is easier, easier, easier

Than building a water-tight wall!

Digging a hole is easier, easier, easier

Than building a water-tight wall!

Now director, designer, and actor must engage their powers of invention even more.

The TAMAKIANS must be shown thinking for themselves. A process needs to be worked out which shows us how they attempt certain actions which they discover can be executed in a simpler way.

A structural device should be assembled on the stage – a pulley system, a truck, something they ingeniously construct which represents their release of imagination and a new found energy.

Great excitement.

As they work, AMULA starts up the encouraging cry:

AMULA Build, my darlings, build!

The cry is picked up by ALUMA.

ALUMA Build, my darlings, build!

Then by LEOJ.

LEOJ Build, my darlings, build!

One by one the cry is picked up by each of the ISLANDERS – it could be a musical chant, or a magnificent hymn specially composed.

At the instant of their success, when the 'engine' is constructed, they turn and show us new faces; till then their frozen look has been that of their masks.

The moment of whipping off masks should be the stunning peak of all the previous theatrical moments.

During the activity we hear AMULA's voice.

AMULA'S VOICE It was thrilling, Fatlips, thrilling. Away went lethargy, away went defeat, peeling off them, like bad skin, falling away from them with their sweat.

As the weeks went by even the little children began to help, forming long chains to shift stones. And I taught them many things, things I didn't realise I knew. Didn't know I'd learned! About leverage and pulley systems, patterns of irrigation, methods of propping up walls. Everything came in useful. And if there was something I'd only half remembered then they'd work out the rest for themselves.

And more – they invented! Invented and improvised and seemed spilling over with ideas of their own for storing and building and cutting down wasted energy.

And I gave them not one bit of magic. Not a jot! I was so happy, can't you imagine it? A whole island coming alive again. It was like discovering a new land. New faces in a new land and you know what else? I gave birth…

> *In the midst of their activity AMULA screams. Birth pains.*
>
> *The ISLANDERS gather round. They cry encouraging sounds at her.*
>
> *'A birth' is enacted and becomes a symbolic birth for them all.*
>
> *The baby's scream coincides with the completion of the construction.*
>
> *Music, sounds and hoorays bring a –*
>
> *FINALE to the second act.*
>
> *Ideally we should be able to 'MIX' immediately into the third act.*

Act Three

The AMERSHAM's cabin.

FATLIPS And there she stayed, lived with one of the islanders. A man called Spiltaf, and had nine children and then –

> *The family lean forward to catch what happened next.*
>
> *FATLIPS enters a reverie in which he absentmindedly sniffs at his snuff.*

SUSAN And then?

FATLIPS And then she left. Like that. As suddenly as she came, as though she'd simply dropped in for a chat. Thirty years later.

> *He drifts into reverie again, mumbling to himself.*

Thirty years later! Thirty!

> *FATLIPS begins to rummage around again in his pockets, and among the things he'd strewn on the table.*
>
> *MR AMERSHAM takes this opportunity of whispering to the rest of the family, except JOEL whose attention is constantly glued to FATLIPS.*

MR AMERSHAM What a lovely madness this old man has.

MRS AMERSHAM Lovely madness? You think that?

MR AMERSHAM But one to be envied, perhaps, not laughed at.

SUSAN Do you mean, dad, that none of his story is true.

MR AMERSHAM Susan – an intelligent girl like you.

SUSAN But Joel believes every word. Look at him? Doesn't doubt a thing.

MR AMERSHAM And it's about him I'm really worried. We must hear the story through to the end and I want no one to contradict it, or show they don't believe it, or we'll have a very distressed and bewildered boy on our hands.

SUSAN But all those things he knew.

MRS AMERSHAM Only a few things and they can be explained away as a simple kind of telepathy.

MR AMERSHAM The old man has excited Joel's imagination over the last few days and I think he's a little feverish…

SUSAN …and liverish, and pale and frail…

MRS AMERSHAM …or oblivious and delirious…

They giggle.

SUSAN You're amused and confused.

MR AMERSHAM You're both sheepish and foolish.

SUSAN While you're distraught and caught – ha!

MR AMERSHAM Stop this. This is – madness.

MRS AMERSHAM Oh dear. I think rhymes like these are a bit of a disease.

MR AMERSHAM Enough!

SUSAN You mean freeze! Ooops!

MR AMERSHAM We'll indulge them but we must not indulge ourselves.

FATLIPS has found another piece of paper.

FATLIPS Ah, here it is.

Over the upper deck we see night coming on, a moon rising, stars appear – all happening while we hear old AMULA'S VOICE, a cello background.

OLD AMULA'S VOICE Oh, dear Fatlips, the mistakes we make. I chose the man who seemed both the gentlest and the hardest worker on the reservoir. But… I don't know…everything about him just didn't go the right way. Not even his name – Spiltaf. A kind man, but then, what's kindness without love?

So I've got a few more years left and this time I'm really going to find the man I love and live the life I've always wanted.

FATLIPS   Which she did! She found me. Old me. Doddery,
          dithery, old Fatlips.

          Sinks into reverie.

          We're going to marry! And that's where I'm off
          to. She lives in this so-called new land. Newland!
          Newland! I don't know why everyone calls it that.
          Whatever you read, whatever you see, even on the
          telly – the Newland! Huh! What's ever new about
          anything!

JOEL   (*Reminding him.*) But something else happened.
          You've forgotten to tell us what.

FATLIPS   (*Surprised, remembering.*) Oh yes. Well. See this?

          He points to a scar on his face.

          Don't laugh, but usually I don't bother to open
          doors, no! Just walk through them. Not when
          anyone's around, mind, but – oh, it just became a
          habit.

          And so, on the day I first heard Amula, I was
          so happy and absorbed talking to her – you can
          imagine we had a lot to talk about – that I didn't
          think and I walked straight through the glass doors
          of Sainsbury's. Yes! Getting my weekly groceries
          I was. Straight through! Only it didn't work. I
          just walked through glass. Cut myself to pieces.
          Shocked me I can tell you. Lost contact with Amula
          immediately. Whooosh! Like that! What was it, I
          wondered? And then I tried to disappear – which
          I do sometimes, though not often, because actually
          I've always liked living as normal a life as I can,
          walking through streets instead of flying....

JOEL   Flying? Flying? You can really fly?

FATLIPS   Course I can fly – didn't do it much because I like
          buses and trains and boats and being with people.
          But the point of this whole story is – it stopped. I
          couldn't walk through the door, I couldn't disappear,
          I couldn't fly and worst of all I lost contact with
          Amula. That was when I understood the magic was

going. On the day I became sixty and fell in love, my magic began to fade. Ironic, isn't it?

> *He sniffs snuff.*

And I'm so sad. Sad, sad, sad.

> *A long, awkward silence.*
>
> *All except JOEL are now convinced the old man in deranged.*
>
> *Suddenly –*

JOEL Could you make me fly?

MR AMERSHAM (*Snapping.*) Joel!

FATLIPS Fly? You? Maybe. A little. (*Conspiratorially.*) Want to try?

JOEL Do I want to try…oh…oh yes!

FATLIPS Come on, then. It's getting stuffy in here, besides. My story's eaten up all the oxygen.

> *He and JOEL leave the cabin for the upper deck.*

MRS AMERSHAM Aren't you going to stop him?

MR AMERSHAM What's the point? We must see it through to the end now.

MRS AMERSHAM But Joel won't fly and he'll be disappointed and I'm very worried about his fever.

MR AMERSHAM First of all Joel's a sensible boy. Secondly, if Fatlips – when Fatlips fails to make him fly he's got a perfect alibi: his magic is gone! Convenient! And Joel will accept it.

SUSAN But supposing a little of the magic trickles back?

> *Her parents regard her with exasperation.*

MR AMERSHAM The fever's reaching you, as well.

SUSAN I only said 'supposing'.

> *All leave.*

SCENE 2

The upper deck.

FATLIPS Now, start here, run, and after a few steps – leap!
And when you come down keep running and then
– another leap. And then again. Run, leap, run, leap.
Like in those dreams. Ever had those flying dreams?

JOEL shakes his head.

You haven't? Well, you've really got something
coming to you. Lovely dream, those are. Flying
dreams. Beautiful. Now off you go.

JOEL does it once. Fails.

JOEL I feel silly.

MR AMERSHAM Of course you do.

*He turns to address FATLIPS with all the authority
he can muster.*

Now – I wish I knew your real surname because
to be frank, well, I feel rather foolish calling you
'Fatlips'. Seems undignified. After all, you're elderly
and I'd like to show respect, but in any case, Mr…
er…

FATLIPS Harrington.

MR AMERSHAM Mr Harrington. I really think the children have had
enough for one day and your stories, well, they're
fascinating, held me completely, don't think we've
ever met a body like you before and I'm sure my
family will agree, but….

SUSAN (*Amazed.*) Oh, Dad. Look!

*During this last exchange FATLIPS had not been
listening to MR AMERSHAM but had strained in great
concentration. So hard that it brought MR AMERSHAM
to cease his flow and he had turned to where SUSAN
was pointing.*

FATLIPS (*Urgently hissing.*) Push! Push! Run, leap, and push!

JOEL had been doing just this and now, with each leap, he is rising higher and higher until, at last, he's airborne.

They watch for a while listening to JOEL's ecstatic cries.

JOEL Oh! Oh! I'm flying. I'm up here flying.

A moment for music...

...till MR AMERSHAM can bear it no longer. He draws FATLIPS aside whispering to him frantically.

MR AMERSHAM Please, please! Bring him down. They're not his own wings. He must have his own wings. Please bring him down. And then make us all forget.

JOEL descends.

A strange moment while memory is erased.

A clock strikes midnight.

The moonlight is eerie.

JOEL Pity. I almost did it.

FATLIPS As I told you, dear boy, magic's gone. Evaporated. I'll have to find my Amula without it, won't I? Ah well, all things must pass. Goodnight. Sleep deep.

JOEL And tight, with peace...

FATLIPS ...and ease. Stay warm...

JOEL ...till dawn.

FATLIPS While I yearn for her return.

JOEL Goodnight.

Their little game over, they smile at one another.

The 'light' glows between them. JOEL has become one of the 'same ones'.

The family descend below deck.

FATLIPS takes up the position where we first encountered him. He waves to them before they go into their cabin.

FATLIPS (*To himself.*) Yes, yes. All things must pass.

The light fades and fades to a small pool on his face, and then – out.

CURTAIN

DENIAL

A play in one act and 21 scenes

Characters

MATTHEW YOUNG
retired businessman. 58 – 60

KAREN YOUNG
his wife, business partner. 55 – 57

JENNY YOUNG
their first daughter. 30 – 32

ABIGAIL YOUNG
their second daughter. 28 – 30

VALERIE MORGAN
a social worker turned therapist. 50s

SANDY CORNWALL
journalist specialising in child abuse cases. 40s

ZIGGY LANDSMAN
friend of KAREN's father. 80s

SETTINGS

– Four.

The YOUNG's lounge

VALERIE's bleak consulting room

SANDY's chaotic den

ZIGGY's study

TIME

Non-sequential.

Apart from the opening film of childhood the play is a mosaic of scenes within a two-year-plus span, but not in sequence.

The film director, Jean-Luc Godard, when asked did he believe a story should have a beginning, middle, and an end replied: yes, but not necessarily in that order.

Denial, had its world premiere at The Bristol Old Vic 16 May 2000 with the following cast

JENNY, Nichola Barber
KAREN, Rosemary McHale
MATTHEW, Jeremy Child
ABIGAIL, Dido Miles
ZIGGY, Bill Wallis
VALERIE, Susan Tracy
SANDY, Ellie Haddington

Director Andy Hay
Set and Costume Designer Tom Piper
Music John O'Hara
Lighting Design Tim Streader
Sound Jason Barnes

I gratefully acknowledge financial assistance during the writing of this play from both 'The Arts Council of England' and 'The Author's Foundation'.

And I'm indebted to Richard Holmes for the title.

SCENE 1

A screen.

Projected upon it is a home movie of a father and daughter aged about five. It seems to be a record of love, delight, innocence.

But – are they halcyon days?

A garden. He is dancing with her in his arms. She leans back; he swings her round and round.

A WOMAN'S VOICE in the background. 'Stop that, Matthew. You'll make her sick'.

When she returns upright he buries his mouth into her neck, and blows loud raspberries. She shrieks with delight, pushes him away.

They drop to the ground. On all fours he plays 'dog'. She crawls away. He grabs her leg. Bites her bum. She turns over. He goes for her belly with his nose.

Growls! Laughter! Shrieks!

Freeze.

BLACK OUT.

SCENE 2

Twenty-four years later.

The shrill voice of the daughter, JENNY, leaving a message on the telephone answer machine.

Her delivery is fast, manic.

JENNY'S VOICE This message is for you, Matthew, father, Matthew fucking father, to let you know that I know, I know, I now know that the man who calls himself my father Matthew fucking father was so fucking fatherly and loving that he loved me like a lover. Like a fucking lover. Ha! Does that make you smile, pet? A fucking lover?

You raped me, Matthew, father, Matthew fucking father, you raped me and then tried to give *me* the responsibility of *your* shame. Well fuck you! I'm not going to take it any longer because it's yours you fucker, you rapist of children.

Remember what you used to do to me? Shall I remind you? When I was two and you were reading stories to me at night you'd get into bed with me and use your fucking fingers wouldn't you? And it really used to hurt, it used to hurt so fucking much you bastard, you.

And then when I was four you took me to that fucking meeting where you watched, you and granddad, you stood at the back, didn't you, you stood at the back watching other men bugger me? I fucking hate you, Matthew, father, Matthew fucking father, for everything you've done to me.

But I'm over it. I'm over it and I'm never ever gonna let you get away with it. So don't ever write to me again, you stupid bastard, and don't ever ever come near your grandchildren again. They're *not* your grandchildren. You *have* no grandchildren. No grandchildren, no daughter, nothing. Guilt and shame, that's what you've got. And that's all, Matthew, father, Matthew fucking father. I'm never ever ever going to forgive you. For anything! Nothing!

SCENE 3

ZIGGY LANDSMAN's study.

An old man, old friend of KAREN's father.

ZIGGY and KAREN. He's there to listen.

KAREN   I've seen her, Ziggy. I needed to see her. It was an ache.

My plan is to catch her as she's taking the children to school. Quarter past eight in the morning. I drive there and wait. I have this pain in me, this pain, here, I have it from the moment I get up – not that I slept, you can imagine. And she comes out of the

door with them, sees me, and – I can understand
this – she gives a scream: 'ahhhh!' I say 'I'm sorry,
Jenny, I didn't mean to frighten you'. 'What are *you*
doing here?' she asks, a bit roughly, so it hurts. And
I tell her 'You must forgive me, Jenny, but this mum,
this mum who loves and misses her daughter had to
come and see her.'

And that's all I was going to say. I said it, touched
her, and turned to walk away. 'I'm taking the
children to school,' she says, 'why don't you get in
the car?' I can't believe my ears. She wants me to
stay with her? So, I get in the car like it's the most
natural thing in the world, and we drive the children
to school with me asking them simple questions
about their teacher and how they're getting on,
and do they like reading – nothing too demanding,
nothing too emotional.

And then I'm left in the car with her. And I'm silent.
Waiting for her. Finally she says: 'Well, you haven't
said anything about how I look.' That mass of
chestnut hair, remember it? Gone! She'd cut it down
to a crew cut. Shocking. But all I say is: 'Oh, your
new hairstyle…'well' I say, 'you've got a beautiful
face so it doesn't matter what hairstyle you have.'
'Yes' she says, 'that's what most people say. It gives
me freedom,' she says. So I say to her, gentle as ever
I could: 'You know, Jenny, freedom doesn't come
with a haircut.' She says nothing.

After a while she begins spouting at me. Her jargon:
'people have to get in touch with their anger, their
inner child…abused children have been robbed
of their childhood…' That sort of thing. And I let
her go on, and I'm thinking all the time of that
childhood, that wonderful childhood, that time of
parties and friends all over the place, and holidays
here, there, and everywhere. And I think 'robbed'?
Funny word.

For two hours I sat in that car, listening, till I think
to myself now it's my turn. And I begin. 'Jenny,' I

begin, 'when you were running the new-age shop your favourite cousin came to see you with her children that you'd never seen – why couldn't you speak with her?' She doesn't answer. 'Jenny,' I say, 'your sister, Abigail, she could never be bothered to celebrate her birthdays, you always organised them *for* her – you loved her. Why have you broken contact?' She doesn't answer. 'Your grandfather, Jenny, you adored him. He's ill, he asks after you, phone him – what will it cost you?' She doesn't answer. 'And me,' I say to her, 'think about *me*, think of the kind of mother *I* was – would I ever have allowed anything in my home? Remember,' I tell her, 'you only get one mother. That's all you get, just one. Think about it.' 'I will,' she says. 'I'll talk to my therapist and think about it. Perhaps' she says, 'we can all meet together'. 'That would be wonderful, Jenny, I say.' 'I'm not promising,' she says. 'No promises.'

Freedom? She can't do anything without this therapist knowing. She shaves her head and chains herself to a therapist. Funny freedom. It makes sense to you?

And as I leave, this terrible pain, here, it's in me, a tightening. I can hardly get to my car.

SCENE 4

The YOUNG's lounge.

MATTHEW in a state of shock and misery.

His wife, KAREN, watching, weighing the words we've just heard, and their impact upon him.

Their younger daughter, ABIGAIL, watching both.

MATTHEW   Why? It's the 'why' I can't understand. I can't understand the 'why'.

KAREN   Matthew, I must ask –

MATTHEW   No. The answer's no.

KAREN   Anything?

MATTHEW   Nothing. Not even the smallest thing.

KAREN   Some gesture that could be misunderstood?

MATTHEW   What can't be misunderstood? Given a touch of envy, ill-will, an inferiority complex – everything can be misunderstood.

KAREN   There must be a reason.

MATTHEW   How can you ask?

KAREN   Think!

MATTHEW   You think. You were around all the time.

KAREN   Not all the time.

MATTHEW   All the crucial times. (*Realising.*) You don't believe me, do you?

KAREN   She's my daughter –

MATTHEW   And I'm her father –

KAREN   Fathers are different –

MATTHEW   – my joy, my hope, my pride –

KAREN   – fraught with dangers, tensions –

MATTHEW   – not a hair, not a blemish –

KAREN   – conflicting messages.

MATTHEW   – not the tiniest harm.

> *Silence.*

You don't believe me.

> *Silence.*

Karen, she talks of meetings. Did you know me go missing to 'meetings'?

> *Silence.*

Your father, Karen, she talks of him watching men bugger her. Your father!

> *Silence.*

And me, would I have stood by to watch even a hair on her head harmed?

> *Silence.*

I would have thrown myself on guns to protect her.

> *Silence.*

I can see it. You don't believe me. You believe there's no smoke without fire.

> *Silence.*

If my wife…

And my younger daughter? (*Beat.*) Abigail?

> *ABIGAIL says nothing.*

God help me.

SCENE 5

ZIGGY's study.

KAREN has fled to him.

They are listening to the end of the tape.

JENNY'S VOICE   …You have no grandchildren. No grandchildren, no daughter, nothing. Guilt and shame, that's what you've got. And that's all, Matthew, father, Matthew fucking father. I'm not ever, ever, ever going to forgive you. For anything! Nothing!

> *Stupefied silence.*

KAREN   Has that voice got anything to do with us?

ZIGGY   Go back to him, Karen.

KAREN   Can you feel that voice has anything to do with us?

ZIGGY   It's not a voice you can trust, go back to Matthew.

KAREN   Who is she? I don't know who she is? Do you know who she is?

ZIGGY   A time like this you need one another.

KAREN   'Get in touch with your anger,' they tell her. 'Anger's the backbone of healing.' My mother was an angry woman, the only thing it did for her was give her cancer.

> *Silence.*

Ziggy, you were in the camps with my father.

ZIGGY   So?

KAREN   You don't like talking about it, I know…

ZIGGY   So?

KAREN   Is there…is it possible…stress…children…memories you've repressed?

ZIGGY   I've tried. I can't. Not even one of them.

KAREN   I'm sorry. I shouldn't have asked.

ZIGGY   But I'll tell you what that voice reminds me of, what I remember most. You'd think it would be the inhumanity of the killings, wouldn't you? It wasn't. The terrible thing about routine murder is that it becomes routine. Liveable with. No, what stands out for me – just for me, not everyone, just for me – was the screaming of the camp guards. Full of self-loathing. They hated themselves, and the more they hated themselves the more they beat us and screamed. That's what stayed with me. All my years as a doctor I watched out for it – this relationship between cruelty and self-contempt.

KAREN   That's what I hear in Jenny's voice – self-contempt. I don't hear Matthew-contempt, I hear Jenny – contempt. (*Beat.*) And how could she accuse her grandfather? She adored him.

ZIGGY   When we were in the camps he used to nag: 'will we make it to be fathers, grandfathers?' 'We'll make it,' I used to assure him, 'we'll make it, we'll make it.'

KAREN   I mean how long has my father got?

        Pause.

ZIGGY   And Abigail?

KAREN   Your Abigail. The lawyer! Investigating. Reserves judgement.

        Silence.

    Jennie could have been anything –

ZIGGY   Not anything. An intellectual she was not.

KAREN   – dominated the business. I used to tell her, husband and wife in the same office? Mistake. Don't do it. Did she listen? 'We're in love!' she tells me, 'we want to be together.' So – they were together – until the staff kept coming to her instead of him and he got jealous.

ZIGGY   It's what happens to over-sized personalities. My grandfather used to warn me: 'Ziggy, never stand out in a crowd.'

KAREN   But if I must be honest there's a 'but'.

ZIGGY   What 'but'?

KAREN   Great personality, everyone asked her for advice, she could talk like she'd known you for years but – she was a bad loser.

ZIGGY   It's true.

KAREN   I hate to say it about my darling daughter, I loved her but – a bad loser and no humour. She had to have the last word. Had to win and had to have the last word. (*Beat.*) We're talking about her like she was dead.

ZIGGY   Karen, go back to Matthew.

KAREN   I'm thinking about it.

ZIGGY   He's lost friends, lost his business, lost his world.

KAREN   I'm thinking about it.

ZIGGY   Phone him. Tell him you're coming home.

KAREN   I'm thinking about it.

ZIGGY   Your father would want it.

    Silence.

    Karen! You're not thinking your father really did…

KAREN   Who knows? The camps affected you all in strange ways.

ZIGGY   (*Angry.*) Talk like that and you can leave my house.

KAREN   Men have mistresses for years and years and the wife is the last one to know about it.

ZIGGY   What's one got to do with the other? You're not thinking straight.

KAREN   I can't think straight.

ZIGGY   You're a strong woman. Try!

KAREN   Strong! Strong! None of us knows anything about
        any of us. There! Is that strong enough for you?

>   *She weeps. He consoles her.*

SCENE 6

>   *The following scenes alternate between two confrontations
>   taking place on different time-scales.*
>
>   The first: *five consultations between VALERIE MORGAN,
>   therapist, and her client, JENNY YOUNG, covering many
>   months.*
>
>   The second: *an interview between VALERIE and the TV
>   journalist, SANDY CORNWALL, taking place over a couple
>   of hours in front of a camcorder.*
>
>   *Both sets of confrontations take place in different parts of a
>   bleak consulting room: with client from behind a desk; with
>   journalist by a low table littered with documents and files.*
>
>   *VALERIE MORGAN, therapist, Welsh, gently spoken, a warm
>   personality.*
>
>   *JENNY YOUNG, client. Suppressed agitation.*
>
>   *The silence between them seems endless.*
>
>   *Finally –*

VALERIE   Not sure I can be of any use to you in silence, pet.

>   *Silence.*

          I'm not one of those therapists who believe silence is
          productive.

>   *Silence.*
>
>   *JENNY scratches her arm, which she'll do every so
>   often.*

          You'll have to say something sooner or later.

JENNY   I'm usually very talkative.

VALERIE   That's promising.

JENNY   Talkative. Organising. Listening. Sympathetic.

VALERIE   Your profession is – ?

JENNY   Was. Sold insurance. I could sell insurance anywhere to anyone.

VALERIE   Insurance to anyone?

JENNY   The right insurance to match the right fear.

VALERIE   Always?

JENNY   Sooner or later. Something right for the right person.

VALERIE   You believe that?

JENNY   Something right for the right person? Yes, I do. Problem is finding the match.

VALERIE   Married?

JENNY   Was. Good-looking, silent, and strange. Wore shoes with heels extra high. Competed with everyone. Even his children.

VALERIE   Children? How many?

JENNY   Two.

VALERIE   Would you like to tell me more?

Silence.

No rush. Therapy is a slow burn.

Silence.

But I often have to remind clients that silence is for lovers.

Silence.

JENNY   His mother said he walked under a lucky star the day he met me.

Silence.

VALERIE   And it costs.

She smiles. JENNY doesn't.

I see I'll have to curb my humour.

JENNY   I don't know where to begin.

VALERIE   Try the beginning, pet.

Silence.

Then, a burst.

JENNY   In the beginning I was born, I was loved, I was happy. I loved my parents, my grandparents, even my younger sister which is unusual I know but it's true. I left school at sixteen, found a good job, got married, had two kids – finished! Simple!

VALERIE   Nothing is simple, Jenny.

JENNY   Yes it is. You're given opportunities, you fuck them up. You're given choices, you make the wrong choice. You think you're one kind of person, you grow up and discover you're not. Simple!

VALERIE   You sure? Why do we fuck-up opportunities? Why do we make wrong choices? Why do we think we are who we're not?

JENNY   That's what I've come here to find out.

VALERIE   Well I'm not going to tell you, if that's what you imagine. You're going to have to talk it through and discover it for yourself. I merely guide you.

JENNY   I don't want guidance I want advice.

VALERIE   I don't advise. Never.

JENNY   What am I paying you for then?

VALERIE   Options – I go through options for you to consider and act upon. And if you're going to view these sessions as getting your money's worth you'd better find yourself another therapist.

JENNY   I'm sorry.

VALERIE   No need to be sorry.

JENNY   I can see you're a tough one.

VALERIE   No not really, pet. Soft as putty inside. But all relationships need boundaries and courtesies to live by.

Silence.

And a little bit of humour helps, too.

Then another sudden outburst.

JENNY   I can't function. I can't fucking function. I used to function like clockwork. More. I used to function happily like clockwork. I was a doer, dependable, the life and fucking soul of wherever I was, whatever

I was doing, and there were forty-six hours in my day.

VALERIE Now?

JENNY Nightmares. Panic. I'm in a state of panic all the time. Or I'm sad. I cry non-stop. I shake. And I eat a lot. I can't stop eating. I eat eat eat then I gag. I look in the mirror and I think you're a young woman of thirty and you look like shit. Worse – you are shit. What have you done with your life? Frightened people into expensive insurance, had a couple of kids, blew a marriage and, and,…

But she can't say it.

VALERIE And?

Silence.

Don't say what you wanted to say, say something else. It'll come later.

Silence.

Tell me about your parents.

Silence.

JENNY And I sleep around.

VALERIE With anybody?

JENNY I need to be taken. I have this need to be wanted, desired.

VALERIE And you have an orgasm each time?

JENNY You must be joking.

VALERIE I try.

JENNY Never! Blokes – they handle you like meat.

VALERIE So why do you persist?

Silence.

Jenny, it's important, this.

Silence.

If you find men handle you like meat why do you seek them out?

Silence.

Jenny?

JENNY   Because I want to be handled like meat.

SCENE 7

Bleak consulting room.

VALERIE is being interviewed by TV journalist SANDY CORNWALL – physically at odds with herself.

A camcorder hovers.

SANDY   So, you qualified as a social worker and began working with battered wives. When did you begin to work with sexually abused children?

VALERIE   I began working with sexually abused children fifteen years ago. In Cardiff. A family of three – girl and two boys. Wayward, difficult, up to all sorts of bloody mischief. You know – stealing, vandalising, bullying, experimenting with drugs – cosy little darlings…

Will I still be in shot if I shift around a bit?

SANDY   Fine. Fine.

VALERIE   Where was I?

SANDY   Cosy little darlings.

VALERIE   Right! Cosy little darlings. Then one day the girl tells me she's been sexually abused by her parents – the zealous, loving kind, you know? So of course we take her in to care at once. But the boys? Ah! Didn't imagine anything happened to boys. Snotty-nosed boys as sexual objects? Didn't know anything about that, and those who should have known – the children's hospitals – knew damn all. Family sit-ins full of embarrassed smiles, helping the offender apologise – solved! All safe now! Let's dance round the Maypole! That's when I upped and went to the States.

SANDY   To do?

VALERIE   To learn more. Worked with a centre treating sexual offenders.

SANDY   So you began working with offenders rather than victims?

VALERIE   Began, yes, until I thought – I can't work with that devious bunch of heathens, they've got a maze where their brains should be. You'd end up screaming to get out of their heads never mind into them!

SANDY   But isn't the offender probably a victim?

VALERIE   Probably. In the distant past. And someone's got to unravel what made them offend. But not Miss Impatience here. The States taught me where my interest lay. In the victims. Got lots of time for victims. But not, I hasten to add, the victim mentality. Big difference. Victims need sorting out, healing. Victim-mentalities need a kick up the arse. It was the healing I was interested in.

>   *Pause.*

>   It's all right for me to be a little crude on telly isn't it? I mean we're not talking cookery and workouts here, and no doubt you can edit me…?

SANDY   You're doing fine. Don't worry.

SCENE 8

Bleak consulting room.
Second consultation.

VALERIE   Have you ever thought about your different selves?

JENNY   Different sides of myself?

VALERIE   No. Different sides are not the same as different selves.

JENNY   What's the difference between the difference?

VALERIE   Your different sides are chained to the same person. When you're split into different selves, each self has its own set of values and behaviour patterns.

JENNY   Need time to wrap my little brain round that one.

VALERIE   You haven't got a little brain, Jenny, and it's not
           difficult to wrap round. Think about it. Different
           selves like different people. All in the one body.

JENNY   Where would I house them all?

VALERIE   Oh, you're so flippant.

JENNY   And why would I house them all? It's hard enough
           living with my one self, why would I want to
           complicate my life creating others?

VALERIE   To run away from the self who's been hurt, perhaps?

JENNY   Who hasn't been hurt?

VALERIE   Perhaps you have an insecure self…

JENNY   Don't we all?

VALERIE   Try not to challenge everything I say, pet. Listen and
           reflect. Consider and then question. You may have
           that insecure self which we all have but do you have
           an arrogant self that lives in contradiction with the
           insecure one? Perhaps you also have a wild self, or a
           self-destructive self, or both, heaped upon the other
           two?

JENNY   Or I may not.

VALERIE   Or you may not. Perfectly true.

           Silence.

           You do like to be in control, don't you, pet?

           Silence. Awkward. Shifting around.

JENNY   These 'selves'. So?

VALERIE   I'm just wondering if I can be of any use to you.

JENNY   I'm listening. Promise.

VALERIE   Yes, but which one of you is listening?

JENNY   Try me!

VALERIE   Ask yourself – do they exist? These different
           personalities within me like different people, are
           they all living in the one mind? Write them down.
           As you recognise one, describe her, give her a
           name – Lucy, Samantha, Sarah, Megan, Carol,
           Tess –

JENNY   Nastasia. I like the name, Nastasia. Don't you? A
        name for an Empress.

VALERIE   Be serious, Jenny. You want my help? Stop being
          flippant, and be serious.

JENNY   I thought you said a little humour helps.

VALERIE   Humour, different from flippancy.

JENNY   What's the difference between the difference?

          VALERIE changes gear.

          *A little music-hall act ensues – perhaps her party-
          pieces?*

VALERIE   My wife and I were happy for twenty years and then
          we met – boboom!

JENNY   Stick to therapy.

VALERIE   I haven't spoken to my wife in eighteen months – I
          don't like to interrupt her – boboom!

JENNY   They're both anti-women.

VALERIE   Only if delivered by men. (*Beat.*) OK, try this:
          women will never be equal to men until they can
          walk down the street with a bald head and a beer-
          gut, and still think they're beautiful.

          I bet you know some.

          JENNY shakes her head.

          You must know *one*.

          Long pause.

JENNY   The secret of a happy marriage –

          – funny session over –

          – remains a secret. Boboom.

          Silence.

VALERIE   You're profoundly unhappy, Jenny. You don't know
          why, I don't know why, but we'll never find out until
          you stop being flippant. Otherwise – look! A door.
          No lock, no key, no guard – you're free to walk.

JENNY   I'm sorry.

VALERIE   We're looking for causes – maybe simple, maybe
          complex.

JENNY   I'm sorry.

VALERIE   Could be painful consequences or no consequences.

JENNY   I'm sorry, sorry.

VALERIE   We don't know. We're looking.

JENNY   Sorry sorry sorry.

VALERIE   I'm not asking you to be sorry, love – there's enough sorrow and pain in the world. I'm asking you to help me help you. It may be that you simply need the love of your family, your parents. We don't know yet. We only know that the courage it takes to heal is no ordinary courage.

SCENE 9

Bleak consulting room.

The interview continues.

SANDY   Can we now talk about the two very different issues of abuse, get them clearly distinguished one from the other?

VALERIE   And they are?

SANDY   The abused child we can see evidence of, and the adult whose memory of abuse might be repressed in the sub-conscious.

VALERIE   Might be?

SANDY   Yes, might be, because the corroboration is vague.

VALERIE   If you've been sexually abused as a child you've been sexually abused whether you identify it then or recover it later as repressed memory.

SANDY   But does scientific evidence exist to prove memory can be repressed? It seems we can forget not repress.

VALERIE   The sub-conscious produces the evidence – depression, lack of energy, self-contempt…

SANDY   All of which could be evidence of pre-menstrual tension.

VALERIE   Experience teaches you to know the difference.

SANDY   I appreciate that but with the abused child you don't
           need to rely on experience only, the evidence is
           visible – bruises, anxiety, disturbance in class – more
           reliable, easier to nail the child abuser.

VALERIE   Easier?

SANDY   Recovered memory on the other hand...

VALERIE   Easier? Do you know how widespread sexual abuse
           of children is? Do you know what barriers the courts
           put in the way before charges can be brought? Do
           you know how difficult it is to get children to stand
           witness? Do you know that less than three per cent
           of those charged get prosecuted? The court system
           stinks so please don't talk to me about 'easier'.

SANDY   I hear that, but –

VALERIE   Imagine, a child enters the world in an instant
           relationship of trust. From the moment of birth a
           mother says 'depend upon me'. She gives breast,
           cleans up the shit, cuddles and comforts and rocks
           to sleep until, one day, the sexual tampering begins,
           and in an instant the bond is broken. Can there be
           any greater betrayal, any more savage rendering
           apart?

SANDY   I share your distress but –

VALERIE   And do you know the vilification I receive?

SANDY   Tell me.

VALERIE   Sneers! They sneer at me – doctors, social workers,
           police –

SANDY   All of them?

VALERIE   Enough of them! The clever ones! The confident,
           cocky ones! Trained in one field, experts in every
           field. Don't you love them? They send me the
           problems they can't cope with but it doesn't stop
           them sneering. I'm a thorn in their side, see. I make
           them get off their arses to do something for the little
           ones. I discomfort them. 'Lady Patronising', 'Mrs
           Sanctimonious', 'Daisy Do-gooder', 'the bitch with
           bitterness in her soul'.

But it's not 'bitterness' it's anger. Because I've seen them, see? The eight-year olds with vaginas burst open by cycle-pumps, young boys with gaping anuses, children who shudder at your touch, implore you with looks, fix terrified eyes upon those intimidating thugs called parents.

SANDY   I do hear you, I promise, but I really am more interested to hear you talk about repressed memories in adults.

VALERIE   And what do you think it did to my life? To my relationship with my husband, my children, my friends? What sweetness and light for me exposed day after day to the cruel adult gratification upon the innocent? So let them sneer. Police, doctors, journalists – the whole damn bloody lot! Sneer to their heart's content –

SANDY   – but it is important not to confuse the two issues, surely?

VALERIE   I'll tell you what's really important – and I hope you don't edit this out – I've walked through the shittiest of lives to give comfort, clear up the mess, face squalor most people walk past, and lead who I could out of relationships horrendous beyond belief. Beyond belief!

SANDY   Scepticism about 'recovered memories' in adults is in no way a denial that sexual abuse of children is widespread.

VALERIE   (*Mocking.*) Oh, it's not is it? Is it not? Really now. Not, indeed!

       Pause.

       And I hope you won't edit out my anger, Pet. You won't will you? Promise? You don't see much anger on telly these days. Everyone's looking to be loved.

SANDY   Can we talk about your childhood? Did your parents –

VALERIE   I would prefer to keep my family out of this interview.

SANDY I was simply curious about their occupations in
order to –

VALERIE If you don't mind. Thank you.

SCENE 10

Bleak consulting room.
Third consultation.

VALERIE Why do you wear glasses?

JENNY What?

VALERIE Glasses. Why do you think you wear them?

JENNY Think? I don't 'think' why I wear glasses. I know
why I wear them – the world is blurred without
them.

VALERIE At what age did your eyes deteriorate?

JENNY For God's sake – I've been wearing glasses since I
was seven.

VALERIE Seven? Your eyesight deteriorated in seven years?

JENNY It happens. The streets are full of kids wearing
glasses.

VALERIE What is it, I often wonder, that we don't want to see
when our eyes deteriorate?

JENNY Nothing! There was nothing I didn't want to see. I
wanted to see everything. I just couldn't.

VALERIE And why is it then that medical science assures us a
relationship exists between mind and body? It does,
pet. I promise you. As certainly as there is a sun in
the sky.

SCENE 11

Bleak consulting room.
The interview continues.

SANDY Can we please concentrate on repressed memories
that have been recovered?

VALERIE What's your question?

SANDY   My question is: should recovered memories be acted
         upon without corroboration?

VALERIE Corroboration is in those symptoms you so breezily
         dismissed before – depression, lack of energy, self-
         contempt.

SANDY   A patient's symptoms can't possibly be evidence of a
         parent's culpability.

VALERIE In my experience it is.

SANDY   But you've listed states and conditions which could
         be accounted for in a dozen different ways: paranoia,
         panic, sexual compulsion, eating compulsion,…
         I mean – I suffer from most of those and I wasn't
         abused as a child.

         Silence.

         VALERIE glares.

         SANDY turns to technician off stage.

         CUT! (*To VALERIE.*) No, I was not!

VALERIE Why are you raising your voice, Pet?

SANDY   Because you have a presumptuous way of looking
         that signals you know what others can't possibly.

VALERIE You've moved from controlled calm to loud
         protestation in two seconds flat – surely we have to
         ask why?

SANDY   I know why.

VALERIE Tell me.

SANDY   Why on earth should I?

VALERIE Then don't.

SANDY   Nothing sinister, nothing complex, just private.

VALERIE I'm not pressing.

SANDY   (*Unable to resist.*) When I was a young woman I
         drank, smoked and battered my poor old body not
         because I was abused as a child but because I wasn't
         loved as an adult. Love – that's what I craved. To
         be wanted, cherished, taken and enjoyed like a
         cherry – sweet, succulent, utterly enjoyed. Even the

silly stone inside. Cherished for the best, forgiven for foolishness.

VALERIE rises and extends her hand.

VALERIE And that's where I think we should call it a day.

SANDY (*Rising, taking hand.*) You do need to be the one in control, don't you?

VALERIE Moi? I'm anybody's for half a smile. Good of you to come to me. Hate television studios.

SCENE 12

Bleak consulting room.
Fourth consultation.

JENNY I was never what you would call an intellectual. My younger sister, Abigail, she was what you'd call an intellectual. I was the one they loved, she was the one they admired.

VALERIE Did that upset you?

JENNY That they loved me?

VALERIE That they didn't admire you.

JENNY I didn't say they didn't admire me.

VALERIE But you did say they admired your sister.

JENNY They loved her too.

VALERIE But they loved you more, and she they admired more?

JENNY Something like that.

VALERIE Would you have preferred it the other way round – to be admired more than loved?

JENNY Let's not take this too far. I was admired plenty – capable, efficient, entrepreneurial.

VALERIE So what precisely was admired about your sister?

JENNY Abigail had a mind. Has a mind. Could read a book of political theory and tell you what it was about.

VALERIE You envied that?

JENNY Wouldn't you?

VALERIE   No. I'm quite pleased to be able to listen to a piece of music and be touched by it.

JENNY   Abigail can do that too.

VALERIE   So you never went to university?

JENNY   No.

VALERIE   Did you want to go?

JENNY   Doesn't everyone?

VALERIE   But some parents don't encourage their children to go.

JENNY   That's true.

VALERIE   But your parents encouraged you to go.

JENNY   Did I say that?

VALERIE   I assume that.

JENNY   Well you assume wrong.

VALERIE   They must have wanted you to learn things. They couldn't not have wanted you to learn things.

JENNY   Of course they wanted me to learn things. What parents don't want their children to learn things?

VALERIE   Especially your parents.

JENNY   Especially my parents. It's that I wasn't bright enough. Or I wasn't bright in an academic sense.

VALERIE   Come now, Jenny. That self-esteem we talked about?

JENNY   Oh, I had gifts. The gift to sell into people's fears, to persuade, encourage, manipulate people into doing what they never thought they would do. But facts? history? abstract ideas? My head is somewhere else. And it worried them, my parents. Which upset me because I love them.

VALERIE   Of course.

JENNY   They were supportive during my divorce.

VALERIE   To their credit.

JENNY   I don't know what I'd've done without them.

        Long pause.

VALERIE   You've stopped.

JENNY I'm not saying I wasn't ambivalent about them.
Especially my father.

VALERIE We're all ambivalent about our fathers, Jenny.

JENNY Especially daughters.

VALERIE Nothing special there.

JENNY Jesus Christ, Valerie. What are you looking for?

VALERIE I'm not looking. You're telling.

JENNY I've got wonderful parents and wonderful
grandparents. What the hell are you looking for?

VALERIE I'm not looking. You're telling.

SCENE 13

*SANDY CORNWALL's cluttered study – part of the converted
hall of a small, Victorian infants school.*

MATTHEW visiting.

SANDY Why, I wonder, do the falsely accusing rant and rave
while the accused rarely show emotion?

MATTHEW Helplessness. How can you prove you didn't do
something?

SANDY Just as you can't prove there are no witches.

MATTHEW Or that people aren't abducted by aliens.

They share a smile.

You live in this?

SANDY Chaotic, huh? What can I do for you?

MATTHEW Your documentary about the accused couple –

SANDY – who hanged themselves –

MATTHEW – we all watched it.

SANDY After which came floods of letters from parents
falsely accused – like sad poems on Christmas day.

MATTHEW You can't be surprised.

SANDY I'm not.

MATTHEW We reach to you for comfort. Not to feel alone. And
because you know Valerie Morgan.

SANDY   Oh yes, I know Valerie Morgan – sardonic sense
        of humour which is seductive, and doesn't use long
        words – which is a bonus.

MATTHEW   You've covered a lot of these court cases?

SANDY   A lot of a lot. And I've come to the conclusion
        there's nothing more destructive than false
        allegations of sexual abuse.

        Pause.

        Where's your wife?

MATTHEW   We're not together just now.

SANDY   Jumped ship has she?

MATTHEW   She's staying with a friend. It's temporary.

SANDY   Doesn't believe you, eh?

MATTHEW   I'm the husband. Children come first.

SANDY   Married how long?

MATTHEW   Thirty-five years.

SANDY   Thirty-five years?

MATTHEW   I understand her.

SANDY   You're generous.

MATTHEW   She's confused.

SANDY   After all those years she's confused?

MATTHEW   Everything's new for us. Such sexual goings on we
        never knew existed.

SANDY   But after thirty-five years?

MATTHEW   She was shattered –

SANDY   Of course. I'm sorry.

MATTHEW   – the story got out, friends divided, lost the business,
        took wild insults –

SANDY   Familiar pattern.

MATTHEW   – no one knows how to look at you.

SANDY   And you don't know how to look at them.

        Pause.

        No, don't worry, you're not alone. (*Beat.*) Are there
        grandparents?

MATTHEW My wife's father. Jenny was his princess. He's very
ill. We haven't told him.

SANDY Why haven't you told him?

Silence.

I see. She's accused him too. A pattern. All the
cases follow a pattern. Daughter goes off the rails,
meets up with a weirdo, mostly they're women I'm
ashamed to say – the kind that's into aromatherapy
or Buddhism or swinging pendulums in search of
the universe's force – and this woman usually knows
just the right therapist who's been a therapist for two
and a half minutes because that's what it's easy to
be these days, you don't need a certificate to set up
in the counselling business, and Bob's your Uncle,
Charlie's your aunt, and your daughter's given an
explanation for every fuck-up she's ever made in her
life. I'm sorry, I swore. Do you mind? It's a bit like
smoking – one should ask before doing it. 'Excuse
me, do you mind if I swear? No? Good! Fuck!
Fuck fuck fuck fuck fuck!' And whatever does that
mean – 'Bob's your uncle Charlie's your aunt'?

MATTHEW You're a bit of a weirdo yourself if you don't mind
me saying.

SANDY Ha! I've got to you. No, I'm not a weirdo. Just weird.
Though I'd prefer to be thought eccentric.

MATTHEW You mean you enjoy not being normal?

SANDY There are no normal people, Mr Young, only those
who haven't been investigated. (*Beat.*) I'm sorry.
(*Beat.*) All I can do is explain things but I can't bring
your daughter back nor advise you how to get her
back.

MATTHEW I understand.

SANDY And here's the good news – your daughter will soon
accuse your wife of complicity. You'll get her back.
Your wife that is.

SCENE 14

Bleak consulting room.

Fifth consultation.

VALERIE Why do you scratch your arm?

JENNY Why does anyone scratch anything? It itches.

VALERIE Remember we once talked about how the body
remembers pain?

JENNY And what pain do you think my arm is
remembering?

Silence.

Why are you looking at me like that?

Considered pause.

VALERIE I'm not sure.

JENNY You? Not sure?

*From here on VALERIE closely watches every
response.*

VALERIE Are you aware how imprecise a science
psychotherapy is?

JENNY Now she tells me.

VALERIE We can prove nothing.

JENNY What am I doing here, then?

VALERIE To talk, reveal yourself, manifest symptoms.

JENNY And have I done?

VALERIE Oh, have you not! But – become a client of six
different therapists in as many months and you'll
be offered six different interpretations of those
symptoms.

JENNY Reassuring, aren't you.

VALERIE I mean another therapist might say you were
demonstrating all the classical symptoms of an incest
victim.

JENNY A what?

VALERIE Incest victim.

JENNY   (*Dismissively.*) I don't have brothers.

        Pregnant pause.

        Slow dawning.

        You're not suggesting –

VALERIE   I'm only putting to you what another therapist might say.

JENNY   I'm not paying another therapist.

VALERIE   Another therapist might –

JENNY   Might?

VALERIE   – might put it to you that you were sexually abused by your father.

JENNY   My father?

VALERIE   Lack of energy, poor self-esteem –

JENNY   My FATHER?

VALERIE   – chronic sadness, sexual compulsion –

JENNY   – itchy arms –

VALERIE   – eating compulsion –

JENNY   You mean greed.

VALERIE   Greed is a judgemental word, we don't make judgements in therapy.

JENNY   You mean I can get away with anything?

VALERIE   Are we being flippant again?

JENNY   Are we being fucking serious here?

VALERIE   A shock, I know.

JENNY   Sexually abused by a father I adore?

VALERIE   Unbelievable, I know.

JENNY   My dad?

VALERIE   Right! A father is a father is a father is a beloved being.

JENNY   Fucking right! Beloved!

VALERIE   But I've spent ten years dealing with victims of incest –

JENNY   You mean you believe it?

VALERIE I don't want to believe it.

JENNY It's absurd.

VALERIE For your sake I'd tell such a therapist to –

JENNY – to go fuck herself!

VALERIE Difficult though I've always felt that to execute.

JENNY Who's being flippant now?

VALERIE Infectious. Sorry.

JENNY I have absolutely no memory of any such thing.

VALERIE Ah!

JENNY Ah?

VALERIE Ah!

JENNY Ah ah ah! What fucking 'ah'?

        Relentless from here on.

VALERIE Whether you remember or not is – for the moment – irrelevant.

JENNY Irrelevant? How can what I don't remember be irrelevant?

VALERIE Ugly memories can be repressed.

JENNY Say something funny.

VALERIE And if they happened when you were a child…?

JENNY I need humour, distraction.

VALERIE … When you were emotionally ill-equipped to deal with them…?

JENNY Be flippant again.

VALERIE …even more so.

JENNY It's not true.

VALERIE The world went blurred for you.

JENNY Not true.

VALERIE The child buried it, the adult has arrived to deal with it.

JENNY It's simply not true.

VALERIE It'll take a long time but –

JENNY It never happened.

VALERIE – but if you don't heal, your symptoms will become dire.

JENNY And what if my symptoms arise from other things?

VALERIE Such as?

JENNY My parents fought, my marriage failed, I used up the money my dad set aside for me –

VALERIE Set aside?

JENNY – savings he'd made from when I was a little girl.

VALERIE Your father set aside money for you?

JENNY Parents do such things, for Christ's sake. He wrote me a note to accompany the cheque: 'This is for you to have a second chance in case you make a mess of the first one.'

VALERIE He knew you'd make a mess of your life?

JENNY The odds must be ten to one that most people will make a mess of their lives.

VALERIE He couldn't perhaps be setting aside money for the little girl about whom he felt guilty?

JENNY Does everything have to mean something else?

VALERIE That's what therapy is about, pet – understanding the meaning of things that distress has forgotten.

JENNY That doesn't make sense. Why should I be distressed only by what I've forgotten rather than what I've remembered?

VALERIE The traumas you've remembered – parents fighting, failed marriage, money misspent – hold no key precisely because you've remembered them. What you remember, you've coped with. What you've suppressed, not remembered, is what you can't cope with. You're in denial. Admirable because it reveals a loving and loyal nature. But as long as you remain loyal to the man who betrayed you –

JENNY If he betrayed me –

VALERIE – you will remain in deep depression. Trust me.

JENNY If he betrayed me –

VALERIE If he betrayed you.

JENNY   If…

VALERIE   Trust me and come out of denial. Come.

JENNY   If. If. If!

VALERIE   Come.

JENNY   If. If. If!

VALERIE   Something is there… Come, lovely. Come. You can
            feel it. I can feel you can feel it.

JENNY   I feel I've just been told I'm terminally ill.

VALERIE   The reverse. You've been told your illness is
            terminal, not you. Come.

JENNY   Why are you smiling?

VALERIE   A problem identified is cause for jubilation. Come.

JENNY   You make it sound like religious revelation.

VALERIE   In a way it is. Come.

JENNY   Makes me feel light-headed.

VALERIE   It's called 'dissociating'.

JENNY   You have names for everything!

VALERIE   That's why language was invented – to give
            everything a name. Come.

JENNY   Dis-sociating.

VALERIE   The sub-conscious protecting you from that which
            you're not yet ready to deal with.

JENNY   This one I'll never be ready to deal with.

VALERIE   Oh, you will. Trust me.

JENNY   You're so certain.

VALERIE   Not everybody can but you will, trust me.

JENNY   Why? Why, why, why? The world is full of
            charlatans, why should I trust anyone but myself?

VALERIE   Because our relationship, Jenny, client and therapist,
            is about trust.

JENNY   Hot! God – why do I feel so hot?

VALERIE   I ask you to take risks, risks that may frighten
            you, leaps in the dark. If you trust me and leap
            – you'll fly.

JENNY   Don't you feel hot?

VALERIE   Flying is healing, and those who trust me heal fastest, and the faster you heal, the sooner therapy ends. It's that simple. And of course – painful.

JENNY   Painful?

VALERIE   I'll see you through it but first –

JENNY   Conditions?

VALERIE   – you've got to leave the flippant adult behind and find your inner child. The innocent child you once were. You need to get in touch with that poor lost inner child that's in us all.

JENNY   Yes. Her. The inner fucking child. Probably the cause of everything going wrong.

VALERIE   No, Jenny. You're not understanding.

JENNY   Every fucking thing going wrong.

VALERIE   You're not listening.

JENNY   I am! I am! There must be a reason. I was happy once, now I'm not. There's got to be some fucking explanation.

VALERIE   But not the inner child, Jenny. She's the real you. The one that was abused. Find her and she'll tell you who was really to blame. It's not your fault, Jenny.

JENNY   Damn fucking right it's not my fault. You don't find people who work as hard as I do, give as much as I do, love as much as I do, achieve as much as I do I do I do. I do! I do!

VALERIE   Shout, Jenny.

JENNY   I've always done.

VALERIE   Let it out, Jenny.

JENNY   I'm so fucking angry with someone.

VALERIE   We'll find them.

JENNY   So furious and fucking angry.

VALERIE   We'll find them, and nail them, and you'll be free of them.

JENNY   I want to be free of them. Whoever they are they've wrecked my life.

VALERIE   Scream it out, Jenny.

JENNY   Wrecked my lovely life.

> *She bangs the table with her fists.*

Wrecked my lovely, lovely life.

> *A batackas – a padded bat – is to hand, carefully positioned by VALERIE.*

> *JENNY reaches for it, beats whatever is around – couch, chair, table.*

Wrecked my one and only life. I had a life. I had a job. I had a home, a family, a future – wrecked, wrecked, wrecked, wrecked! I'm so angry. The world was mine. I've lost it. The world was fucking mine. I want to kill. I'm so furious and fucking angry. I want to kill, kill, kill! Wrecked, wrecked, wrecked…

> *Scream and rage until exhausted.*

> *She throws the bat down, sobbing.*

> *VALERIE waits till gradually JENNY reaches out, approaches, falls into her arms.*

VALERIE   There, there, Pet. There, there. We'll find them. Trust Valerie. We'll find them. I think you're very brave. Soon you'll realise how brave you've been. We'll find them. There, there.

> *Slowly there has faded up the last lines of JENNY's message to MATTHEW.*

JENNY'S VOICE   … You have no grandchildren. No grandchildren, no daughter, nothing. Guilt and shame, that's what you've got. And that's all, Matthew, father, Matthew fucking father. I'm never ever ever ever gonna forgive you. For anything! Nothing!

SCENE 15

SANDY's chaotic study.

Her meeting with MATTHEW continues.

MATTHEW Your first feeling is horror. Like your doctor tells you you're terminal. It's difficult to grasp. One day you've got a life ahead of you, no final fence in sight, the next – the fence has been fast-forwarded. You're over the other side. With the doomed ones. One minute you're a functioning family, your daughter's at the end of a phone talking, listening, sharing – the next, she's a stranger and you're an outcast. She's an accuser and you're on trial – those agonising doubts: what did I do? What could I possibly have done? And then – when you can't find anything really heinous to cause such a rift you forget about yourself and you start thinking about your child. My daughter – if she's made such dreadful accusations she must be dreadfully unhappy. My agony can be nothing compared to what she must be going through. Poor Jenny…

    Holds back tears.

    Silence.

Incomprehensible. We were such a happy family.

SANDY Ha!

MATTHEW How can happiness cause such misery? It makes no sense to me. A happy family.

SANDY A happy family! Fatal! Worst thing! Few encounters more dispiriting than those with happy families. Let me tell you a story.

    She's trying to change his mood.

One day last year my eldest son, he was thirteen then, was standing outside his school talking to some friends. He's a big lad – long hair, bright, confident, and with those irritatingly happy eyes. Two boys approached. One kicked him in the backside the other told him to get stuffed. He ignored them. That

really irritated them. They called to him again. 'Get
stuffed!' This time he said obligingly 'all right, I will'.
Which of course irritated them even more. And one
of them drew back a heavy ringed fist and smashed
into my son's right eye.

MATTHEW Good God! He –?

SANDY No – he's alright. A bruise, a gash. Healed now.
But it made me realise – there exists a certain kind
of mean mind that hates the sight of happiness.
In anyone or any form. Loathes it. Difficult to
comprehend how such a mind functions. What
could there possibly be in the nature of happiness
to arouse such hostility, such a demonic desire to
destroy it? 'Because it's not mine'? 'I hate them being
happy because I'm not happy'? Could it be that?
Does one person's happiness highlight another's
failure? Is that it? Too dazzling? 'Stars must fall! The
mighty laid low! The achievers denied! The whole
God-blessèd edifice of joy brought down to ease the
pain of my miserable, insignificant life. How dare
you love your parents when mine were unlovable?
How dare your eyes sparkle with confidence and
happiness? Happiness? You want happiness? I'll give
you happiness.' Wham!

And so it begins – the murderous, insidious,
dismantling of your cherished kith, kin, and hearth.
Bit by painful bit until you're made to feel guilty
for adoring those who gave you birth, those who
nourished you with affection, watched over your
fevers, reassured you through lean doubts. So it
begins.

Silence.

MATTHEW How many children?

SANDY Two.

MATTHEW You been accused?

SANDY Too young.

MATTHEW So why – ?

SANDY   'Any man's death diminishes me.'

MATTHEW   You're a bit too educated for this old man.

SANDY   John Donne. 'Devotions.'

SCENE 16

Bleak consulting room.

JENNY with her fierce sister, ABIGAIL.

JENNY   It's true.

ABIGAIL   You know they're devastated.

JENNY   The truth is the truth – devastating.

ABIGAIL   And how did you come across this 'truth'?

JENNY   I found out.

ABIGAIL   'Found out'? How 'found out'? Someone told you? They were watching?

JENNY   Take me seriously, Abbie. Take me very, very seriously.

ABIGAIL   I don't understand the 'found out' bit. You didn't know?

JENNY   I'd repressed the memory.

ABIGAIL   How can you repress a memory like that?

JENNY   Awful things happen. You want to forget them.

ABIGAIL   I know. I'm trying all the time to forget that people hurt me, that life isn't lovely, that not everyone is kind and intelligent, that….

JENNY   Are you going to be a supportive sister or not?

ABIGAIL   I'm sorry. You 'found out'.

JENNY   I've been in therapy.

ABIGAIL now understands where she is.

ABIGAIL   Here?

JENNY   Yes.

ABIGAIL   Not exactly conducive for confession.

JENNY   You don't confess to a room, you confess to a person.

ABIGAIL   How long?

JENNY   Over two years.

ABIGAIL And your therapist has helped you remember –

JENNY   – dad's abuse.

ABIGAIL Which you'd somehow forgotten.

JENNY   If you've come to sneer at me with your fucking
         intellectual superiority, then –

ABIGAIL I'm sorry. Really. It's serious.

JENNY   You're damn fucking right it's serious.

ABIGAIL Jenny – just one thing. Can we drop the eff word?

JENNY   But you always –

ABIGAIL Not always. And now – never. Hardly ever. Under
         extreme duress, but rarely.

JENNY   Why?

ABIGAIL It's to do with prisons.

JENNY   Oh, Christ – it's one of your fuc – one of your
         esoteric – is that the right word – one of your
         esoteric theories?

ABIGAIL No. Simple, really. I'm trying not to get hooked
         on certain words. Like drugs and ideologies and
         jargon and Gods – you become chained to them.
         'Absolutely'. 'Know what I mean?' 'This moment
         in time'. 'Yer know' – junk language. My bête
         noire for this year is 'basically'. I'm at war with
         the word 'basically'. Everyone's using it from pop
         stars to politicians and judges. I spend hours in the
         courtroom listening as the word flies from witness to
         QC, from QC to accused – like an influenza germ.
         It's not easy but let's try to have a conversation
         without hiccups and crutches. 'Know what I mean?'

JENNY   What irritates me about you is what I also adore
         about you.

         Hugs her sister.

ABIGAIL I adore you, too. I just wish you had a sense of
         humour.

JENNY   What the fu–. Sorry. What on earth are you talking
         about?

ABIGAIL You've always been so – intense about life.

  JENNY Are you telling me I never laugh?

ABIGAIL I think I am.

  JENNY That's not fair. I'm always smiling.

ABIGAIL True. Smiling. Your features smile but your eyes don't laugh.

  JENNY What do my eyes do, then?

ABIGAIL They're a constant, singleminded. You have the most single-minded eyes I know.

  JENNY In this life –

ABIGAIL I know, I know – in this life it's kill or be killed.

  JENNY More or less.

ABIGAIL OK. You've put me in serious mode.

        Pause.

  JENNY I've recovered memories.

ABIGAIL You've recovered memories.

  JENNY At first I dismissed the idea as outrageous. Like you. My father? Never! Impossible! Then I went under hypnosis. Images came to me – wild, bizarre. I thought I was inventing them but one particular image returned – the incinerator. Remember it? We used to take garbage to the bottom of the garden where the incinerator was? Why did it keep coming back to me? The incinerator – why?

ABIGAIL Who conducted these sessions?

  JENNY My therapist, Valerie Morgan.

ABIGAIL She's expert? Experienced?

  JENNY You'd love her, Abigail. She's warm, human, sympathetic, sardonic –

ABIGAIL Sardonic.

  JENNY And she laughs a lot.

ABIGAIL She laughs a lot sardonically and she's persuaded you that you were abused by your father.

JENNY   She's taken me back into my past. Powerful.
         Disturbing. All sorts of memories unearthed going
         back to when I was two. Our parents –

ABIGAIL Parents?

JENNY   Yes. Parents!

ABIGAIL You think our mother was involved…?

JENNY   She stood by. Complied. She was complicit in
         everything that went on.

ABIGAIL I think I could get very angry, Jenny.

JENNY   And you know what? They did it to you, too.

         *ABIGAIL slaps her sister's face. Immediately regrets
         it. Clasps her.*

ABIGAIL Sorry. Sorry. I'm so sorry. I didn't mean that. I didn't
         mean –

         JENNY is forgiving and tender.

JENNY   It's exactly what I wanted to do to Valerie – thump
         her. Just that. Beat her with my fists. Her, anyone.
         But mostly – dad.

ABIGAIL Jenny, if I could take that back and do penance, I
         would. But I can't – not for one minute, not for one
         second – believe daddy touched me. What am I
         saying? I know he didn't touch me.

JENNY   You're in denial.

ABIGAIL In what?

JENNY   It's all right. A natural reaction. Happens all the
         time. The memory of the event is so awful our first
         impulse is to deny it. But once you've passed denial
         you reach recovery.

ABIGAIL You have the air of a missionary. 'Stop denying
         Christ and you'll reach a state of grace.'

JENNY   What's wrong with a state of grace?

ABIGAIL If we were talking about religious faith – nothing.
         But we're talking about our mother and father.
         You're asking me to believe degeneracy in our
         parents, you're not asking me to have faith in divine
         existence.

JENNY   I'm asking you to get in touch with your inner child.

ABIGAIL   My inner who?

JENNY   The child in you is crying out to be known. Know her!

ABIGAIL   (*Pacifying the demented.*) Jenny, Jenny.

JENNY   The child in you is hurting – find the courage to heal her.

ABIGAIL   That incinerator –

JENNY   The inner child needs avenging or she'll never have peace –

ABIGAIL   Fuck 'the inner child', tell me about the incinerator.

JENNY   – and until the inner child has peace you won't have peace.

ABIGAIL   What 'inner child'? My 'inner child' was a pain in the arse – have you forgotten? Loud, bumptious, selfish, a liar to get her own way, illiterate till the age of seven. Yes! Seven! I couldn't read until I was seven. Remember? Who needs an inner child like that? Give me back my lovely childhood, yes, my youth, my chance to start again – yes! Yes, yes yes! But the 'inner child'? Spare me – and tell me about that incinerator.

JENNY   You're far too clever, Abigail. For your own good – too clever.

ABIGAIL   I shall never understand how anyone can be 'far too clever for their good'. Tell me about the bloody incinerator.

JENNY   I took it to the incinerator and burned it.

ABIGAIL   Burned what?

JENNY   Our foetus – his and mine.

ABIGAIL   Whose and yours? Whose? Whose?

JENNY   Dad's.

ABIGAIL   What?

JENNY   Our baby.

ABIGAIL   WHAT?

JENNY   I aborted our baby –

ABIGAIL   (*Her lawyer voice.*) What age?

JENNY   Twelve, Abbie, I was only twelve.

> *ABIGAIL pauses to make swift mental calculations.*

ABIGAIL   Jenny, the incinerator was gone when you were twelve. Dad's business took off two years earlier. The entire garden was re-laid.

JENNY   You're in denial, Abbie.

ABIGAIL   No incinerator, Jenny, no incinerator.

JENNY   You're in denial.

ABIGAIL   And you expect me to believe you repressed what happened aged twelve?

JENNY   Denial, denial. You're in denial.

ABIGAIL   And you're in deep shit.

JENNY   Sever contact with the family, you'll never recover unless you get out.

ABIGAIL   Recover from what? There's nothing I want to recover from.

JENNY   Find the family you've chosen, not the one you've been lumbered with.

ABIGAIL   I like the one I've been lumbered with – even you, you nutter.

JENNY   Oh, Abbie. I feel so sad for you.

ABIGAIL   You feel sad for me?

JENNY   Sad, sad, sad. Here – let me hold you. Hugs are good. They help. Good, good. Hugs are good. There, there…

> *She enfolds her sister, rocks her.*

SCENE 17

YOUNG's lounge.

KAREN and MATTHEW.

KAREN is in a state of shock, as was MATTHEW in Scene 4.

She is recovering from tears. In her hand a letter.

KAREN   Me! Me! She's accused me!

MATTHEW   At least we're together again.

KAREN   We've lost a daughter – what matter if 'we're together again'?

MATTHEW   Don't snap, darling.

KAREN   She's accused ME!

> *The tears return.*
>
> *He holds her.*
>
> *She recovers.*
>
> *She looks at the letter.*

How do you disprove such things? (*Reads.*)

… and when you had finished washing me you passed me to dad, and when he washed me he passed me back to you to be washed again, as though I was not clean enough…

We played games with her. What is she remembering? We played games with her in the bath, like most normal parents.

…You knew, didn't you? And once you knew you joined in. Sleeping in mum and dad's bed was never the same again…

> *Deep shock.*
>
> *Struggles to understand, to speak.*
>
> *Her features contort; her lips seem unable to form words.*

I can't…but she…what can I…she…can't…

> *MATTHEW can only watch, stand by, leave her to work through.*
>
> *The effort exhausts her.*

Finally –

I think I now know what it means to be struck dumb.

They exchange smiles.

Forgive me, Matthew.

He kisses her forehead.

We must see her.

MATTHEW How? She doesn't answer letters and her therapist has forbidden her to go near us.

KAREN How did we let it come to this? A stranger, someone who's known her only a few years? It doesn't make sense. We have history – what does the therapist have? We have memories – what does bloody Morgan have? We have blood-ties and love-ties and looking-after-her-through-illness-ties. What does fucking few-year-old, jumped-up, half-educated, self-righteous fucking Mrs Coming-from-nowhere have?

MATTHEW You're swearing.

KAREN I know I'm fucking swearing. You think I can't hear myself fucking swearing?

MATTHEW You never swear.

KAREN I've never been so fucking furious in my life that's why I'm swearing. Sexually abused my daughter? My own daughter? She'll never find a more upright woman than me. Swear? I want to murder her that trumped-up Morgan nonentity. I want to drag her by the hair and haul her up and down the road with a placard round her neck saying 'I break up happy families'.

MATTHEW Karen –

KAREN 'I break up happy families'.

MATTHEW Karen –

KAREN 'Stone me – I break up happy families'.

MATTHEW Karen, listen to me.

She stops to look at him as though she hadn't known he'd been there.

Maybe we couldn't have been such a happy family.

KAREN   What?

MATTHEW   We did something wrong.

KAREN   We did some…?

MATTHEW   Don't look at me so surprised. There has to be a reason. A daughter divorces, sells up everything takes off with her children, squanders her money on no good spongers who play the tarot cards, and then makes wild accusations of sexual abuse. There has to be a reason.

KAREN   Give me one. Just one.

MATTHEW   We were too demanding?

KAREN   We had expectations – not the same thing. And if we hadn't had expectations we'd have been accused of indifference. Not good enough. Another.

MATTHEW   We quarrelled too loudly.

KAREN   It's true. You shouted. When the business had problems you shouted at me like a maniac. Used to frighten me. I confess, I was frightened.

MATTHEW   So perhaps…

KAREN   Because you shouted? Your daughter accuses you of sticking a finger in her because you shouted at me? Not good enough. Another.

MATTHEW   We were too careful –

KAREN   With what? Money? Love? Praise? What 'careful'? Not good enough. Another.

MATTHEW   Claustrophobic. We were too close. Always wanting to know about each other. Maybe we didn't give each other enough space?

KAREN   We gave them a room of their own. From the start. You and me, too. All four of us had places to run away from each other.

MATTHEW   You can be oppressive even through closed doors.

KAREN   Oppressive?

MATTHEW   Love is oppressive. It's a fact. It's the fountain of the best kind of happiness but, paradoxically, it's oppressive.

KAREN   Did they have chains on their feet? Did we bribe them with riches?

MATTHEW   Perhaps our love was too greedy, too insistent.

KAREN   The only thing I ever insisted on was they should never come home alone, not even in a taxi. Stay in a friend's home. I oppressed them with that. Not good enough. Another.

MATTHEW   I don't know. I can't explain it. I'm scratching around for explanations – the question came off the top of my head.

    Silence.

KAREN   We must plan. From now on I'm going to write to her every week – I don't care if she doesn't reply.

MATTHEW   It'll take more than weekly letters to solve this one, Karen.

KAREN   Food. I'll send her food parcels every week, with special goodies for the children.

MATTHEW   She'll give the food away.

KAREN   Perhaps we can pay someone to work where she's working, befriend her, gain Jenny's confidence by pretending she too is a victim of child abuse.

MATTHEW   Karen, this is wild talk.

KAREN   She might be angry at first but then she'd be grateful.

MATTHEW   She's lost her self-esteem – that's the problem needs solving. Even if deep in her heart she knows she was never abused how can she face the world after she's lost everything she ever achieved?

KAREN   Then maybe someone should persuade her to set up in business again, regain self-esteem, get strong again. Then she'll be able to face the world. People are reasonable from a position of strength.

MATTHEW   Which is why you're not being reasonable. You're in no position of strength. You've been accused of something against which there is no defence. You're talking wild things, Karen.

KAREN   I'm wild! I'm wild! We've lost a daughter – I'm wild!

SCENE 18

Bleak consulting room.

ABIGAIL stands confronting a seated VALERIE.

ABIGAIL I want my sister back.

VALERIE Why don't you sit down?

ABIGAIL I don't want to sit down, I want my sister back.

VALERIE I'm running a therapy clinic not a prison.

ABIGAIL You've got Jenny dependent on you, that's prison in my book, and I'm a lawyer.

VALERIE I do think you'd be more comfortable sitting.

ABIGAIL I don't want to be more comfortable sitting, I want my sister out of here and in the hands of a qualified psychiatrist, which you most definitely are not.

VALERIE There are those who say psychiatry is a patriarchal conspiracy to deprive women of power.

ABIGAIL Please, I've not come here to debate –

VALERIE No! You've come here to be rude.

        Held.

ABIGAIL I'm sorry. Forgive me.

        Silence.

My sister's absurd accusations have driven nails through the heart of our family.

VALERIE Are you certain you won't sit down?

        ABIGAIL sits.

Jenny tells me you're of an intellectual bent.

ABIGAIL I don't think you can have an 'intellectual bent'. She just thinks I'm clever.

VALERIE I can see she's right.

ABIGAIL Why does my sister refer me to you?

VALERIE She's put herself in my care.

ABIGAIL Then you must have advised her not to see me again.

VALERIE I don't advise, I try to find out what my clients want.

ABIGAIL   If they know what they want why do they need you?

VALERIE   They don't always know that they know.

ABIGAIL   Which leaves them wide wide open to manipulation.

VALERIE   By me?

No response.

Manipulation? By me?

No response.

Abigail, this is not an institution. I run a clinic in
an ill-equipped, bleak room, which is all the social
services can afford for people who've led such
battered lives you wouldn't credit. Your sister is
her own person who makes her own decisions.
I'm seeing you because *she* asked me to see you.
I wouldn't have – my duty is to my client not my
client's family. But because my duty is to my client
I'm acceding to my client's wish. I'm seeing you.
How can I help?

ABIGAIL   My sister was once a happily married, successful,
much loved, much depended upon human being.
But something has happened. Something alien has
happened. Someone has come into her life and
talked her into beliefs without foundation.

VALERIE   Beliefs?

ABIGAIL   About her state of mind.

VALERIE   And how do you imagine it's possible to talk people
into beliefs without foundation?

ABIGAIL   It happens. Your first big failure – you become
uncertain about yourself, vulnerable. You need
explanations. Someone comes along bursting with
explanations – this is to blame, that's to blame,
him or her or it – anything but yourself. And the
therapist knows – better than anyone – that you
don't tell a client they are to blame because then the
client lumps the therapist together with everyone
who's ever been judgmental. The client doesn't
want to be judged, she wants to be let off the hook.

You let her off the hook. The relief is palpable, and dependency takes over.

VALERIE   Got it all neatly tied up and explained, haven't you?

ABIGAIL   I've read, consulted memory experts, and I think.

VALERIE   Why do I feel you've done more than 'think consulted read'?

Silence.

ABIGAIL   Astute, aren't you. All right – I know about dependency. I had a boy friend. I became dependent on him.

VALERIE   Want to tell me about it?

ABIGAIL   (*Sardonically.*) How much will it cost?

VALERIE   Your sister is my client. She pays.

ABIGAIL   You mean she's paying for this meeting?

VALERIE   Do you imagine I'm a rich bitch therapist who can afford time without payment –?

ABIGAIL   So, to help my sister you said: 'I'll see Abigail but someone has to pay for the session', and my sister said: 'you can't ask Abigail to pay, she'll blow your fucking head off so I'll pay.'

VALERIE   (*Reasonably.*) Why are you so hostile?

ABIGAIL   I'm angry and hostile because my sister is talking about incest within our family.

VALERIE   It could be you're angry and hostile because you know incest occurred.

ABIGAIL   'Could be, could be!' It 'could be' you're looking for vicarious pleasures.

VALERIE   I think you'd better leave.

ABIGAIL   It could also be that it didn't occur, or that if Jenny declared it occurred then she was doing so for self-dramatisation, to make herself interesting, to create alibis for her failures. It could even be that if it did occur it was because my sister seduced her father into making it occur – an unlikely image to wrap my imagination around but – could be. Welcome to the

land of comfortable 'could be's. Choose whichever
suits your need, your personality, your therapist.

VALERIE Aren't you a little worried about the implications of
your verbal violence?

ABIGAIL And what would those implications be?

VALERIE Denial?

ABIGAIL Ah! 'Denial'. The cosy jargon of psychobabble.

VALERIE Ah! 'Psychobabble' – the cosy jargon of truth-
avoidance.

ABIGAIL Yes! It does occur to me that I could be in denial.
I could also be impatient with stupidity, furious for
intellectual dishonesty, contemptuous for cant!

VALERIE I really do think we'd better bring this to a close,
we're not getting anywhere.

She stands, offers her hand.

ABIGAIL No, wait.

VALERIE What for?

ABIGAIL I'm a lawyer. I also charge. (*Smiling.*) Even for letters
I'm asked to write.

VALERIE (*Sitting.*) Well at least I don't charge for letters.

Silence.

ABIGAIL Let's talk about dependency. That boy friend
I had – the focus of my life for four years,
married, of course! We never learn. I shared and
trusted everything to him – dreams, sins, sexual
fantasies – he was a good listener, sympathetic, and
bright with it.

So, I became dependent. Mother, father, brother,
teacher, lover all in one. Fine. Until it turns out he
has problems he's never dealt with, and I realise I'm
not his mistress, I'm his revenge. And I'm helpless. I
don't want him but I need him.

VALERIE Did you ever ask yourself how come you needed
such dependency?

ABIGAIL Not because my father abused me.

VALERIE I didn't say that.

ABIGAIL   You would have done sooner or later.

VALERIE   Not at all. You're not my client. I'm concerned with
          Jenny's unhappiness and so I'm interested in yours.

ABIGAIL   I didn't say I was unhappy.

VALERIE   You've just told me a story about an unhealthy
          dependency.

ABIGAIL   Isn't all dependency unhealthy?

VALERIE   Yes, but what are its roots? Find the cause, the
          dependency ends. I'm interested in why a woman
          needs to depend, lacks confidence, is unhappy.

ABIGAIL   Who knows why a woman is unhappy, why she
          can't hold a life, a marriage together? Could be
          all sorts of reasons. She makes love clumsily, she's
          boring, humourless, over-powering. Some women
          talk their men out of existence, others boss them
          into oblivion. And we all know about the woman
          who marries for the wrong reason. One morning she
          wakes up with a man snoring at her side. 'Is this who
          I depend upon? Is this the man who once gazed at
          me adoringly?' Mistake! Terrible mistake. A mistake
          like that can knock the bottom out of self-confidence.
          Most people disappoint themselves a little, women
          are prone to do it totally. Sexual abuse in childhood
          is one of a thousand possibilities for unhappiness.
          Take your pick.

          Silence.

VALERIE   What would you like me to tell your sister?

ABIGAIL   My little speech didn't impress you?

VALERIE   I've heard it before.

ABIGAIL   OK I'm not original. That's no response.

          No response.

          Attaching blame to oneself undermines the
          profession, huh?

          VALERIE looks at her watch.

          My time's up?

VALERIE   I do have other clients.

ABIGAIL   Tell my sister I miss her, that mum and dad are heart-broken and will never, never recover, that we all make mistakes and there's no shame in that, that it takes courage to admit you've been wrong but you're stronger in the end, and that I'm there for her forever. Tell her these things.

>*Silence.*

You won't tell her any of these things will you?

>*Silence.*

Of all the good therapists in the world she had to choose you.

>*VALERIE rises, extends her hand.*

>*ABIGAIL rises but doesn't take it.*

Not a rich bitch therapist. A dangerous bitch therapist.

SCENE 19

SANDY's chaotic study.

KAREN and MATTHEW.

SANDY   The two of you?

KAREN   No. Just me. Mother, mother's daughter, daughter's therapist.

SANDY   Where?

KAREN   The Community Day Centre. She has a room there.

SANDY   I know it. Bleak.

MATTHEW   Bleak hour, too. Nine o'clock at night.

SANDY   And your daughter will be in a constant state of bleak rage. Can you believe it? The idea that women can repress what happened to them? Can you imagine silencing women? Women can't wait to talk to each other.

KAREN   How does the Morgan woman have this power?

SANDY   She deals in half-truths, jargon. Like cheap music – it gets to you. (*Beat.*) You want me to tell you what will take place at the confrontation. I can only tell you

what other parents have told me. You'll be asked
by Valerie to say what you want to say, then you'll
say it – and Jenny will listen because she's been
told she must listen without interrupting. When
you're finished, Valerie will ask Jenny what she
wants to say, and here – I'm afraid – you might get
very upset. Jenny won't talk naturally. She'll have
rehearsed with Valerie a list of abuses – all very
distressing. Let her finish. Don't show surprise, anger
or contempt. And when she's finished try to touch
her and tell her you love her. If she flinches don't
protest. Just reassure her you're there, whenever
she's ready to return.

And I don't suppose you'll do half the things I
advise.

MATTHEW   Karen, you sure you want to go through with this?

KAREN   I'm sure.

MATTHEW   You sure you're sure?

KAREN   I'm sure I'm sure.

SANDY   One last thing – Jenny sees herself as a survivor not
a victim.

SCENE 20

YOUNG's lounge.

MATTHEW, KAREN, ZIGGY, ABIGAIL.

ZIGGY   A survivor of what?

MATTHEW   Of 'lost' memory.

ZIGGY   I don't understand. How can you be a survivor of
what you've forgotten? I'm a survivor. A survivor of
what I've never forgotten. Of what I couldn't forget.

Silence.

ABIGAIL   I'm worried.

KAREN   About what?

ABIGAIL   The confrontation.

KAREN   You think I'm not?

ABIGAIL I've met this Morgan woman.

KAREN She's my daughter. She's been imprisoned.

ABIGAIL This confrontation is not a wise move.

KAREN I can't stop fighting to release her from prison.

ABIGAIL Mother, listen to me. Admitting you're wrong is difficult for anyone let alone Jenny.

KAREN It's taken a long time to set up this meeting, Abbie. I'm going. Nine o'clock this stupid mum is going to be there. Dad will drive me and wait outside, and I'll go meet this Morgan woman and talk to my daughter. Come – I'll show you what's in the fridge.

Both leave. KAREN stops halfway and returns.

Why is it that children fight you for an independence you haven't denied them? I shall never understand. Never.

Finally leaves.

MATTHEW You're not saying much, Ziggy.

ZIGGY But don't think I haven't thought, me and my granddaughter – there but for the grace of God. And it only takes one question: Just one: 'what happens when you're alone with her?' A wicked question. The accusation is in the question. Lots of things happen. I love being alone with her. We sit at a table, read books together, I ask her to name the orange, the ladder, the lion, the bear. And on her bedroom wall is a long sheet with a colourful alphabet and pictures. A is for Apple, B is for Bath, C is for Cup, D is for Dog. And we draw pictures and colour in colouring books. I get more pleasure out of it than she does, and I kiss her and bite her and stroke her and hug her and hold her and dance with her. I can't get enough of her. She's a delight and she's delighted. Everything has to be done a dozen times. Innocent. Until someone asks 'how innocent? When you're alone with her how innocent?' Wicked questions. Innocent? Innocent? Of course innocent. But tell me, whose honour is not defenceless before

the whispering of wicked questions? Don't think
I haven't thought about it. 'How innocent?' Don't
think I haven't thought.

    Silence.

SCENE 21

*Bleak consultation room, but this time we can see the corridor
leading to it, and the front door of the building.*

VALERIE and an anxious JENNY.

VALERIE We're not nervous now, are we?

JENNY If it had been my father I might have been.

VALERIE I don't think we could have gone on refusing to see
your mother.

JENNY She's strong, my mother.

VALERIE So are we, aren't we?

JENNY I don't know what I'd have done without you,
Valerie.

VALERIE Let's have none of that. It's work.

JENNY Not meetings with my mother.

VALERIE Oh well, the extra-mural sessions are to do with
friendship.

JENNY Not friendship, Valerie. Family. You're family. One
I've chosen, not that I was lumbered with.

VALERIE Right, pet, and frequently the best.

    Silence.

We *are* nervous, aren't we?

JENNY I feel hot, so hot.

VALERIE Winter outside, tropics inside. They never get the
bloody balance right.

    Silence.

Shall we go over it again?

    *Towards the end of this next passage, KAREN and
    MATTHEW approach the front door.*

*He ascertains she'll be all right. She assures him, and
pushes him out of sight.*

Remember – it's you who've chosen the time and
place, and it's you who've set the agenda. She – is
coming to you, not you to her. You didn't ask to
come into the world and no one is on this planet to
make their mother and father happy. No contract
exists, you are totally and utterly independent. All
this gives you strength, Jenny. Hold on to it.

Silence.

Don't be nervous, pet – you've written down what
you want to say, and you've delivered it to me three
times: you don't want *revenge*, you just want them to
know what it is *you* know.

Pause.

And try not to use the eff word, right?

JENNY nods.

I'll do the talking to begin with. Not much. 'What is
it you want to say?', basically. And you let her talk.
No interruption. Promise?

Another nod.

Your turn will come. Promise?

JENNY nods.

KAREN rings the bell.

VALERIE to JENNY – a look: 'ready?'

JENNY nods.

VALERIE moves to the front door.

*KAREN enters in a rush, to get out of the cold. VALERIE
points the direction.*

KAREN enters the room, VALERIE behind.

Mother and daughter confront each other.

*KAREN is nervous but outwardly calm and gentle. Steps
forward.*

KAREN Hello, darling.

JENNY steps back.

JENNY Hi.

KAREN 'Hi'?

> *KAREN turns to VALERIE. They shake hands.*

Hello, I'm Jenny's mother, Karen. We didn't introduce ourselves at the front door. So cold. How do you do? I'm very pleased to meet you, and I must tell you that I'm happy we could arrange a meeting. I always think it's better talking than not talking, don't you agree?

VALERIE It's not my role to agree or disagree.

KAREN Oh, dear! Can I sit?

> *VALERIE points to a chair.*

(*To JENNY.*) I don't suppose she'll charge extra for that.

> *KAREN hopes her daughter will share her smile. She doesn't.*
>
> *Long silence.*

VALERIE Right, Mrs Young. You've got the meeting you wanted – what is it you want to say?

KAREN Oh, you mean I must talk first? There's a special order for these meetings?

VALERIE No special order but –

KAREN Let Jenny speak. I've come to hear what my daughter wants to say to me.

VALERIE I don't think so, Mrs Young. You wanted to be here. It was you not Jenny who asked for this meeting.

KAREN I know, but –

VALERIE But nothing, Mrs Young. Your daughter is in my care, I don't normally see the relatives of my clients but in this case I've made an exception after careful thought together with Jenny. It was she who made the decision to agree to your request, and I'm here to ensure that no unfair advantage is taken of her.

KAREN Excuse me. I don't really understand what you're saying. It's a strange language to me. 'Unfair advantage'? What 'unfair advantage'? I'm her mother. We were friends Jenny and me. I was friends with both my daughters. They were very loving, and this loving daughter I'm not allowed to see, and I don't know why, and I don't know how she got here. One minute she was my daughter full of plans and chatter and laughing, concerned about this one in the family and that one in the family, next minute – she's gone. She's someone else.

VALERIE These things don't happen in a minute, Mrs Young. Cause and effect, cause and effect.

KAREN What 'cause and effect, cause and effect'?

JENNY can't hold back a smile at her mother's gentle mockery.

VALERIE is momentarily unnerved.

VALERIE Something very serious has happened in your daughter's life, Mrs Young. I don't think –

KAREN You don't have to tell me something very serious has happened in my daughter's life. I've been living for many months now with the heartache of 'something very serious in my daughter's life'. I don't know anything about you, Mrs Morgan, but you don't know anything about me so please don't snap like I'm a prisoner in a dock. Whatever you've made Jenny think, I'm not on trial here. I'm here to understand. Help me.

It was the marriage – a marriage not even her husband's mother thought was the right match. But Jenny insisted – she was in love. Your daughter says she's in love – you go with it. All the way. Right, Jenny? Our blessing and support all the way. You ran a business – we helped you. The children came – we began laying down for their education. You started to have problems – we listened, we advised.

And then the marriage sours, and everything goes wrong. The business collapses, divorce, debts, wild love affairs – all of them with boyfriends who had problems. One of them introduces you to a woman who persuades you that a new-age shop will solve your problems so you sell your house and go into partnership with her. Then she tells you therapy will solve your problems so you meet first one therapist then another. This one says she can help then that one says she can help and on the way everyone gets a bit of you until (*Turning to VALERIE.*) she meets you, Mrs Morgan, who tells her hypno-therapy will help, and I'm sure you're a very respectable qualified therapist who knows what she's doing but the next thing we hear – these accusations.

JENNY And true.

VALERIE Jenny –

JENNY Every one of them true.

VALERIE Jenny –

JENNY You stood by and let them happen –

VALERIE Jenny –

JENNY – so you fucking know they're true.

VALERIE JENNY!

KAREN And she never swore.

       Silence.

VALERIE Have you said all you want to say?

KAREN Not really. Give me a week, give me a month, a lifetime – I might say all I want to say.

VALERIE We don't have a week or a month, not even many more minutes, Mrs Young.

KAREN Do you fully understand who you've got under your care, Mrs Morgan? You think you've just got my daughter, don't you? Let me tell you – you've got her parents, her sister, her children, her grandfather, her friends – we're all in your care. Nothing, no one has been the same since this happened. You have a grave responsibility, Mrs Morgan. My daughter is eaten up with her anger, I can see it. Her eyes are burning from all the anger and fury in her. Look at her – anger, bitterness, hatred from I don't know where and I don't know why. And I've got to tell you

something, Mrs Morgan, anger and bitterness and
hatred in my book are neither helpful nor healthy.
I don't know what you hoped for, encouraging all
this anger, but it's doing damage to her, your client,
it's doing damage to her. Never mind about me, us,
the family – your client, look to your client. I don't
see recovery there, Mrs Morgan. You must excuse
me, I'm not an expert in these things but I do not see
what you could call recovery.

VALERIE   Are you finished now, Mrs Young?

KAREN   No. I'm not. But thank you.

VALERIE   Your turn now, Jenny.

In a gush, parrot-like.

JENNY   There's nothing more important than woman's self-
esteem. For centuries we've lived in a patriarchal
society dictated to by men taught by men living
by men's rules and laws and so women have been
conditioned to accept and obey and be silent. Not
any longer. We take no shit from anyone and that
means you and the man who calls himself my father
Matthew fucking father and who was so fucking
fatherly and loving that he loved me like a lover
from the age of two your fucking husband. Did you
ever know I hated myself? Did you ever ask? You
didn't did you? Why did my marriage fail? Why did
the business fail? Why did I go to pieces? It shocked
you but you never asked why. And why didn't you
ask why? Because you were afraid of the answers.
You knew the answers and you were afraid of
them. My father raped me. My own father Matthew
fucking father raped me. And my grandfather the
old man with his hands all over me and you knew
you my mother the one who should have looked
over me and after me and protected me and you
didn't you failed me you all failed me and I am filled
with so much anger for a stolen life and a robbed
childhood and the pain and the humiliation and the
betrayal and the loss of self-esteem. But no more, no

more negative thoughts – the truth is out. No more creeping into corners – the truth is out. No more shame and head-hanging and bended knees and yes daddy goodnight daddy. The truth is out. Out out out!

Oh it's so hot in here I feel so hot.

As she talks she pulls a pullover off over her head.

When her face is next visible we see it is deeply, deeply tormented.

She beats her breast with fists, and screams – a howl of utter misery and despair.

KAREN is distressed to the point of collapse.

VALERIE is more unnerved than ever. She had not expected this.

But it is JENNY's words that arrest them.

JENNY Family! Family! I need family. I need my family.

Both women, in this instant, share a common concern for the unhappy soul before them.

The commonality is brief. VALERIE returns to being a therapist.

VALERIE Breathe, Jenny. Breathe deeply. Let it out slowly. Good girl. Good. Slowly, slowly, pet, slowly.

JENNY breathes deeply many times, and calms down.

JENNY It happened, mum. It really happened.

KAREN Jenny, nothing heals with anger.

Silence.

VALERIE I think you'd better go now.

KAREN doesn't move.

KAREN Daddy's here. Will you see him?

Long pause.

What will she answer?

JENNY Yes.

KAREN leaves instantly.

VALERIE   Now wait a minute, Jenny, I think we should talk this over. (*Calls.*) Mrs Young! (*To JENNY.*) This is not what you want.

VALERIE leaves.

MATTHEW enters followed by KAREN, followed by VALERIE.

Father confronts daughter.

Both women alert, animal-like. What will happen?

MATTHEW   Hello, Jenny. How are you, sweetheart?

JENNY   Don't 'sweetheart' me, dad. Don't come here to 'sweetheart' me and soften me and try to confuse me with your patriarchal authority. I'm beyond your patriarchal authority beyond your reach forever and forever and forever after what you did to me all you did to me all you fucking did to me. You raped me! Tampered and raped me and she knew and said nothing and you robbed me of my childhood O I'm so hot it's so hot in here I feel so hot.

MATTHEW   (*Slowly, tenderly.*) Jenny, not this father. Not in a million years, to you, to anyone. Not this father.

He reaches to touch her arm.

Just remember – we love you.

VALERIE   Right. That's it.

MATTHEW   No. That's not it.

VALERIE   Out!

MATTHEW   Please, don't raise your voice to me, Mrs Morgan. That's not quite 'it'. I have something I want to say to you.

VALERIE   Out, out!

MATTHEW   It's a confession of guilt.

This holds her.

It is now JENNY's turn to be unnerved.

VALERIE   Confession?

MATTHEW   I bit their bums.

> *KAREN raises a cautionary hand – they won't understand.*

VALERIE   You what?   .

MATTHEW   I bit their bums.

VALERIE   You bit…

MATTHEW   No, let me finish. It gets even worse.

> *KAREN, as the story progresses, smiles until she finds the memory too overwhelming, and flees.*

We *both* bit their bums. Even worser – we let them bite our bums. Jenny's right – we tampered with her. We used to have bum-biting days. The girls would run away and hide and we'd go after them, and when we found them we'd bite their bums. Then *we* would hide, and they'd look for us and when they found us they'd bite *our* bums. And everyone squealed, and everyone shrieked. Got hiccups from shrieking and squealing, and laughing and fearing. Clothed, of course.

VALERIE   I think you should leave now.

MATTHEW   Why? It gets worse. My worst of worstest confessions. I loved, absolutely loved bathing them – splashing them, squirting them, blowing bubbles for them, and then – rubbing them in with baby oil. Rubbing their poor little chapped thighs and groins with soothing oils. And as I did it I lingered over it, and looked into their eyes and kept bending down to kiss them. Their face, their belly, their fat arms, their toes. This little piggy went to market, this little piggy stayed at home, this little piggy ate all the roast beef, and this little piggy had none. But this little piggy went inky pinky ponky poo – and we tickled them. Tickle, tickle, tickled them. Terrible – no? Oh, we tampered with them all right. And I tell you what, Mrs Therapist, give me back their childhood and the young man I once was and I'd have those glorious bum-biting days all over again. All over again.

> *He turns to see what effect his words have had on JENNY.*

Her back is to him. She is on the edge.

KAREN has fled.

VALERIE   Out!

He moves to the door.

MATTHEW   Tell me, Mrs Morgan, where were you trained?

Unceremoniously she pushes him through the door.

VALERIE   Out, out, out!

She turns with concern to her client.

Before MATTHEW and KAREN move off she arranges her husband's scarf and they become engaged in the most incongruous and touching exchange.

KAREN   You know, darling, the last little piggy didn't go 'inky pinky ponky poo'. You didn't remember right.

MATTHEW   I didn't?

KAREN   No, darling. The last little piggy went 'wee wee wee wee wee wee wee all the way home!'

MATTHEW   It went 'wee wee wee wee wee wee wee wee' not 'inky pinky ponky poo'?

KAREN   Yes, darling. 'Wee wee wee wee wee wee wee all the way home'.

MATTHEW   How could I have forgotten?

KAREN   (*Taking his arm.*) You've forgotten, you've forgotten. It happens. The details. One forgets the details. Gets them wrong.

They move but KAREN stops one more time.

VALERIE   Jenny?

KAREN   And what if we're dead and she recants and there's no one to say 'sorry' to?

MATTHEW   Don't think I haven't thought about it. Don't think I haven't thought.

KAREN releases a deflated sigh.

They've gone.

VALERIE   Jenny?

JENNY howls.

Jenny?

She turns to face VALERIE – haunted, confused, uncertain.

END

THE ROCKING HORSE KID

Characters

MARVIN SIMPSON
retired professor of philosophy, aged around 75

ZELDA,
his wife, aged around 74

CLARA MASON,
widowed, retired pharmacist, aged approaching 75,
South African

AGNES STONE,
lecturer in philology, aged around 45

DAPHNE STONE,
her mother, aged around 65

RAMBO PHILLIPS,
(finally nick-named RIDER) West Indian black
6th former, aged 18.

WOMAN ON BUS,
aged around 25

WAITRESS IN CAFÉ,
French, aged around 23

PEDESTRIAN,
female, around 74

SETTINGS

Brighton around the early 2000s

WOMAN ON A BUS and WAITRESS can be played by same actress.

DAPHNE and PEDESTRIAN can be played by same actress.

Music by Benjamin Till.

Note: 'This is a pre-production draft, before changes which are inevitable during rehearsal'.

12 September 2008 Blaendigeddi.

Prologue

A VOICE SINGING

>Rock me, fly me, rocking horse
>Around the world
>Rock me, fly me, rocking horse
>Before the fall
>Climb me to the sky
>There is no force
>They can apply
>To fly you one way
>And me another
>We are tougher
>Than them all.
>Rock me, fly me, rocking horse
>Before the fall
>Before the fall.

>>*An ethereal voice utters, like a voice in our heads:*

All shall be well and all shall be well, and all manner of things shall be well.

SCENE 1

A road in Upper Clapton, London. Autumn.

MARVIN appears. He's tired, he's been walking. Mumbles to himself.

MARVIN   It's a long road, Cazenove Road. From Alkham Road to the Upper Clapton Road – a long road.

>*A female PEDESTRIAN approaches.*

PED   Excuse me, can you tell me where Cazenove Road is?

MARVIN: You're on top of it, dear lady, here, on the right. I've just come from there myself.

PED   You live there?

MARVIN   Used to. Many years ago. (*Beat. Coolly.*) My son was killed here.

PED Oh!

MARVIN Just there, just before Cazenove Road meets the Upper Clapton Road.

He was walking up it when a crazy kid, who'd stolen a car, swerved from the main road too fast. Couldn't turn sharply enough. Mounted the pavement where my son was walking –

PED Oh, I'm so sorry –

MARVIN Smashed into him.

PED So, so sorry.

MARVIN Didn't stand a chance.

PED To lose a child …

MARVIN A boy of seventeen.

PED And you revisit the spot?

MARVIN I feel the need, yes, every so often.

PED I can understand.

MARVIN Used to be every week in the beginning. Then we moved to Brighton on the south coast. It's four times a year now. Sometimes five.

PED So *you* laid those flowers?

MARVIN But I don't come just to lay flowers.

PED Oh?

MARVIN No, I come to walk the road and look at everything he might have looked at for the last time. I think to myself – he saw this before he died, and that. Perhaps he was looking at that chestnut tree on the left, full of leaves in the spring, and conkers in the autumn.

PED What was his name?

MARVIN Jonty. His name was Jonty.

Look, here, the car smashed into him here. Just as he was about to turn left and catch the bus to Manor House underground station, home to Swiss Cottage. It's a long road, Cazenove Road, and I walk it from the corner of Alkham Road where he went once a week to sing in a choir, right up to here – where he sang no more.

I look at everything he might have looked at for the last time. That old house there with its grey stone and carved Victorian emblems. He loved architectural conceits, the gargoyles, the fruit, the curled leaves. And those street lamps. He saw those. Perhaps he saw all these things up till here. And here, a step away, he saw no more.

PED   That's so heart-breaking.

MARVIN   Here – he was alive, vibrant, curious; beyond – nothing, blackness. Stand here – everything to live for. A couple of steps forward – emptiness. A life finished. Smash! Just like that. (*Weeping.*) A precious life. My boy's one and only precious life. Just like that.

     Pause.

Forgive me.

PED   No need.

MARVIN   Public spectacle and all that.

PED   No need at all.

MARVIN   (*Pointing.*) There. Cazenove Road, there. Goodbye.

     They part their separate ways.

SCENE 2

CLARA in her garden.

CLARA   You're still lonely, Clara. You've created rituals for yourself but you're still lonely.

I sit here in my garden, and I realise how much I love life. So many objects surround me. Some lovely, some sad, photos of Joburg, photos of demonstrations, of dead friends, Zulu carvings, paintings of the High Veldt – each a special memory. I watch day by day the orchids I bought last year, wondering if a second growth will appear. It excites me. I can make things grow but it doesn't stop me feeling lonely. Seventy-five years old in ten days time – my ankles aren't swollen, my eye-sight's not bad, my hearing's OK, I can still walk without a stick, and thank God I don't need medication for anything, and – I can make things grow. I would just like to kiss someone goodnight and wake up saying 'good morning'.

On the other hand Jack's been dead so long I don't know that I could stand another body around the place. (*Beat.*) Seventy-five… Is this what it means to be seventy-five? Frightened of change? Deaf to new voices? Needing to be alone? (*Beat.*) But oh, to kiss someone goodnight and wake up saying 'good morning'…

SCENE 3

AGNES at her desk. Essays waiting to be read.

AGNES   We were in a restaurant. Very expensive. He wanted to buy me a special dinner for a 'special occasion' he said. We were at the coffee stage. He drank his little espresso, held the cup in the air for a split second, laid it back in the saucer with a harshness I don't think he intended. I think he intended resolve. And he said: 'I'm leaving you, Agnes. I've fallen in love with another woman. The bill is paid. Goodbye.' And he stood up and left.

Just like that. From nowhere. So I was too shocked to say anything. My gaze just followed him to the door as he went through it, and I thought, absurdly, that it was a joke and that he'd soon return with his gorgeous grin. But he didn't and I just sat there with a deep blush on my face hoping no other customer had heard and that my blush had not been noticed.

The waiter approached and handed me an envelope. My hands were shaking and I dropped the corner of the letter into the coffee.

Dear Agnes, it said. *It had to be like this, swift and sharp with no time for recrimination, and in a public place to avoid a shouting match. It had been wonderful and then it had not been wonderful. I'm sorry. You will find the settlement generous. It's no consolation now but broken hearts mend. Paul.*

'It had been wonderful and then it had not been wonderful.'

> *Bitterly considers.*

SCENE 4

Part of a sports hall – a sliver of a wall with netball net.
RAMBO is practising.

RAMBO   Rambo! Yeah! My family actually did christen me Rambo. Don't much look like him though. All them muscles – too heavy to carry around, man.

> *He's not very good. Gives up.*

Hate the sodding game. Hate all sport if the truth be known.

> *Finds a chair to Rap Tap on.*

Try looking for me
But I'm not there
I'm a hole in di wall
I'm not anywhere.
Di other guys
Di gangsta guys
Des easy to see
Des overflowing
Wid murderous
Murderous
Bom diddy bom diddy
Bom bom bom
I used dem words
To fill a gap
I'm gonna cool it now
Cos I hate rap

Cos I hate 50 Cent[1] and rap
Cos rap is a trap
An easy trap
A 50 Cent trap
For a sap sap sap.

Drumming stops.

Tries the ball in the net again.

Everyone thinks I should love rap 'cos I'm black.
Don't! Can't help it. Wish I could. It ain't easy hating
rap when you're black, you know. Puts you on the
outside. In the cold. Cold and lonely in the cold
outside. Can't help it. Wish I could. Need friends.

Gives up aiming the ball.

Where you going in your life, Rambo? What you
good at, Rambo? You ain't good at nothing 'cept
messing 'bout in stables. You earn couple shekels
clearing out stables in a riding school, but you ain't
never rid a horse. 'Cept once. That once. You'd
like to own one though wouldn't you? A horse of
your own. But how you gonna get you a horse,
Rambo? You gotta work, man, to get you a horse,
man. Horses don't grow on trees you know. Work,
Rambo, work! When you finished school you gotta
work to get you a horse. To get you *any*thing you
gotta work.

SCENE 5 – A FLASH BACK

Interior of a church.

Organ music and slide of a stained glass window will do.

MARVIN   What shall we do with his rocking horse, Zelda?

ZELDA   Keep it, Marvin. What else can we do with it? I don't
want to give it to charity.

MARVIN   We'll put it in the window.

ZELDA   Bit shabby.

---

1   50 Cent is the name of a rap singer

MARVIN   No matter. It might give pleasure to passers by.
          Provide a talking point, like walking a dog in the
          park. Remember that Chekhov story? *The Lady with
          the Dog*?

ZELDA   That was a love-story, sweetheart; our son's rocking
          horse in the window is not going to lead to a love
          story.

MARVIN   You don't know what a rocking horse in the window
          will lead to.

          Music swells a little.

          Seventeen years old! What does God want with a
          seventeen year old boy in the delight of his life? I
          knew there was a good reason never to believe in
          Him.

          Music fades.

SCENE 6 – A CHANGE OF MOOD

A bus pulls up at a stop.

*Four passengers board: AGNES; her mother, DAPHNE; a
MOTHER and BABY; RAMBO*

DAPHNE   Here, Agnes. There's a seat for the two of us.

AGNES   I'm standing, mother. There's a woman here with a
          baby.

WOMAN   Oh, that's kind. Thank you.

DAPHNE   Should be the men who stand.

WOMAN   Should be, should be. They never do, though.

RAMBO   Here, I'll stand, miss. You sit with your mother

WOMAN   Well, I was soon proved wrong, wasn't I!

RAMBO   I don't like the word 'never', see. 'Never' stops good
          things happening.

AGNES   (*Whispering.*) He'll go far that one will.

RAMBO   I heard that, miss. Think so?

AGNES   I didn't mean you to hear it.

RAMBO   But do you?

AGNES   Think you'll go far?

RAMBO   Yeah.

AGNES   Well, if you go on denying the possibility of 'never', you might.

RAMBO   I've got promise, you mean?

AGNES   Yes, I could mean that.

RAMBO   I've been told that before, you know. 'Promise'. I like that word – 'promise'

DAPHNE   Better than 'never', that's for sure.

>   *Pause.*

RAMBO   What about 'never say never'?

DAPHNE   Ha! Answer that one, daughter.

AGNES   'Never say never' is the one time 'never' works.

RAMBO   Because two negatives make a positive, right?

AGNES   (*Further impressed.*) Right!

RAMBO   So, she's your daughter, then!

DAPHNE   She is indeed.

RAMBO   Look more like sisters to me.

AGNES   Oh, please…

DAPHNE   Please, what? Compliments don't come my way every day, Agnes.

AGNES   But not from a kid.

RAMBO   I don't pay compliments, lady. I say what I see – and I'm no kid, nither.

DAPHNE   Now look, you've upset him.

RAMBO   Nah! I'm not upset. Take more than names to upset me. I'm not that type.

AGNES   What type is that?

RAMBO   I'm not the type that looks for insults round every corner and demands respect all the time. You gotta earn respect is what I think; you can't demand it. And I look at you and think that's a good and handsome woman. Am I right, daughter? Am I right about your ma there?

AGNES   You are, indeed. But why do you talk about 'types'? Everyone's an individual.

RAMBO   But a type of individual. The frightened-of-his-shadow type; the no-girl-can-resist-me type; the brainy-and-quiet type, the victim type, the stupid-and-loud type. There ought to be a book written about types so's you know where you belong.

AGNES   And which type would you belong to?

RAMBO   I bet you think I'd belong to a black-roots-type.

AGNES   You don't?

RAMBO   Tell you a story. An' I don't mind anyone else listening, niver. I once got into a scrape at school defending a poor little white kid against three big black boys. And they turned on me and screamed 'where are your roots, black boy? Doncha know where you belong? Roots, man, roots, remember your roots.' And I screamed back 'my roots is justice, blood. My roots is intelligence.' They laid me out flat and left me for dead.

DAPHNE   Oh, look, Agnes, that window again with the rocking horse in it.

RAMBO   A rocking horse? Where? Where?

DAPHNE   There, look, there!

RAMBO   Oh, yes. Wow! That's a beaute. Always wanted a rocking horse – ever since I played on one in a nursery. A little wooden thing it was, falling to pieces because all the other kids treated it rough. Not me. I'd sit on it and imagine myself riding across deserts, through forests, up mountains.

AGNES   Got a strong imagination, have you?

RAMBO   Yeah! But what I really want is a real horse.

DAPHNE   Like horses do you?

RAMBO   Love 'em.

DAPHNE   I used to ride horses when I was a girl.

RAMBO   I work a few hours a week in some riding stables.

DAPHNE   I loved the smell of them.

RAMBO   And the feel of them, too.

DAPHNE   Brush them down, do you?

RAMBO   Yeah, they love that.

AGNES   Where would you ride your horse?

RAMBO   Oh, I don't know.

DAPHNE   Round the race tracks?

RAMBO   Nah! Hate competing for things. Prefer aiming for things.

AGNES   Over fields, then?

RAMBO   Yeah. And up mountains.

AGNES   And through forests.

RAMBO   And over deserts. Different places. Round the world

AGNES   Round the world? Ambitious.

RAMBO   Yeah! Why not. Round the world. Just thought of it. I mean people sail round the world, fly solo round the world, drive round the world in a car or a motor bike. No one's ever done the world on a horse.

AGNES   Then maybe you'll be the one.

RAMBO   Maybe! (*Reminding her.*) Never say never!

DAPHNE   I love bus rides, train rides. Meet all sorts.

   Music.

AGNES   (*To herself.*) Wish I had more students like him around me. He's got something. His eyes. His smile. I see a spark. I've seen it before – he's immediate, he's there. He enters and he's there. The other passengers were gripped by his story. I watched them. Wonder what kind of a life he's going to make for himself. Will he ever get to ride a horse around the world? He's not afraid to stand above the crowd. Admirable but dangerous. Will the crowd drag him down and hang him high? None of your business, Agnes. Yet he does cry out to be looked after. Not by you though. Protected. Not by you, though!

SCENE 7

A lounge in the house of MARVIN and ZELDA.
Late afternoon.

ZELDA Oh, dear. Dozed off again.

MARVIN I think you should leave me, Zelda. I can't be good to live with as I grow grouchier.

ZELDA I'm a tired, old woman of seventy-five, Marvin, where would I go?

MARVIN You have sisters.

ZELDA And you're a tired old man of seventy-five. Who would look after you?

MARVIN I can look after myself.

ZELDA Four times a year you go to Cazenove Road, and every time you return you tell me I should leave you. How many more times, sweetheart, tell me, how many more times?

MARVIN You don't deserve a grouchy old mourner like me.

ZELDA That's only one small part of you.

MARVIN List me the others.

ZELDA You're just fishing, you old fraud, you.

MARVIN No, Zellie, I'm not. I'm being serious. As I've grown older I've understood less and less how I'm perceived. I've no sense of myself, no idea what more you see in me

      Pause.

ZELDA Kindness, intellect, passion, tenderness, touch of gaiety now and then – lots! All sorts. Not bad for fifty years of marriage.

MARVIN That long?

ZELDA The Golden one soon. What a lot we've lived through.

MARVIN And has anything really changed?

ZELDA The internet?

MARVIN Externally, yes. But I fear human nature is a
        constant. The Internet doesn't change human nature,
        human nature shapes the Internet.

ZELDA   Twenty-five years old when we met.

MARVIN Were we ever twenty-five years old?

ZELDA   I think so, sweetheart. Bicycles, weekend camping,
        baked beans on toast smelling of burnt wood,
        roasted chestnuts, groceries from a van…

MARVIN The rag-and-bone man.

ZELDA   The ping of the ticket-collector on the tram, the
        trolley bus.

MARVIN The air-raid siren.

ZELDA   The all-clear.

        Pause as the memories sink in.

MARVIN Jonty will never know twenty-five years old.

        Silence.

        I'm sorry, Zellie. That's what growing old is
        about – accumulating loss. Loss of innocence, loss
        of youth, loss of parents, friends, appetites. The
        inevitable cycle, natural. Except the loss of children,
        that's unnatural. I'm sorry. I will never recover.

ZELDA   You keep saying that. Keep saying it and it'll become
        self-fulfilling. You will recover. Before you die you
        will recover. Somehow. I'll see to it. We'll find
        something to recharge your life.

MARVIN Like what?

ZELDA   Oh, I don't know. It'll come to us, to you, or to me,
        one of us. Life's like that – a slow dawning. Why
        don't you take up writing your diary again?

MARVIN To put what in it? Nothing happens to retired
        professors of philosophy, and I've no patience for
        the boring details of living

ZELDA   You used to have a lot of patience for 'the boring
        details of living'. 'Truth resides in the detail,' you
        used to say.

MARVIN That's not why I wrote a diary.

ZELDA   Why *did* you write a diary?

MARVIN   To prove to myself that I existed the day before.

ZELDA   Philosophers!

MARVIN   Not really, Zellie. If I'd been a real philosopher I'd
have added one tiny argument, one insight, one
important something to illuminate one tiny part of
the darkness. Nothing! I added nothing.

ZELDA   You taught your students not to judge things through
the prism of a religion, or an ideology. That was an
important something.

MARVIN   It was nothing. Just words. We lived through a world
war, economic cycles, the birth of Europe which
may or may not be a good thing, the backward
stride into religious fundamentalism, and I've neither
added to, nor shaped, nor protested about any of
that.

ZELDA   I thought you thought Europe was a good thing.

MARVIN   Did I?

ZELDA   Yes, darling. You've forgotten. It was me
who questioned it because I'd always felt
European – steeped in European literature and
European music. What did we need a Union for, I
wondered?

MARVIN   To prevent another European war.

ZELDA   So we go elsewhere for our wars. Progress!!
Pause.

MARVIN   Fifty years! The Golden One. (*Beat.*) I'm glad it was
you, Zellie.

ZELDA   How would you like a drink?

MARVIN   Isn't it too early?

ZELDA   It's never too early for something you want.

MARVIN   You know what we rarely drink these days?

ZELDA   Tell me.

MARVIN   Sherry.

ZELDA   You always viewed sherry as a boring middle-class
drink? Facile view I always thought.

MARVIN   And philosophy warns against such facile views.

ZELDA   I mean the only people who are boring are boring people.

MARVIN   Right!

ZELDA   And you find them everywhere.

MARVIN   Every-bloody-where.

ZELDA   Sherry, then?

MARVIN   Sherry!

She sets up the glasses.

Do you remember Pat Burke?

ZELDA   Overweight and intimidatingly clever.

MARVIN   But you liked her.

ZELDA   I liked clever people. Still do. (*Beat.*) Here you are, sweetheart. One Medium dry.

MARVIN   She used to start her day reading essays – Hazlitt, Montaigne, Orwell, nothing heavy. Then she'd go on to a novel; then a chapter or two of history, and finally a chapter of philosophy. It was a way of bringing her brain up to fever pitch in preparation for her students. When she told me that was how she woke up to the world I tried it myself. Never got past the first essay. Had to go straight to philosophy.

ZELDA   (*Lovingly.*) See! I could never leave you, Marvin.

MARVIN   Still think you should.

SCENE 8

A bus.

AGNES seated. CLARA boards.

CLARA approaches AGNES.

CLARA   Excuse me, do you mind if I sit next to you?

AGNES   Please do.

CLARA   I couldn't help overhearing you and your mother talking the other day in the bus.

AGNES   (*Uncertain where this is leading.*) Ye-es.

CLARA   And that young black boy stood up for the other mother and child.

AGNES   Oh, yes, I remember.

CLARA   And your mother flirted with him.

AGNES   She does tend to take over.

CLARA   Impressive young man, wasn't he!

AGNES   Immediate, yes.

CLARA   But uncertain. He'd say something then look to see how you were reacting.

AGNES   And people did react. They were drawn to him.

CLARA   And you were talking about a toy rocking horse in the window of a certain house that this route passes.

AGNES   Yes, I remember.

CLARA   I've looked at that horse for years.

AGNES   Does it have a history?

CLARA   I think so but I don't know for sure. I'd love to be able to find out though. Do you live in Brighton or Hove?

AGNES   Hove, actually.

CLARA   Long?

AGNES   Two years.

CLARA   Live with your mother?

AGNES   No. She visits every now and then.

CLARA   I must say your mother is a very attractive woman.

AGNES   And doesn't she know it! The boy on the bus was right – good and handsome.

CLARA   If I was as attractive I think I'd flirt with a younger man, but at seventy-five – your mother's not seventy-five is she?

AGNES   Sixty-five.

CLARA   My problem is I don't feel seventy-five. The head and heart is stuck at thirty-five but it's the poor old body… And I feel I have so much to give. You're not seventy-five of course but I bet you don't feel your age.

AGNES None of us do.

CLARA Married?

AGNES Was.

CLARA Ah, 'was'! (*Beat.*) Sure you don't mind me asking?

AGNES Not so far, providing you don't ask me about 'was'. Still a little tender in that place.

CLARA But this route – ?

AGNES I take it to work.

CLARA From Hove to Brighton?

AGNES I'm a lecturer in philology at Sussex University.

CLARA I thought you might be – a lecturer, that is.

AGNES Do I look so professorial?

CLARA No, it was the way you spoke with that young man – supportively.

AGNES It's a tough, bewildering world they're going out to. They need a lot of support and reassurance. (*Beat.*) Oh, look. The beautiful rocking horse. How large it looms in the window. In fact it seems to have grown.

CLARA You've noticed.

AGNES But it can't have.

CLARA Indeed it can't. But it seems to. Grow one day, seem smaller on another.

AGNES Why do you think that is?

CLARA I'm not sure. I think it has to do with mood. Grows if you're happy, shrinks when the world's too much for you. You must be in a good mood. Getting over your break-up perhaps?

AGNES And why does it loom large for you?

CLARA Perhaps because I've plucked up courage to talk to you. I live alone but I enjoy company, you see, and I still have appetites for living and delights. Just no one to share the delights with, no familiar body around the place.

AGNES I'm rather pleased to have no familiar body around the place.

CLARA   That's the difference between a husband dying and a
        husband fleeing. Sorry. That was intrusive.

AGNES   No, no…

CLARA   I'm normally shy.

AGNES   It's all right.

CLARA   But sometimes a personality strikes me and I feel
        I should strike up a conversation with that person.
        Mostly I don't. But you – you with that boy, I
        thought 'there's a woman I'd like to know'.

        Uneasy moment.

AGNES   (*A little anxious.*) Thank you. That's flattering. (*Beat.*)
        Tell me what you know about the rocking horse?

CLARA   I've lived in Brighton since I was forty-three. I've
        been on and off this bus over thirty years but that
        rocking horse wasn't there when I arrived, and I
        only first noticed it a couple of years later. It was
        in and out of the window for the first ten years,
        sometimes away for long periods, three or four
        weeks, but it always came back. And then one day it
        was gone, and didn't come back for six months, and
        when it did it had been re-painted. And there it's
        been ever since.

AGNES   What a strange story.

CLARA   Not really a story at all. Or rather only half the story.
        The other half lies behind that front door.

AGNES   Have you ever seen any one go in or come out of
        that front door?

CLARA   Yes as a matter of fact – come out. A stooped, elderly
        man and an upright elderly woman.

AGNES   Oh, forgive me, my stop's coming up.

CLARA   Mine, too. Look, have you got time to have coffee
        with an old woman? I've got my rituals like most
        people, and one of them is to have a coffee and
        pastry in my favourite coffee shop. Treat's on me.

AGNES   As a matter of fact I do have time. I'm ridiculously
        early for all my appointments. I have a dread of

being late. It's such an insult to keep someone waiting, don't you think?

CLARA   I do, I do! Come on, then, quick, or he'll drive off before we get to the door.

    They make it in time.

    Doors closing.

CLARA   (*To herself.*) 'Make friends,' say my friends. But that's easier said than done. Older women are too desperate, younger women are scared because they see themselves in a few years' time. But this younger one doesn't seem scared. Perhaps because she can see I'm not desperate. I can make things grow, my orchid is showing a second growth, I can make things grow, and that gives me confidence. Perhaps she can see the confidence. We're drawn to confidence, aren't we, Clara?

SCENE 9

The lounge.

MARVIN and ZELDA.

MARVIN   You should leave me, Zellie.

ZELDA   That's twice you've told me in a couple of days.

MARVIN   Twice?

ZELDA   Twice! And you've started calling me 'Zellie'? You haven't called me that in years.

MARVIN   There's a lot I haven't done in years.

ZELDA   Guilt, Marvin, grief and guilt, a lethal mixture. Get rid of it.

MARVIN   I want to hold him and I can't.

ZELDA   I know, sweetheart, I know.

MARVIN   My son's not here to be held.

ZELDA   Do you imagine I don't miss a son to hold?

MARVIN   It's such an ache.

ZELDA   Here, let's hold on to each other instead.

MARVIN Such an ache.

          Weeps.

ZELDA I know, darling, I know. Hush… Ssssh.

          Comforts him.

MARVIN Look at me, I've become a foolish weepy. I used to be strong and wise, once.

ZELDA You know what they say: within every wise man is an idiot trying to get out and betray him.

MARVIN Who said? I bet you don't know who said. I bet you said. I bet you made that up just to make me smile.

ZELDA Good thing to smile.

MARVIN I know, Zellie, I know. Used to do a lot of it myself.

ZELDA You're smiling now old man.

MARVIN I'm not!

ZELDA You are!

MARVIN I'm not, I'm not!

ZELDA You are, you are! (*Giggles.*) Look at yourself. A big grin from ear to ear. Ha, ha! Ho, ho! Look at him! From ear to ear! (*In the wake of her merriment.*) Marvin! I have an idea. Let's drive off somewhere.

MARVIN Drive off? Where? Drive off where?

ZELDA I don't know. When we were younger you used often to say 'I'd like to get into a red sports car with an open top and just go off'. Let's just go off, Marvin. Pack a bag, open the car door, start the engine and – off! No plans, where the fancy takes us. Vroom! See the world. Vroom, vroom.

MARVIN We don't have a red sports car, vroom vroom!

ZELDA MARVIN! Really! You're so exasperatingly pedantic sometimes.

MARVIN You're asking me to be the younger man I no longer am. I can't change.

ZELDA People don't change, but they do find different parts of themselves.

MARVIN I'm too old to go looking.

Pause.

Zellie, can you remember the name of the woman
who made the rocking horse?

ZELDA Wendy. She used to make rocking horses from the
photos people gave her of their favourite horse.
Jonty didn't have a horse, favourite or otherwise.

MARVIN I know.

ZELDA You were afraid he might have an accident.

MARVIN I know, Oh don't I know.

The irony is unspoken.

SCENE 10

A café.

Low hum of conversations.

Tinkle of cups.

Music is Baroque.

AGNES Oh, my God! Look at that array – fruit tarts, Mille
Feuilles –,

CLARA – chocolate éclairs –

AGNES And look at those prices!

CLARA No, don't look at those prices. I told you, the treat's
on me.

WAITRESS approaches.

WAITRESS (*French accent.*) What can I get for you ladies?

CLARA Cappuccino for me, please. And for my friend – I'm
sorry I don't know your n –

AGNES Agnes. Agnes Stone.

CLARA And I'm Clara Mason. How do you do.

AGNES How do you do.

CLARA Pleased to meet you.

WAITRESS And my name is Mirabelle. How do you do. I would
love to serve you.

AGNES I'll also have a cappuccino.

WAITRESS Two cappuccinos. Anything else I can get for you?

AGNES I don't think I can resist that Mille Feuilles.

WAITRESS One Mille Feuilles.

CLARA And I shall go wild and have a chocolate éclair.

WAITRESS Two cappuccinos, one Mille Feuilles and one wild chocolate éclair. Merci! Enjoy your conversation.

WAITRESS leaves.

CLARA Was she being cheeky or friendly?

AGNES Friendly I think. She just didn't understand that 'enjoy your conversation' is not the same as 'enjoy your meal'.

Atmosphere sinks in.

AGNES I see why you make a ritual of having coffee here. Nice ambience –

CLARA I'm afraid since becoming a widow I've had to create many rituals for myself.

AGNES What are your other ones?

CLARA Cinema once a week. Once a week to London for theatre. Eat out a couple of times. Swim every morning, and – sssh! don't tell anyone, a half-hour doze most afternoons.

AGNES Who doesn't doze when they can?

CLARA And sometimes in the theatre, too.

AGNES Oh, sin of sins!

CLARA I mean when those lights go down it's bedtime isn't it? And the actors mumble so, or talk to each other as though they're in a small room together with no one else around, and I want to shout out to them 'hey, I'm here, too, and I've paid good money to hear words'. But we don't do that sort of thing these days do we, more's the pity.

AGNES Children? Grandchildren?

CLARA Sadly, not. But I have nieces and nephews.

AGNES What did your husband do?

CLARA   Pharmacist. We ran a large chemist shop in the back streets away from the competition. We were both pharmacists, and when we sold it we had enough to buy a flat for renting out. Pays for the pastries!

AGNES   When did you leave South Africa?

CLARA   You heard the accent.

AGNES   Unmistakable, actually.

CLARA   Nineteen seventy-six. After Soweto. The black kids didn't want to learn Afrikaans so they rioted and got shot. We might've stayed on to become part of the protest movement but we later heard the kids had stoned to death one of our friends who'd devoted his life to social work among the blacks. And we'd already served time in prison for giving sanctuary to rebel leaders so it looked like becoming a mess chemists couldn't help solve.

AGNES   Do you regret leaving?

CLARA   Yes and no, like most decisions in life. But I miss being involved with something.

AGNES   Did your husband wonder about the rocking horse?

CLARA   Of course. He tended to be dismissive. 'They had children', he said, 'they had children and the children grew up and left home and one day they'll come and take it away for their own children.' No sense of mystery my old man.

AGNES   Why was it repainted?

CLARA   Precisely! Why was it repainted?

AGNES   Your husband said?

CLARA   'It became an eye-sore so they re-painted it. Women!' he said, 'why do they make mysteries out of the simple things in life.'

WAITRESS returns to lay order on table.

WAITRESS   Two cappuccinos, nice and frothy. One Mille Feuilles very rich but very tasty. One wild chocolate éclair, and one wild bill.

CLARA   Thank you.

WAITRESS Enjoy!

        WAITRESS leaves.

AGNES I hate that. 'Enjoy'. I don't know why. After all, it's a simple order – 'enjoy'. Perhaps that's what irritates me. It's an order more than a polite request. 'Enjoy or else!' Lazy, unfinished!

CLARA Like 'bless'. Another piece of verbal laziness. (*Mockingly.*) 'Ah, bless!'

AGNES And sentimental, too.

CLARA Yes! Yes! Let's see, what else irritates us.

AGNES I get irritated by people who write and sign themselves 'me'.

CLARA Me too!

AGNES And I hate hearing students greet each other 'hello you'.

CLARA Me, too, me, too! Oh, what fun. I haven't had a bitching session like this in ages.

AGNES Nor me!

CLARA I'm so pleased you agreed to have a coffee with me. You do still have time, don't you? Not in a rush?

AGNES All right so far.

CLARA Daily companionship with a partner – there isn't anything quite like it, is there!

AGNES When it works.

CLARA Which yours didn't? (*Beat.*) I hope we do get to know each other better.

AGNES I'm afraid I'm not the best company these days.

CLARA Melancholic, I can see it. I was, too, after Jack died. Loss! Freud observed: the most profoundly depressing emotion is loss. And life is full of it from start to finish. You lose dreams, homes, husbands, hopes. I think the worst loss must be parents because suddenly you're an orphan, on your own, no one at the end of that phone like there used to be.

AGNES But you haven't lost the appetite for living, you say.

CLARA   Oh, no! Never! You're talking to a woman who doesn't ever want to die. And when I do I want to be buried on my back so that I can look up at the sky and stars and the trees going through their seasons.

AGNES   Does my melancholy really show? I'm sorry.

CLARA   Don't be sorry, please.

AGNES   I try to hide it, I really do. There's something embarrassingly banal about unhappiness. Everyone's unhappy and it's –

CLARA   (*Suddenly.*) Wait! Look! That boy! Your boy in the bus. He's just passed the window.

AGNES   No, don't, Clara. I don't want to get involved…

CLARA   Back in a tick.

     Rushes into street.

AGNES   (*To herself.*) What in God's name am I letting myself in for? Why did I agree to have coffee with a stranger? I'm not ready for a social life. And yet I like her. At least she won't break my heart. 'Broken hearts mend' he wrote. He was wrong, the broken heart doesn't mend. You put it together like a precious, broken cup that never looks right, that looks wonky, that looks like what it is: a broken cup stuck together with glue. You feel as though if you pick it up the tea will run the other way. You can never quite trust it to function as it once did.

SCENE 10 A

The street outside café.

CLARA   (*Calling out.*) Hello!

RAMBO   (*Startled and defensive.*) It's alright, ma'am. I'm on my way to college now.

CLARA   No, don't run off. I've got a friend of yours here.

RAMBO   A friend of mine?

CLARA   I was in the bus the other day. You stood up for a mother and her baby and you got into conversation with two women.

RAMBO   Right! One of them said I had promise.

CLARA   She's in the café. And you talked about 'types'.

RAMBO   I thought a lot about her after that.

CLARA   You playing truant?

RAMBO   You don't play truant when you're in a sixth form college, man, you just don't turn up for lectures.

CLARA   Fancy a coffee and pastry?

RAMBO   A what?

CLARA   I'm paying.

> *Pause.*

Something sweet something free?

RAMBO   Can't say 'no' to that can I!

CLARA   Come on then.

SCENE 10 (CONTINUING)

Inside cafe again.

AGNES   (*To herself.*) 'It had been wonderful and then it had not been wonderful'. Is that the story of all marriages in a nutshell, I wonder? 'It had been wonderful and then it had not been wonderful.' Ha! Simple!

> *RAMBO and CLARA appear.*

AGNES   We meet again.

RAMBO   Coincidence or not? I tell you, man, life gets weirder every day. Last week, a Monday it was, I bumped into a cousin I hadn't seen all year – which if you knew the West Indian community is difficult to do. Then I bump into him again on Tuesday, and again on Thursday.

CLARA   Think it means something 'weird'?

RAMBO   Nah! Means nothing. I hate all that looking for
          hidden meanings. Life is what you see and what you
          see is what you get, is what I think.

                    Catches sight of the Mille Feuilles.

          What's that?

AGNES   A Mille Feuilles.

RAMBO   Mill what?

AGNES   Feuilles. French for 'leaves'. Mille Feuilles – a
          thousand leaves. Made by rolling and folding dough
          four or five times over butter so the heat makes the
          butter rise which makes the dough rise. It's called
          puff-pastry. Puffs up!

RAMBO   Wicked! How come you know about things like that,
          then?

AGNES   I was a drop-out before I decided to go back to
          education and get a degree. One of my drop-out jobs
          was working in a bakery in Paris.

RAMBO   Cool!

                    WAITRESS approaches.

WAITRESS And what's the handsome black boy having?

RAMBO   Handsome? You reckon?

WAITRESS If I didn't have a boyfriend …

RAMBO   Hang about! Young people these days!

WAITRESS Espresso? Americano? Pastry?

RAMBO   Cappuccino and one of those.

WAITRESS Cappuccino and one Milles Feuilles. Thank you.

                    WAITRESS leaves.

RAMBO   Wicked!

CLARA   God! They make me feel so old.

AGNES   You studying for A levels?

RAMBO   Yeah!

AGNES   Failed them first time?

RAMBO   Yeah! Got to take them again.

CLARA   What are your weak subjects?

RAMBO Maths and science.

AGNES Lots walking away from those two.

RAMBO Not much good in English, niver.

CLARA Nor me, but I soared in maths. Know lots of games with numbers.

AGNES Do your parents help?

RAMBO What? You're joking. They work all the time. I'm a latch-key kid, man, been one for years, can't you tell?

CLARA Ever get into trouble?

RAMBO Why, because I'm black?

CLARA Don't be edgy. I know what prison is like.

RAMBO You done time, then?

AGNES Did time.

RAMBO Did time.

AGNES (*To herself.*) What on earth am I doing bothering to correct this boy?

CLARA For a good cause, though. Anti-apartheid.

RAMBO Anti-a-what?

CLARA Apartheid. Separating blacks from whites. South Africa

AGNES (*To herself.*) Good God! How quickly important words get forgotten!

CLARA What were you done for?

RAMBO I didn't say I was done. (*Beat.*) For stealing a horse.

AGNES Stealing a horse?!

CLARA I hope you didn't hurt it.

RAMBO Nah! Didn't really steal it, niver. I muck out stables in a riding school for pocket money, and one night I borrowed one to try and ride it.

CLARA And could you?

RAMBO Yeah! Over the Sussex Downs. Bare back, too, man. Come naturally, like.

CLARA And you'd never ridden before?

RAMBO Never! But I had to chose an evening when the boss come back to check on something, didn't I! Saw a horse missing, and called the Feds.

AGNES Took you to court?

RAMBO Nah! Good boss. Let me off with a warning, didn't 'e. 'Cos I brought it back, see. No damage. And he rang my mum who come down and apologised for me, saying I was a good boy, which I am, just stupid.

AGNES You don't sound stupid to me.

RAMBO At school things I am. Trust. Stupid.

CLARA No one else around to help you with homework?

RAMBO My dad says his responsibility is to put food on the table. Teaching is for teachers.

AGNES What does he do?

RAMBO Tunes pianos and plays in a jazz band.

AGNES And your mum?

RAMBO Accountant for a record company.

CLARA (*To herself.*) Don't do it, Clara. Your routines, your rhythms, your rituals will all be shot to pieces. Don't make any offers of help. Don't be seventy-five and daft.

    To RAMBO.

    How would you like me to help you with science and maths?

RAMBO Don't you work?

CLARA Retired. And Agnes here lectures in English.

AGNES No, no, please. Count me out.

CLARA We could all meet at my house.

RAMBO Hold on, guys.

CLARA I'll cook great food!

RAMBO I'm not looking for handouts, you know.

CLARA Who's talking about handouts! I know things you need to know – it's *you* who's handing me the opportunity to be useful.

AGNES   Forgive me if I sound selfish but I teach all the time,
        I get fed up with it, honestly.

CLARA   Oh, come on Agnes.

AGNES   I need breaks.

CLARA   You need taking out of yourself.

RAMBO   And I need to have a think. I ain't never been
        offered anything like this before.

CLARA   We'll all have fun together.

AGNES   And I'm not exactly in an altruistic state of mind…

CLARA   Nothing like altruism to mend a broken heart.

AGNES   Please! Clara!

CLARA   Sorry, bloody tactless. But we can all go out together.

RAMBO   You got a broken heart, then?

CLARA   We could got to theatres, movies…

RAMBO   Oh yeah? And who'll pay?

AGNES   I'm not ready.

RAMBO   See, she's not certain either.

CLARA   Concerts, exhibitions…

RAMBO   She's not ready and I'm not ready.

CLARA   Doesn't the prospect excite you?

RAMBO   You, not her.

CLARA   Don't let your ex win twice – to break your heart
        and then not leave you alone to mend it.

AGNES   Well…

RAMBO   Hello! Does anyone hear me?

AGNES   I suppose…

RAMBO   Do I have a say in this?

AGNES   I do miss a purpose in life.

CLARA   And what's life about if not purpose!

RAMBO   (*To himself.*) Is this weird or is this weird? Two smart
        white women – one old enough to be my mother,
        the other old enough to be my grandmother, offering
        to help me. Why? I don't know them. What's in it
        for them? Weird, I would say it's weird.

To them.

Why would you women do this? You ain't got designs on my body have you?

CLARA Oh, well, if you're worried about being…

RAMBO No, no! But you can understand, right? All of a sudden two strange white women offering a strange boy, a strange black boy help, well it is a bit…er …you know…er…

AGNES Overwhelming?

CLARA Unusual?

RAMBO I was thinking scary.

AGNES Perhaps your politeness on the bus made an impression on us.

RAMBO (*To himself.*) Now then, guy, you can't creep through life being suspicious of everything. These women see you. 'Promise' said one. 'Perceptive' said another. 'Politeness'. 'Made an impression'. Can't be bad. You was looking for respect – the best kind, this, 'cos of who you are, not 'cos like some guys strapped with a gun in their hand. I mean – go for it, Rambo.

CLARA So if your dad plays in a jazz band you must play an instrument.

RAMBO Nah, I'm a listener. Listening is enough for me.

AGNES What do you listen to?

RAMBO What's playing now – stuff like that.

AGNES Baroque?

RAMBO That what it's called?

AGNES I thought you would have liked rap.

RAMBO 'Cos I'm black? I hate rap.

AGNES Hate it?

RAMBO Not all blacks are the same, you know.

AGNES What don't you like about rap?

RAMBO Boring! Monotonous! My dad when he tunes pianos hits all the notes, one by one and each one is different, and he plays chords and each chord is

different. So I grew to like variety. I like rainbows,
different colours, different sounds. You walk the
street and you see everyone's different. Drive you
crazy if everyone looked the same. So I don't like
my music to be the same, I like colours, like the
rainbow. My mum asks me what I'm gonna do
with my life and I tell her 'mum, I'm gonna live a
rainbow life'. She think I'm crazy.

CLARA (*To herself.*) Listen to him, Clara. This is no mistake
you're making. On the other hand you may be
missing a cause in your life but aren't you too old for
causes. No one's ever too old for causes. You don't
want your last years to be selfish last years, do you,
Clara? On the other 'other hand' what do you know
about A level syllabuses? Well, we'll find out won't
we! We'll ask questions and find out.

SCENE 11 – THE TRIP

*NOTE: Scenes eleven to twenty-one inclusive are offered
impressionistically, a montage helped along with our music
played at a busy, energetic, jazzy pace.*

The sea front, Dieppe.

*The air is full of fantastically shaped kites. It's the bi-annual
Kite Festival.*

ZELDA Oh, Marvin, what shapes! Look at those shapes – a
firefly, a giant squid, a dragon. And that one
there – look, three painted panels like stained glass
windows. How lucky to have coincided with a Kite
Festival.

MARVIN Haven't gone far, though, have we? Haven't exactly
leapt into a red sports car and raced vroom vroom
through Europe. Dieppe! A few miles across the
English channel!

ZELDA You miss the point! We didn't plan it, we didn't
even know such a festival existed. And here we are,
looking out to sea and at those glorious kites.

SCENE 12 – TEACHING

We move between CLARA's room and AGNES's room.
CLARA's room.

CLARA … What you must remember, Rambo, is that science is not merely a list of chemicals to be learned by heart, it's an attempt to describe and explain the world.

RAMBO Like art does?

CLARA Exactly! A famous professor, Bronowski his name was, suggested that art and science were two sides of the same coin.

RAMBO So which side does religion belong to?

CLARA Religion?

RAMBO Well doesn't religion also try to describe and explain the world?

CLARA You're not going to let me get away with anything, are you?

RAMBO Like you don't let me get away with anything.

CLARA Religion invites faith in the inexplicable. Some people are comfortable with that. They need it. I don't – I find faith unreliable.

RAMBO You want explanations for everything?

CLARA 'Fraid so.

RAMBO Yeah, I'm a bit like that. Drives my mum crazy that I don't go to church with her. Doesn't make for an easy life, though, does it! So much can't be explained.

CLARA Yet!

AGNES's room.

AGNES Language – one of the greatest engines – probably the greatest engine invented by man.

RAMBO You mean 'human kind' please, Miss, like you keep telling me.

AGNES You aren't going to let me get away with anything, are you?

RAMBO   Like Clara doesn't let me get away with anything.

AGNES   Language, the greatest engine invented by humankind.

RAMBO   An 'engine'?

AGNES   An engine, yes! To drive you through a complex world. A well-constructed sentence is like a well-constructed engine – purrs with pleasure, takes you places.

RAMBO   So you think language is only a journey?

AGNES   I didn't say that. I said it was an engine that would take you on a journey.

RAMBO   The greatest invention?

AGNES   Yes.

RAMBO   More important than the wheel?

AGNES   I think so.

RAMBO   More important than DNA?

AGNES   Nothing, nothing, nothing could happen without language. We were born to think and explain our way through life. Language shapes thought, language names thought, language illustrates thought, defines it. Our only hope for sanity and peace.

RAMBO   Providing everyone knows that.

AGNES   Meaning?

RAMBO   Well, problem is not everyone knows what language can do, so – no language no power of thought. No power of thought – guns! Easier! Pull a trigger – bang! Problem solved!

AGNES   Until someone else pulls a trigger in revenge – problem back again. (*Beat.*) And DNA was not an invention it was a discovery, the basic structure of the molecule of heredity waiting for two scientists to discover it.

RAMBO   Who?

AGNES   Crick and Watson.

RAMBO   Crick and Watson?

AGNES Francis Crick and James Watson. Won the Nobel
       Prize for it.

RAMBO When?

AGNES Don't know the year. Look it up.

RAMBO Will do. James Crick and Francis Watson.

AGNES No! Francis Crick and James Watson.

RAMBO Just testing!

SCENE 13 – THE TRIP (CONT)

The Kite Festival.

MARVIN and ZELDA.

MARVIN Kites! Whoever thought there could be such an array
        of differently conceived kites.

ZELDA   And from all over, look – Chile, Ukraine, Korea,
        China, Malaysia – everywhere! Did you know such a
        festival existed, Marvin?

MARVIN No, Zellie, I must admit. Festivals of music, drama,
        poetry but not one of kites. I'd have been very
        disparaging about the notion of a kite festival, I
        confess.

ZELDA   But to see them, to actually see such stunning
        creations doing all sorts of turns and dances in the
        air just by pulling the strings in a certain way.

MARVIN Ingenious I must admit.

ZELDA   Look at that one, an enormous mobile of fluttering
        birds. Exhilarating!

MARVIN Jonty would have been exhilarated, for sure!

ZELDA   Marvin, stop it! Stop relating everything to our dead
        son. Let this holiday be for us. We haven't had such
        a break in years. Let it be a second honeymoon.
        For us!

SCENE 14 – TEACHING (CONT)

CLARA and RAMBO.

CLARA   An arithmetical progression is?

RAMBO   Two, four, six, eight, ten, twelve.

CLARA   Right! A geometrical progression is?

RAMBO   Three, six, twelve, twenty-four, forty-eight.

CLARA   Right!

RAMBO   Wow! I'm learning, I'm learning!

CLARA   Never mind about 'wow I'm learning'. There's a long way to go. Now, the square on the…

RAMBO   I know! Don't tell me, I know, I know! The square on the hypotenuse is equal to the sum of the squares on the other two sides. You think I don't work when I'm on my own?

CLARA   I'm impressed.

RAMBO   No you're not, you're surprised.

CLARA   It's true, I'm surprised.

RAMBO   And amazed.

CLARA   Amazed and surprised! That's the reward of teaching you, Rambo – you pay dividends in amazement.

SCENE 15 – THE TRIP (CONT)

In their car.

MARVIN   Where are you proposing we go next, Zellie?

ZELDA   Oh, I don't know. Just drive until we see a sign pointing to a village we fancy the name of, or until we see a river, or a hill, or a forest that grabs our eyes. That's what you taught your students: look at what people do, look at the buildings they build, the landscapes they cultivate, that will tell you the truth about them. So just drive, sweetheart, and look hard.

MARVIN   We might be in time for the festival of Avignon.

ZELDA   That's the spirit, we might.

MARVIN   (*Enthusiasm rising.*) And do you realise that we've never been to Venice?

ZELDA   Venice! How did we miss Venice?

MARVIN 'The City of light'!

ZELDA 'Queen of the Adriatic'.

MARVIN 'Serenissima'!

SCENE 16 – TEACHING (CONT)

AGNES and RAMBO.

AGNES … A simile is when you compare something to something else. 'Shall I compare thee to a summer's day?' 'A summer's day' is a simile. A metaphor is something that stands in for something else. Why is 'He's the king of the castle' a metaphorical statement?

RAMBO Because he's not a king and there's no castle but he's in charge.

AGNES Correct! Give me another simile.

RAMBO You have a head of hair like silk.

AGNES Good, but corny.

RAMBO You mean I have to be original as well as informed?

AGNES Nothing wrong with being original.

RAMBO Gets up people's nose, that's all.

AGNES Come on, another simile.

RAMBO She looked at me like thunder.

AGNES Almost. Try to link 'She' with 'thunder' which is what you intend.

RAMBO She looked at me with eyes like thunder

AGNES Better. One more.

RAMBO My blood is a twin branched scarlet tree.

AGNES That's chilling, but it's a metaphor. A simile should refer only to a noun and not a phrase like 'twin branched scarlet tree'. Where'd it come from?

RAMBO A poem I read the other day.

AGNES Whose?

RAMBO Can't remember. Charley somebody. I'll learn it for you if you like.

AGNES   I'd very much like.

SCENE 17 – THE TRIP (CONT)

Venice.

MARVIN and ZELDA in a gondola.

MARVIN   Of course we can't see the *original* Venice, Venice as it was in the fifteenth century. Ruskin knew the real Venice. He kept coming back looking for what it once was like before they began building haphazardly, hiding the vistas, breaking up the original design.

ZELDA   Did you know that in the sixteenth century Venice was one of the known world's most populated city?

MARVIN   And he wrote about it, Ruskin: *The Stones of Venice.*

ZELDA   Now there are only about 70,000 inhabitants and 21 million tourists.

MARVIN   The original stones of Venice. Ruskin discovered them. What a work!

ZELDA   What I'd really love to see is the Palio race in Siena.

SCENE 18 – TEACHING (CONT)

CLARA and RAMBO.

RAMBO   Give me a succinct description of the purpose of science.

CLARA   To discover what things are and how they work.

RAMBO   Thank you. That'll do nicely. Succinct!

CLARA   Another thing to remember is that science is not merely a subject to be studied in school, it's to do with your life, with you! People who die of sclerosis of the liver haven't understood the destructive effect alcohol has on it.

RAMBO   I don't drink, do I!

CLARA   Glad to hear it.

RAMBO   Bet you do, though.

CLARA   I tipple now and then, yes.

RAMBO   Science didn't do you much good then!

CLARA   We're talking about excess here.

RAMBO   What intrigues me is how it all began.

CLARA   What, life?

RAMBO   Nah! *Thinking* about life. Who was the first man to think scientifically, I wonder?

CLARA   Could've been a woman.

RAMBO   Could've been. Was it?

CLARA   We don't know. Can't know. Early history is murky but we do know there was a Sumerian priestess called Enheduana who's thought to be the first named author in all of world literature. She wrote hymns, poems, to a Goddess called Inanna some four thousand years ago. But if you want to go back to the beginning, to the Middle Stone Age –

RAMBO   How long ago was that?

CLARA   Some two hundred thousand years ago.

RAMBO   Jesus Christ!

CLARA   Want me to go on?

RAMBO   And there were people around then?

CLARA   Sort of.

RAMBO   How d'yers know about such things?

CLARA   I thought I was going to be an archaeologist before I realised I was better suited to pharmacy.

RAMBO   Didn't like getting your nails dirty, eh?

CLARA   Do you want me to go on or not?

RAMBO   Sorry. The Middle Stone Age. See I was listening.

CLARA   The Middle Stone Age is talked about as producing sophisticated stone tools – can't see women conjuring up those. Both genders hunted and gathered – hard work but not much call for thought there. Then people began looking after their old ones – you can bet women were involved in that! The archaeologists then found evidence of rituals,

religious or not we're not sure but it's safe to guess
that women were involved in those since the early
gods were goddesses – mother earth, fertility and
all that.

RAMBO   So the first gods were goddesses?

CLARA   I don't know. Sorry. I'm out of touch. Look up the
internet.

RAMBO   Therefore it makes no difference if I ask who was the
first man to think scientifically!

CLARA   I just object to the assumption.

RAMBO   OK. Let's ask it that way. Who was the first woman
to think scientifically, I wonder?

CLARA   How about who was the first 'person'?

RAMBO   OK. Who was the first person to think scientifically?

CLARA   I suspect that before the 'thinking' person there was
the 'frightened' person.

RAMBO   Fear before thought?

CLARA   'Fraid so.

RAMBO   So the first thinker was the first person who stopped
being afraid?

CLARA   So it seems to me.

        Pause.

RAMBO   I don't think I like using the word 'person', it makes
a person seem grey, without features, without energy.
'Man' has energy attached to it; 'woman' has power
attached to it. 'Person' is non-descript.

CLARA   And how did you come across the word 'succinct'?

RAMBO   Agnes is building my vocabulary isn't she? Every
time we meet I have to bring along three new
words and she gives me three new words, and she
makes me write sentences including them to show I
understand their meaning.

SCENE 19 – THE TRIP (CONT)

Siena – the Palio.

Sound of horses thundering round the square in Siena.

MARVIN   Magnificent! Those costumes, banners, those horses – and they have to ride bareback.

ZELDA   Looks painful to me.

MARVIN   And they say the race is rigged.

ZELDA   Can't be! All that splendour – corrupt?

MARVIN   I'm afraid it can be, Zellie. That's what was wrong with my lectures to those poor students. When you travel you only see what people have done, not how they've behaved.

ZELDA   Not true! Places have atmospheres which are created by people.

> *FADE up thundering horses, briefly, then – sound of crowds and horses' hooves retreating behind which…*

MARVIN   Jonty would have been excited by that race.

ZELDA   Marvin, stop it! Jonty is dead. Gone! Dead and gone! I grieve for him as much as you do – I carried him, remember? I gave birth to him, I bled for him, I nearly died for him, but my grief has found its place. Everything has its place in my heart: grief for my son, love for you, love of literature, love of music, all things. All things have their place. You've got to find the right place, Marvin, or you'll not only kill your capacity for joy, you'll kill mine, too, and I won't have it. I just won't. Jonty wouldn't have wanted it and I don't want it. It's only when you find a place for your grief that all will be well.

MARVIN   'All shall be well, and all shall be well, and all manner of things shall be well.'

ZELDA   Whose words are those?

MARVIN   St Julian of Norwich. Why is that such an astonishing assembly? So few words, seven of them, just repeated – and they're so comforting.

SCENE 20 – TEACHING (ENDING)

AGNES and RAMBO.

They shout words across to each other as though hurling snowballs.

RAMBO Intimidate!

AGNES Cherish!

RAMBO Infrastructure!

AGNES Concept!

RAMBO Tyranny!

AGNES Courtesy!

RAMBO Respect!

AGNES Aesthetics!

RAMBO Utopia!

AGNES Choice!

RAMBO Compassion!

   Pause.

AGNES Talk to me about Utopia.

RAMBO UTOPIA is an imaginary country where everything is perfect. Different people conceive different kinds of UTOPIAS. The one where people are perfect, the one where relationships are perfect, the one where laws are perfect, organisation of transport, farming, hospitals, buildings every part of our lives is perfectly organised. Not a real place, can't be, not ever, 'cos it's impossible to achieve perfection in anything. But perfection is something most of us strive for. Even though it's impossible to achieve nevertheless it is good to imagine and strive for.

SCENE 21 – THE TRIP (ENDING)

MARVIN and ZELDA in their car.

MARVIN An astonishing assembly! 'All shall be well, and all shall be well, and all manner of things shall be well.'

   Music ends.

SCENE 22

RAMBO is reading to AGNES an essay she has set him.

RAMBO 'So there I was riding this horse galloping fast just hanging on to its neck. And she let me. She let me hang on there. She trusted me. We was comfortable together, like we'd always known one another. Galloping! Galloping! But it wasn't like galloping, it was almost as if we was flying. Her feet didn't seem to touch the ground. We was a couple. "Go on," I whispered in her ear, "go on, fly me, lovely." She liked my voice, I could feel it. "I'm flying," she said. She talked back to me. "I'm flying. For you I'm flying." And I could swear that if only I'd known the right way to twist her head or pull her mane or grip her belly with my legs she really *would* have flown for me, galloping on air, up into that starry sky, all the way to the moon.'

> *Long pause.*

AGNES And that's all your own work?

RAMBO Well who else could have written it? (*Beat.*) After all these months you still uncertain about me?

AGNES I'm sorry, Rambo – Christ! I wish that wasn't your name. Can't we find a nickname for you?

RAMBO How about Rider? Which is what I want to be.

AGNES Rider! Excellent! From now on – Rider. (*Beat.*) I'm sorry I always seem to be doubting you. It's just that –

RIDER Just that what?

AGNES It's just that you've improved by leaps and bounds. Clara says your skill in maths is picking up speedily, too.

RIDER And no one can be that clever.

AGNES Well they can be, but –

RIDER But not a black boy.

> *Silence.*

A moment of tension.

You said in the bus that I showed promise.

AGNES   But you've shown more than promise, you've shown achievement, and in a short time. That piece of writing…

RIDER   You liked it?

AGNES   Very much. The language is pretty good, the structure is good.

RIDER   You want me to be a writer, don't you!

AGNES   It's not me that wants anything, Rambo.

RIDER   Rider.

AGNES   Rider. It's your talent that's revealing itself.

RIDER   I don't want to be a writer.

AGNES   There's a book I want you to read.

RIDER   I don't want to write!

AGNES   *Travels with a Donkey in the Cevennes*, by Robert Louis Stevenson.

RIDER   I-do-not-want-to-write. End of conversation.

AGNES   The donkey carried his pack, and that part of France interested him because of the Protestant uprising against the Catholics that took place there.

RIDER   Protestants against Catholics in France? I thought that was Ireland.

AGNES   Ah, dear Rider. If only! The I-am-holier-than-thou conflicts continue the world over.

RIDER   There! Another type! The 'holier-than-thou' type. You find them everywhere.

AGNES   You're right. There are no frontiers to stupidity.

RIDER   Can't I just ride a horse around the world without writing about it?

AGNES   You could, but it would be a waste of experience. You could write about the types you met, and the bits of journalism could help pay your way.

RIDER   I just hate writing.

AGNES   So do most writers. (*Beat.*) And by the way it's 'we *were* comfortable together' not 'we was'.

RIDER   See! I'd get it all wrong.

AGNES   No you wouldn't. You'd learn, as you've been learning.

>   *Pause.*

RIDER   'Oh, mother my mouth is full of stars'.

AGNES   What?

RIDER   The poem.

AGNES   Which poem?

RIDER   Forgotten already? The metaphor I thought was a simile 'my blood is a twin-branched scarlet tree...'

AGNES   Oh, yes.

RIDER   'Oh mother my mouth is full of stars...'

AGNES   (*To herself.*) Will he ever understand how he makes people feel?

RIDER   'As cartridges in a tray.'

AGNES   I fear for him.

RIDER   'My blood is a twin-branched scarlet tree'

AGNES   His kind of cleverness attracts hostility.

RIDER   'And it runs all runs away.
>   Oh cooks to the galley is sounded off
>   And the lads are down in the mess
>   But I lie down by the forward gun
>   With a bullet in my breast.'

>   *He's trying to remember the next lines.*

AGNES   He'll be the type they'll want to punch, the achiever they'll want to bring down, the truth-teller they'll want to execute. The bright-eyed clever one! The who-does-he-think-he-is one!

RIDER   'Don't send me a parcel at Christmas time
>   Of socks and nutty and wine
>   And don't depend on a long weekend
>   By the Great Western line.'

AGNES But what joy he gives, what reassurance that all
       might be well with the world.

RIDER 'Farewell Aggie-Western. The barracks at Guz,
       Hang my tiddley suit on the door
       I'm sewn up neat in a canvas sheet
       And I shan't be home no more.'[1]

AGNES (*Still to herself.*) Oh, Rider, Rider, Rider – will they let
       you go round the world on a horse?

RIDER Like it?

AGNES Loved it.

SCENE 23

The House.

MARVIN and ZELDA back in their routine.

ZELDA Afternoon sherry coming up!

MARVIN Home! Nothing like it.

ZELDA Still smells musty, though.

MARVIN I can't smell anything.

ZELDA Men never can.

MARVIN Men! Men! I know! We can't have babies, we don't
       see dust, we can't make washing machines work. But
       just remember – men die women survive!

ZELDA You are in good spirits, sweetheart. Dusting your
       books, sorting your papers, being opinionated again.

MARVIN Because of you, Zellie, because of you. That trip was
       a tonic.

ZELDA Everything was new for you that's why.

MARVIN 'And there is nothing new under the sun!' says
       Ecclesiastes who was wrong, wrong, wrong – the
       morbid old bugger.

ZELDA Listen to him! The one always dismissive of people
       who reinvented the wheel.

---

1   *'Song of the Dying Gunner'* by Charles Causley

MARVIN   Well I was wrong, then, wasn't I! Wrong, wrong, wrong! Everyone should be allowed to reinvent the wheel. I even think we were born to reinvent the wheel. To build as though there'd been no cathedrals; write poetry as though there'd been no Milton, plays as though no Shakespeare, compose as though no Handel, paint as though Turner never held a brush …

ZELDA   Whoa! Whoa!

MARVIN   …and to live as though no one had ever lived before.

ZELDA   That trip seems to have been more than a tonic. It's made you high.

MARVIN   I tell you, 'And there is nothing new under the sun' is a wail, a moan. It denies astonishment in the name of wisdom. What, come upon The Grand Canyon and not be astonished because others have been astonished before you? Not to be awed by great minds because there have always been great minds?

ZELDA   Hold on, sweetheart, you'll give yourself a heart attack.

MARVIN   Hush, Zellie, I'm on a roll. I tell you – everything is new under the sun to those who confront it for the first time. Like love. No lover thinks his love is stale because Romeo once poured out his heart to Juliet. Nor should he. Every lover is the first lover ever. That festival of kites in Dieppe, that gondola in Venice, that Palio race in Sienna – we were the first ones ever to see them. They happened specially for us. Let EVERYone reinvent the wheel!

ZELDA   Marvin! Think about what you're saying. If everyone only reinvented the wheel there'd be no progress.

MARVIN   (*Still high.*) I think I'm ready for Jonty's room.

ZELDA   You haven't been there since –

MARVIN   – since he died. I know, Zellie.

ZELDA   I'm worried about you. You've come back a little unhinged.

MARVIN   I'm being everything you want me to be and you're calling me unhinged? Can't you see what's happened? I've been focused on grief for his lost life when I should have been thinking of ways to celebrate the short life he *had*.

ZELDA   You had his portrait painted on his rocking horse.

MARVIN   But that comforted only us.

ZELDA   (*Warning.*) His room is as he left it… I only dust it now and then, can't let the dust accumulate…

MARVIN   I know, Zellie, I know. I'm prepared for it.

SCENE 24

The café.

CLARA, AGNES, RIDER – all in high spirits.

AGNES   More than pastries today, mes amis. A dinner! A celebratory dinner for the boy who's passed his A levels against the odds.

CLARA   A toast! To the boy who hated to say 'never' – Rider Philips!

ALL   Never say never!

Clink glasses.

RIDER   Why am I suddenly frightened? You're going to expect things of me. What if I don't deliver? And what if those A levels are a flash in the pan? What if that's all I've got and there's no more?

CLARA   Doubts, Rider, they're called doubts. Nothing wrong with doubts.

RIDER   We're born with brains like a jug of water aren't we! Some of us are born with the jug only half filled, and some with only a quarter filled. Einstein was born with his jug full, and Shakespeare, too. Full jugs! Not many like them though, is there? What if my jug is only A levels full and no more?

CLARA   And only the best people suffer from doubts.

AGNES   Another toast – to chance encounters.

ALL Chance encounters!

Clink.

RIDER One more, one more –

CLARA Oh, we'll have many more before the evening's out –

RIDER To the rocking horse kid whose rocking-horse brought us together.

ALL To the rocking horse kid!

Clink.

RIDER You know what I'd like to do?

CLARA Tell us.

RIDER No, no. You wouldn't approve.

AGNES Try us.

RIDER You'd veto me.

CLARA Risk it.

RIDER I'd like to knock on the door and speak to the people the other side, ask them about that rocking horse.

CLARA Great idea! We should all go.

AGNES I'm not so sure.

RIDER See! A veto.

AGNES The rocking-horse may be associated with a painful memory.

RIDER Yeah. Maybe Agnes is right. I'd hate being an intruder.

CLARA No! I don't agree. Even if it is associated with pain people enjoy having others being interested in them.

AGNES Not all people. We could have the door slammed in our face.

RIDER Aren't you curious?

AGNES Of course I am but privacy is privacy.

CLARA How private can it be if they stick it in the window for the entire world to gaze at?

RIDER Right! It's almost an invitation to knock at the door.

AGNES But imagine how oppressive it is for them to
have people constantly knocking any time of day
intruding upon their lives.

CLARA If it had been an oppressive experience they'd have
removed the rocking horse from the window.

RIDER They might even enjoy people intruding on them. I
say we risk it.

AGNES I'm not convinced.

RIDER Buy them some flowers and risk it.

AGNES Let's eat first and think about it.

CLARA This dinner's on me by the way.

AGNES No, you and I will share it so that Rider is the guest
of us both.

RIDER I wish I could be taking you out for a meal after all
the help you've given me. I've given you nothing.

AGNES Oh, yes you have, you most certainly have – the
pleasure of seeing you fulfil your potential.

CLARA Happens to only a few.

AGNES You're on the way to becoming a role model for
others. You're the future, Rider. That's a grave
responsibility.

RIDER But there's nothing from me to you.

AGNES That's the way of the world. Jill gives to Jack who
gives to John who give to Jane.

CLARA As our family and friends –

AGNES – and teachers –

CLARA – gave to us.

AGNES And now we've been allowed to give to you –

CLARA And you can give to others.

AGNES The world works that way. Now let yourself be
fussed over. May not happen again.

RIDER You mean passing A levels is all a black boy can
achieve?

AGNES Give it a rest, Rider.

RIDER Teasing, teasing!

CLARA   Let's order. I'm starving. We'll talk about Rider's
             university future when our stomachs are full.

RIDER   I don't want to go to university, I want to ride round
             the world on a horse.

CLARA   Pick up your menu and order.

RIDER   You women are something else.

CLARA   Order!

SCENE 25

The House. JONTY's room.
ZELDA enters.

ZELDA   Marvin? Marvin, you look awful.

MARVIN   Did you know he kept a diary?

ZELDA   You shouldn't have come up here.

MARVIN   He was so clever.

ZELDA   He had a clever father.

MARVIN   He had a stupid father. Listen. (*Reads.*)

             'My father teaches philosophy. He talks to me
             sometimes about the philosophy he teaches. I don't
             always understand what he's saying because he
             doesn't seem to know how to untie the knots in the
             rope that he's trying to hand on to me. 'Philosophy
             is a rope,' he says 'to haul yourself out of the abyss
             into the light of meaning.' He keeps talking about
             the meaning of life, but I don't believe there *is* any
             meaning to life, there's just purpose: to do good
             – in a word, a deed, a chair made, a tree planted,
             the poor fed, in love. The purpose in life is to love,
             there's nothing more powerful.'

             Has difficulty holding back tears.

             That was our son, Zellie. Aren't you proud to be his
             mother?

ZELDA   I've always been proud to be his mother as I've
             always been proud to be your wife.

MARVIN I'm going to plant trees, Zellie, or feed the poor, or
        commission a piece of music, or find a student to
        give a scholarship in Jonty's name.

ZELDA   We don't have money, Marvin.

MARVIN We've got some savings.

ZELDA   For the rest of our retirement, Marvin? Please, don't
        let me live my last days worrying about money.
        Jonty wouldn't want you to celebrate his memory by
        relegating his mother to the poor house.

MARVIN I'd be prepared to sell the rocking-horse.

ZELDA   Good thing! At last!

MARVIN And I'll sell my books. There are some valuable
        volumes on those shelves. I'll never read them again.
        Sell my books and cease grieving. You'll go with me
        on that won't you, Zellie?

ZELDA   As I've gone with you on everything in our
        marriage.

MARVIN That's not true.

ZELDA   Everything.

MARVIN But everything I've ever wanted you've somehow
        persuaded me to want.

ZELDA   Found me out, have you, sweetheart?

MARVIN I love you, Zellie.

ZELDA   And I love you, old man.

MARIVN I don't think I've said that in a long while.

ZELDA   No you haven't.

MARVIN (*Quoting.*) 'There is no meaning there's just purpose:
        in a word, a deed, a chair made, the poor fed, in
        love ...'

        Music, melding into laughter.

SCENE 26

The Café.

CLARA What finally turned Rider on to maths was when I showed him the magic of numbers.

AGNES Magic of numbers?

RIDER Yeah. You think numbers are just for calculating things.

AGNES That's all I want to think of them as. My eyes glaze over if you start explaining mathematical theories to me.

RIDER Not theories. We'll give her something simple shall we? Did you know there was such a thing as 'perfect numbers'?

AGNES No, and don't try to explain what they are.

RIDER (*Ignoring her.*) All perfect numbers are equal to their true division.

AGNES See my eyes glazing over?

RIDER For example, take the number six. Six can be divided by one, two and three – which also add up to six. Twenty-eight is another perfect number.

AGNES Stop!

RIDER It was when Clara turned me on to the games you can play with numbers that I took off with maths A level. The games opened the door to understanding. Bingo! That's all I wanted you to know.

AGNES And I'm thrilled, Rider, I really am thrilled with what you've achieved.

RIDER So when are we going to knock at the rocking-horse door?

AGNES And say what?

RIDER 'Hello, mister. I hope we're not disturbing you but we're three people who didn't know each other until we started talking on a bus about that rocking-horse in your window. And we all admired it and became friends and now we're dead curious to know the

story behind it. (*Beat.*) Oh, and here's a bunch of
flowers for your missus.

AGNES   And you think he'll believe us?

CLARA   Why not? It's a very pretty speech and we don't look
threatening do we?

AGNES   Three strangers at your doorstep?

RIDER   Agnes, I have four aims in my life and while eating
this meal and listening to your praises of me for
both of which I'm truly thankful oh Lord, and when
I'm the success you think I'll be I'll buy you both
a meal and sing your praises, and – where was I?
Agnes, you didn't warn me about getting lost in long
sentences.

AGNES   'And while eating this meal.'

RIDER   And while eating this meal – thank you – I've been
turning over in my mind all the preparation and
research I must carry out. I mean can a horse be
ridden that far?

AGNES   How many hours a day can you make the poor beast
ride?

CLARA   Will you have to change horses? And, good God!
how many times?

RIDER   And what do I feed her on?

AGNES   'Her'?

RIDER   Has to be a 'her'. Women are more reliable.

CLARA   You'll probably have to take whatever you can get.

RIDER   And I'll have to learn horse language, and read up
about the signs of horse illness. I mean I've got this
ambition, this longing to ride a horse round the
world but I know nothing about horses and nothing
about the world. Where do I go from Brighton?
North, south, east, west?

AGNES   You might have to find a sponsor – a newspaper like
the *Mirror*, or a horse breeder.

CLARA   Or a horse magazine.

RIDER   So now I've got five not four aims in my life: to find out the story of the rocking horse kid; to work and save a lot of money; to learn all about horses; to find a sponsor, and then – to do it! To actually do it, to go round the world on a grey steed.

CLARA   Why 'grey'?

RIDER   Grey and black, man – elegant.

AGNES   The title of your book, perhaps: *Black Man on a Grey Steed.*

RIDER   You won't get me writing no books. That's a promise.

CLARA   Don't make promises for your future self – he may not forgive you.

AGNES   And how many times must I tell you? Two negatives make a positive.

CLARA   As in maths.

AGNES   'You won't get me writing any books'.

RIDER   (*Laughing.*) Look how easy it is to wind her up.

AGNES AND RIDER (*Together.*) 'If I won't get you writing *no* books then I *will* get you writing *some* books. How many times must I tell you…'

> *RIDER and AGNES deliver their lines together in a jumble of gaiety.*

SCENE TWENTY-SEVEN

This last scene is a duet between those in the house and those outside.

Inside House.

ZELDA   Look at all this post.

MARVIN   I've wasted a lot of time these last years, haven't I, Zellie?

ZELDA   I don't know that they were wasted, sweetheart. 'Misspent' might be more accurate.

MARVIN   Amounts to the same thing.

ZELDA   Except 'wasted' suggests nothing was done; 'misspent' suggests something was done but mistakenly so.

MARVIN   Am I mistaken in my quest for purpose as Jonty would have it, rather than meaning?

ZELDA   Not mistaken, just romantic.

MARVIN   Me? Romantic? I'm getting all these responses to my adverts.

ZELDA   Of course you are, sweetheart. You're offering an interesting sum of money, and it's romantic of you to ignore the surge of bounty hunters, crack-pots and bankrupts, and still go on hoping. Otherwise fine!

      Walking to the House.

CLARA   Now, we're agreed we let Rider talk first, and if he makes a mess of it Agnes butts in, and I'm the reserve cavalry.

RIDER   (*Rehearsing.*) Hello, mister –

AGNES   'Sir.' 'Hello, sir', suggests more respect.

RIDER   I can't say 'hello, sir'. 'Sir' doesn't go with 'hello'. How about 'excuse me, sir, I hope we're not bothering you' –

AGNES   'Disturbing you'.

RIDER   'I hope we're not disturbing you' ….

CLARA   Oh, yes, that's better, that's good.

      Inside House.

      MARVIN enters from another visit to JONTY's room.

MARVIN   I've just read more of his diary, Zellie.

ZELDA   Are you sure you should have done that, sweetheart?

MARVIN   No, I'm not sure. (*Beat.*) Do you think our love was oppressive to him?

ZELDA   No, I don't. Not our love, but your intellectual expectations of him might have been. Why do you ask?

MARVIN His diary is full of his thoughts about the conflict between a loving family and the tyranny of family life.

ZELDA And he writes that we were tyrannical for him?

MARVIN No, but the conflict between love and freedom-from-love seems to have preoccupied him. (*Beat.*) Did you feel oppressed by my love, Zellie?

ZELDA No, sweetheart. I learned very early on that the paradox of love is that it liberates the spirit by binding it.

MARVIN Need to think about that one, you clever old thing.

Arriving at house gate.

AGNES I'm still not convinced this is the right thing to do. I think we should about turn, go for a drink, and leave these poor people in peace.

RIDER Do you really think so?

CLARA Well I don't think so. Our intentions are honourable, good-neighbourly.

AGNES Three people on your doorstep is intimidating.

RIDER Agnes, if I don't fulfil this first aim I'll never fulfil the others.

AGNES Then I think you two should knock at the door and I'll go wait in the car. One old, one young.

CLARA No – we're a team. We've developed an aura by now. It'll show and be reassuring.

RIDER Hey, look, there's no bell just an old fashioned knocker. One knock? Two? Three?

AGNES Three will sound too insistent.

RIDER Three might, but rat-a-tat-tat won't.

AGNES Rat-a-tat-tat will sound like a police knock.

RIDER We don't want that. We want the door opened not hidden behind. For me it will be – da dum! – a door opening on to the world.

Inside House.

MARVIN   Zellie, I want to go to Cazenove Road one more
         time. One last look at what was his last look. Will
         you come with me?

ZELDA   I'm not sure, Marvin.

MARVIN   To finally exorcise our son's ghost?

ZELDA   He was your ghost not mine.

MARVIN   And then I'll find the right place for my grief, as you
         want me to. Please? 'All shall be well...'

ZELDA   And you believe Jonty's 'purpose' will come
         knocking at our door, just like that?

> *Outside, front door.*

> *RIDER's six knocks – pah pom! pah pom! pah pom!*

MARVIN   ...'and all shall be well, and all manner of things
         shall be well.'

> *END.*

WHEN GOD WANTED A SON

For Nuria Espert dear friend, great actress, rising metteuse-en-scene du monde, in whose house by the sea I finished this play.

Characters

MARTHA
  aged fifty-two

JOSHUA
  aged fifty-five, her estranged husband

CONNIE
  aged twenty-seven, their daughter

Time: the present

When God Wanted a Son, completed in October 1986, received its first airing as a reading to raise funds for the Jackson's Lane Community Theatre on 19 February 1989. The actors were

MARTHA, Elizabeth Spriggs

JOSHUA, John Savident

CONNIE, Nichola McAuliffe

It was narrated and directed by the author.

World premiere 6th February to 9 March 1997 at The New End Theatre, Hampstead, London, with

CONNIE, Julie Clare

MARTHA, Jacqueline Pearce

JOSHUA, Lawrence Weber

Director Spencer Butler

Designer Andy Wilson

Act One

A rough cabaret club.

CONNIE, 'apprentice' comedienne, stands before her audience fearing the worst. Her material seems to amuse only her. Prominently hanging round her neck is a gold chain from which hangs a Star of David. Her 'audience' is not us but a gathering slightly offstage.

CONNIE Poland, 1875. Moshe Ben Levy. The richest Jew in his village. Comes the Cossack pogroms. Moshe's store – no chance. Burned to the ground. Stock looted, son murdered, daughter abducted, wife dead from a broken heart. Poor Moshe Ben Levy. Down to his last crust of bread, his last pat of butter, the last leaves of tea, the sugar gone. You couldn't get lower than Moshe was in that year of 1875, in the heart of Poland, the heart of winter, heart' broken and cold. Surely this was the end.

He places the last of his logs on the fire, fills the kettle for the last leaves of tea, toasts his last crust of bread, butters it with the last pat of butter – then, as though God hasn't punished him enough for sins he can't remember committing – the last of his calamities.

The water boils. He reaches for the kettle. He's shivering from the cold. He's clumsy. Brushes against the last piece of toast buttered with the last pat of butter – plop! To the floor! The filthy floor!

Now, everyone knows that toast falls butter side down. Always. Without fail. But not this day. This day – a miracle! Moshe's toast, which should have fallen butter side down, falls butter side up!

Is this an omen? A sign that his luck is about to change? He rushes off to the Rabbi.

'Rabbi, Rabbi. You know me, Moshe Ben Levy,
once rich now poor, my son murdered, my daughter
abducted, my wife dead from broken heart. But,
Rabbi, this morning, this morning I knocked my
toast to the floor and it landed butter side up! A
miracle! Everyone knows that toast falls butter side
down, always, without fail. Tell me, is it an omen? Is
my luck about to change?'

The Rabbi thinks and thinks and says: 'I have not
wisdom enough to interpret this sign alone. I must
confer with the other Rabbis. Return tomorrow
morning. You will have our answer.'

Moshe falls asleep only for one hour before the sun
rises. All night his imagination is on fire with visions
of a new life. Without washing or changing his shirt,
pausing only to gabble his morning prayers, Moshe
Ben Levy hurries to the Rabbi's house. The Rabbi
emerges tired from a room full of tired Rabbis, grey
and numb with the meaning of life.

'Rabbi, Rabbi,' cries the eager, demented Moshe.
'Tell me, the miracle, what does it mean? My toast
landed butter side up – is it an omen? Is my luck
about to change?'

His language is Yiddish, of course.

The Rabbi replies. Also in Yiddish of course. 'We
have stayed awake all night. Seven of us. The wisest
in the district. We have prayed, we have argued,
we have referred to the holy books. One of us even
dipped into the Cabbala to search for the meaning of
your toast which landed butter side up. And we have
concluded – (despair and sadness) – you must have
buttered your toast on the wrong side.'

> CONNIE *cups her mouth and yells as though she were
> one of the audience.*

(*Yelling to right.*) Gerroff! Women shouldn't tell jokes!
You've never told a good joke and you never will tell
a good joke! (*No longer audience.*) Thank you, thank
you. I thought you'd like that one.

She smiles ingratiatingly, a smile of gratitude which turns into contempt.

SCENE 2

The 'office' of MARTHA.

A room in her house. She speculates in stocks and shares. On the wall are three huge sheets. On each sheet is a graph. They are graphs of the daily movements in value of the stocks of three different public companies. They are named: CENTRAL CEMENT PLC, VIENNESE RESTAURANTS PLC, NATIONAL GARDENS PLC.

MARTHA is scanning the pages of the Financial Times. *Round her neck, very prominently, hangs a gold chain with a heavy cross.*

MARTHA   (*Reading.*) 'Argyl Construction… Bounty and Buildings… B, H, C, Carlyle Construction… ah! Central Cement: 575 to 577, up two points.

> *She marks the graph up two points. Returns to the paper.*

Now, catering… A… B… C… S… T… U… V… Vacations International, Various Holidays… Viennese Restaurants: 353 to 350. Down three? Mmm. Is it the coffee they're not drinking or the cakes they're not eating?

> *She marks the graph down three points. Returns to the paper.*

Now National Gardens… Leisure, leisure, leisure… Ah! Leisure…

SCENE 3

Cabaret club.

CONNIE   All right! All right! So I'm not funny. I'm funny but not very funny. You don't like my jokes so let's play a game instead. Let's divide the world. I believe the world's divided into those who are clever and

massacred, and those who are stupid and do the
massacring. (*Pause*.) Come on now, you tell me how
you think the world is divided. (*Beat*.) I believe
the world's divided into those who are clever and
massacred, and those who are stupid and do the
massacring. How do you think it's divided?

>   *Silence.*

You want another example? Right. Here's another
example. I believe the world's divided into those
who applaud achievement and those who begrudge
it – pah pom!

>   *Silence.*

Thank you, thank you. I thought you'd like that one.

SCENE 4

A young girl's room.

*Unchanged. The signs of toddlerhood through to young
womanhood are there. It's CONNIE's room.*

*MARTHA opens the door to let in her daughter. CONNIE
regards her past.*

MARTHA I didn't want to change it, then I did, then I didn't,
then I did… Finally, well, you can see. I didn't.

CONNIE Except for my montage.

MARTHA I tried, but you glued, it. (*Beat*.) Didn't you ever
think it would have to come down?

>   *No response.*

'His' room I dismantled. Utterly! Call me if you want
anything.

CONNIE Thanks, Mum.

MARTHA And don't start crying as soon as my back is turned.

>   *She leaves. CONNIE moves around her old room
>   picking up this and that. On the walls are pinned
>   scraps of paper, some of which are written upon,
>   some typed.*

CONNIE (*Reading.*) 'Don't you think men overrate the
necessity of humouring everybody's nonsense till
they get despised by the very fools they humour?'
George Eliot.

That was when Dad thought I was going to be an
MP.

(*Reading.*) 'A man may take to drink because he feels
himself to be a failure, and then fail all the more
completely because he drinks. It is rather the same
thing that is happening to the English language. It
becomes ugly and inaccurate because our thoughts
are foolish, but the slovenliness of our language
makes it easier for us to have foolish thoughts.'
George Orwell.

That was when Dad thought I was going to become
a philologist.

(*Beat.*) Or a dipsomaniac!

(*Reading*) 'Are you saying what you mean? Is what
you mean worth saying? Are you saying it with
poetry, imagination and style?'

And that was when he thought I was going to be a
writer.

*She finds her old toy telephone. Should she? Hesitant,
sheepish, she dials.*

Hello? God? Is that you? Wasn't sure you'd still be
there. It's Connie. Didn't recognize the voice?

She hops, arms akimbo in the one-liner joke routine.

Once a con always a Connie! Pah pom! No? Well,
perhaps my voice is changed. Got a moment? To
talk?

Long pause.

Tell me, why wasn't I any of those things? (*She
weeps.*)

SCENE 5

MARTHA's office.

MARTHA alone.

MARTHA All money is worth twice its value. (*Thinks about that.*)
I know that means *some*thing. (*Beat.*) But what? I
have a hundred pounds. I spend twenty. Not only do
I no longer have a hundred pounds but in addition
I'm left with only eighty pounds. (*Thinks about that.*)
Stupid! That's merely describing the same state in a
different way. (*Beat.*) And you now possess twenty
pounds' worth of goods. (*Pause.*) And yet – all money
is worth twice its value. I feel it. You have both got
it and haven't not got it. To be aware of that is the
secret of wealth; I'm convinced of it.

(*She picks up the* Financial Times. *Scans it. It's another
day.*) Central Cement: 577 to 578. Up one point.
Interesting… (*She marks the graph up one point.*)

Viennese Restaurants…

SCENE 6

CONNIE's room.

*MARTHA enters with a tray on which are a pot of tea, a jug
of milk, a sugar bowl, ornate silver tongs, a plate with two
kinds of thinly sliced triple-decker sandwiches – the crusts cut
away, sliced into triangles.*

MARTHA I thought when you came through the door: this girl
needs looking after but I'm not going to spoil her.
And here I am –

CONNIE – spoiling me.

MARTHA You don't know what it's like when your children
leave home.

CONNIE I know what it's like for the child!

MARTHA It's not simply the empty house, or that your
usefulness is over. It's not that their company
is missed – though God knows it is missed. It's

imagining them lonely. I cried for days when you left.

CONNIE   So did I!

MARTHA   And felt helpless.

CONNIE   So did I!

MARTHA   That's a special pain – to feel helpless about your child.

CONNIE   Cried, couldn't sleep, heard every noise, feared every movement.

MARTHA   Children don't leave, parents are abandoned.

CONNIE   (*Reading a note on the wall.*) 'It grows dark, boys, you may go.'

MARTHA   Who said that?

CONNIE   The last words of the Great Master of the High School of Edinburgh.

MARTHA   Not sure I always approved of your fa – (*Beat.*) 'his' little notes to you.

CONNIE   Yes, you were sure. You never approved.

MARTHA   I suspect advice offered through other people's words. Especially if it's pinned on walls.

CONNIE   Oh, you're so English about things.

MARTHA   I don't know any other way to be about things. (*Changing the subject.*) You going to guess the fillings?

CONNIE   How many kinds?

MARTHA   Two.

> *CONNIE picks one triangle. Eats. Considers.*

CONNIE   Sardines, for sure.

MARTHA   No mistaking that.

CONNIE   Not Spanish onions. Spring onions.

MARTHA   Clever.

CONNIE   Do I detect garlic vinegar rather than malt?

MARTHA   You do.

CONNIE   No salt, I'm glad to say, there's enough in the brine – but – you've peppered it.

MARTHA   Yes.

CONNIE   And there's something else, something – unusual.
It's, it's – must have another bite. (*Bites.*) It's – good
God! It's alcoholic. Sherry! You've soaked your
onions in dry sherry. That's crazy!

MARTHA   But is it tasty?

CONNIE   Well – it's – a surprise.

MARTHA   Which is what I always wanted to be, surprising.

CONNIE   I've learned a new game. 'Dividing the world.'
Example. I believe the world is divided into those
who surprise you and those who don't. Your turn.

MARTHA   I need another example.

CONNIE   You can be humorous about it, too. I believe the
world is divided into those who squeeze their
toothpaste from the bottom up, and those who
squeeze their toothpaste from the middle.

MARTHA   I don't see the point of that.

CONNIE   The point is to make the most important perception
ever about the human condition. There are only
those who squeeze their toothpaste from the bottom
up, and those who squeeze their toothpaste from
the middle. All other divisions between people are
trivial, irrelevant. (*Pause.*) You can be serious about it
if you like: I believe the world is divided into those
who are sick and those who are healthy.

MARTHA   You haven't guessed the other filling.

CONNIE   You never liked the games I brought home.

MARTHA   They were too clever by half.

CONNIE   Only the English use 'clever' as an insult.

MARTHA   (*Edgy.*) Why do you keep talking about 'the English'
as though you were something else?

CONNIE   (*Herself curious.*) Not sure.

MARTHA   'His' is not the only ancient tribe.

CONNIE   It's just that –

MARTHA   My family also go back centuries, you know.

CONNIE   I didn't mean…

MARTHA   Centuries! (*Beat.*) And half of you is me, remember.

CONNIE   (*To change the subject.*) I believe the world is divided
          into those who are grateful the bottle's half full and
          those who complain the bottle's half empty.

MARTHA   Monopoly and Scrabble, those are my games.

CONNIE   That's because you know how to spell and you love
          money.

MARTHA   (*Too violently.*) I hate money.

CONNIE   Ha!

MARTHA   I loathe any talk about money.

CONNIE   Ha!

MARTHA   Loathe it!

CONNIE   (*Diverting her.*) I believe the world is divided into
          those who are fat and those who are thin.

MARTHA   (*As a way of taking control of herself.*) I believe the
          world is divided into those who are tall and those
          who are short.

CONNIE   Good! I believe the world is divided into those who
          listen and those who talk.

MARTHA   You haven't guessed the other filling.

CONNIE   (*Biting into second pile of sandwiches.*) Oh well, easy –
          very crispy bacon.

MARTHA   Obviously.

CONNIE   And obviously cabbage in mayonnaise.

MARTHA   But what kind of mayonnaise?

CONNIE   You mean it's not from a bottle?

          (*MARTHA is disdainful. Preens herself.*) Ah! You *made* it.
              MARTHA nods. Happy.
          With egg yolk and oil and – er – (*Amazed.*) lemon
          juice?
              Happy MARTHA nods.
          Without curdling it?
              Beaming MARTHA nods.

Clever old you. (*Beat.*) Red peppers and –
er – chicken!

MARTHA (*Triumphant.*) Turkey!

CONNIE Shit!

MARTHA I believe the world is divided into those who curse
life and those who caress it.

CONNIE Very good. But is it true?

MARTHA It also has to be true?

CONNIE Mother! Did you notice how you sang that line?
(*Imitates her going up on 'true'.*) 'It also has to be true?'
Like Dad would have sung it.

MARTHA Nonsense. How else can you 'sing' it?

CONNIE 'Does it have to be true?' 'Has it got to be true?'

MARTHA What's the difference?

CONNIE Think about it.

MARTHA You and him! You and him and your theories!

CONNIE Very interesting theories they are, too.

MARTHA (*Viciously mocking.*) 'You don't really mean what
you're saying,' he'd tell people. 'The sound you're
making doesn't match your words.' To their face!
Insult them! Thought he knew what they didn't
about themselves.

CONNIE The best people are uncomfortable to have around.

MARTHA You and him! Insufferable pair!

CONNIE How do you think Dad divided the world?

MARTHA I try not to think anything about your fa – about
'him'

CONNIE Not succeeding, are you?

MARTHA If you're going to talk about…

CONNIE I think about him all the time.

> *MARTHA rises to go.*

No, stay. Oh, Mother, why am I making such a mess
of my life?

MARTHA (*Contempt for her chosen vocation.*) Comedienne!

CONNIE   I always made them laugh at school.

MARTHA   What makes children laugh embarrasses adults.

CONNIE   Where I tell jokes they're not adults.

MARTHA   But they think they are.

CONNIE   (*Yelling.*) Gerrout! Gerrup! Gerroff! (*Beat.*) It's my
          father's humour, that's the problem.

MARTHA   His humour, his values, his arrogance were always
          the problems.

CONNIE   For God's sake, name him. Father. He's my father.

MARTHA   Analysing, probing, taking me apart. He was good at
          taking things apart, but could he put them together
          again?

CONNIE   Ah! You believe the world is divided into those who
          destroy and those who build.

MARTHA   And he never mixed with my family. Had no
          patience for them. Too dull for him.

CONNIE   I believe the world is divided into those who
          surrender and those who survive.

MARTHA   I believe the world is divided into those who are
          Jer – into those who are 'them' and those who are
          'us'.

          She abruptly gathers the tea things and storms off.
          CONNIE picks up the toy phone. Dials.

CONNIE   Hello, God? We have a problem.

SCENE 7

CONNIE's room.

Through the darkness comes a man's voice on a tape recorder.
Lights up to reveal CONNIE listening to a tape of her father
JOSHUA, speaking. CONNIE's lips move to JOSHUA's voice.
She pretends she's him giving a lecture. She has played the
tape to herself many, many times.

MARTHA in the background in shadow.

VOICE OF JOSHUA It seems to me we reveal our true meaning through the musicality of what we say rather than through the words we use.

Each word is carried on a note. The words add up to meaning.

The notes add up to meaning.

Sometimes the meaning of a word coincides with the meaning of a note. Sometimes they're different. Sometimes they're at variance with each other.

Example: Take a simple fact which one person wants to communicate to another: one and one is two.

If you say: 'One and one is two' you are doing more than communicating a mathematical verity. You are also saying, 'You were wrong before.'

Listen: 'One and one is two.' The music is the same as: 'You were wrong.' 'You were not right.' There is even an element of scolding in the music.

Or, again, it may be that we are sensitive, and other people's slow wit embarrasses us. And so we sing 'apology' into our voice.

Listen: 'One and one is too-oo.' Meaning, 'I feel terrible telling you this but – one and one is too-oo.' The 'two' is delivered in two syllables: 'too-oo' and the second syllable goes up. 'One and one is too-oo.' The music of apology.

Now, take the 'two' down and what do we have? 'One and one is two.' The music of impatience. 'One and one is two.'

Emphasize the word 'two' in yet another way and you can make the melody say, 'You're a fool as well.' Listen: 'One and one is two.' Meaning, 'Not three, you fool.'

You can even add a further layer on to those five words. You not only think the person is a fool, but you also show contempt. Listen 'One and one is two.' Meaning, 'Will this stupid person never get it right? One and one is two.' Sigh! The music of contempt.

I will now rephrase my first sentence. It seems to me we reveal not simply our true meaning through the musicality of what we say rather than through the words we use but also our true personality.

CONNIE switches off the tape.

SCENE 8

CONNIE's room.

She plays with her old teddy bear. It sits in a chair facing her, a bib round its neck. A plate of the sandwiches has been left behind. She sits waiting for it to eat. And sits.

Picks up and offers a sandwich. No response. She feels his forehead. Is concerned. Takes his pulse. More concern. Finds doctor's outfit. Applies stethoscope. An ailing teddy. She sighs sadly at the pain of it all.

MARTHA in shadow in the background.

SCENE 9

MARTHA's office.

MARTHA   All money is worth twice its value.

Turns it over and over, willing it to make sense.

All money is worth twice its value.

She marks her charts from the Financial Times.

All money is worth twice its value.

All money is…

SCENE 10

CONNIE's room.

Through the darkness comes JOSHUA's voice repeating the end of the recording.

Lights up on CONNIE *who has been listening to it again.*
MARTHA in shadow in the background.

VOICE OF JOSHUA … I will rephrase my first sentence. It seems to
me we reveal not simply our true meaning through
the musicality of what we say rather than through
the words we use but also our true personality.

CONNIE switches off the tape.

CONNIE Dogs sniff one another out. Humans listen to each
other's musicality. (*Thinks about it.*) But what about
those of us who are tone-deaf, Dad? Will we always
fuck up our relationships? (*Beat.*) Unless we can
interpret eyes. (*Beat.*) Or facial muscles. (*Beat.*) Or
body movements. (*Thinks about it.*) Pity those deaf
and blind.

She repeats the mathematical fact again and again,
imbuing it with: anger, incredulity, delighted discovery,
sadness, defiance, simple fact.

One and one is two!

One and one is two?

And so on…

SCENE 11

MARTHA's office.

MARTHA What I have I am also not without. I am *twice*
blessed: for possessing and for not having been
dispossessed.

Every state is *two* states. I know I'm right, It is
important to understand: all money is worth twice its
value.

All money is…

SCENE 12

CONNIE's room.

She stands with a packet of old cigarette cards in her hand. She is spinning them down in a game where one card must rain down and cover another. She is an expert.

MARTHA in shadow in the background.

Abruptly CONNIE stops her play.

CONNIE Give up your toys, Connie. Give them up.

SCENE 13

CONNIE's room.

CONNIE on the toy phone. MARTHA in shadow in the background.

CONNIE You should have trusted me, Billy Boy. There was evidence enough. I'd hit days of chaos, that's all. Couldn't you tell? Every gal hits her days of chaos. Most have it every three years. The menstrual cycle of despair.

Let me tell you about the ages of women. Age the first: little girl.

Little girl in awe of loud-mouthed male intimidation. Sometimes little girl in competition with loud-mouthed male intimidation. Sometimes little girl turns intimidator and leads squad of mocking girls to diminish male pride.

Age the second: breasts! Little girl with big breasts. A new confidence or a new intimidation? Should she be afraid to be stared at or should she use them to command attention? I used them to command attention. Breasts turned me into woman. Nothing turned boy into man. I was ahead.

But not for long. Age the third: young woman! and – pah pom!

Male expectations! Which were either crude or unfathomable. He groped you or demanded you

appear in a certain way. From which followed –
chaos. And so the menstrual cycle of despair began,
Billy Boy. One day I was busy trying to be what I
thought you wanted me to be. Next day I was as
unfeminine as possible. If he wants me he'll have to
take me for who I am not what I look like.

Stupid woman! I hadn't understood that *what* I look
like reveals who I am. As everything does. The
way I walk, talk, gesticulate, think about the world.
Stupid woman! Stupid theories! I bristled with
them. You must have felt you were making love to a
porcupine, Billy Boy. Bit of a pain in the arse, was I?

Here, I have a Norfolk joke for you. An old, old
widow called on her parson with a problem.
'Parson,' she say, 'Parson, I see my dead husband
today, sitting in his ole chair next to the fire. What
do it mean d'yer think?' 'Could mean many things,'
say the Parson. 'What do you think it means?' 'Well,'
say the ole dear, 'they do say it could mean rain.'
Oh, Billy. Boy, you should've persevered. I'm not
arrogant. It's just that half of me is my father's child.

(*She puts down the phone. Drifts to another note on the
wall. Reading.*) 'If you think education is expensive
you should try ignorance!'

SCENE 14

CONNIE's room.

MARTHA and CONNIE. Evening. Drinks.

MARTHA My favourite game is inventing haikus.

CONNIE What exactly is a haiku?

MARTHA A Japanese three-lined poem in which the first and
third lines have five syllables and the middle one has
seven.

CONNIE Example?

MARTHA Well, (*Coyly.*) one of my best was:

I buy you flowers

Letters return on the scent

Where will it all end?

> *She repeats it tapping out the syllables with her finger.*

I buy you flowers. Five.

Letters return on the scent. Seven.

Where will it all end? Five.

That last line. Gave me a shiver when I first wrote it. 'Where will it all end?' Very mysterious. Could mean great happiness or great – sadness.

CONNIE   That's not a game it's an – art form!

MARTHA   It's a game if you play it with someone else and see whose comes out best.

CONNIE   Who's to judge?

MARTHA   Well, honest couples usually agree on what's self-evident.

CONNIE   And were you and Dad an honest couple?

MARTHA   Who said anything about playing with your fa – with 'him'?

CONNIE   Oh, Mother! You didn't compose haikus with your local priest.

MARTHA   It might have been a lover.

CONNIE   Before or during?

MARTHA   Either.

CONNIE   Some women are temperamentally suited to adultery, for others it's as inconceivable as a flying hippopotamus.

MARTHA   And you're saying I'm a hippopotamus that can't fly?

CONNIE   Well, you confessed: 'I always wanted to be unpredictable,' you said. Meaning you never were.

MARTHA   (*Harshly.*) I said 'surprising'. 'Surprising' I said, not 'unpredictable'. I said, 'I always wanted to be surprising.' (*Beat.*) And who says I never were? Was.

CONNIE   Soaking spring onions in dry sherry?

MARTHA (*Caught.*) I was frightened of where it would all end.

    CONNIE doesn't want to press her point. Struggles
    with a haiku instead.

CONNIE Drink wine with me discuss art.

MARTHA More than five syllables there.

CONNIE Drink wine discuss art.

MARTHA Five. Good.

CONNIE Drink wine discuss art
    Illuminate life for me
    'Where will it all end?'

MARTHA Bit heavy.

CONNIE Heavy?

MARTHA 'Discussing art and illuminating life.' Heavy. Try
again.

CONNIE (*Struggling.*) Er – 'Wine loosens up my limbs.' No. Six
there.

    Wine loosens my limbs.
    A button falls from off my blouse.

    No. Eight there.

    A button falls from my blouse.

    Better.

    Where will it all end?

    There! Lighter for you?

    Wine loosens my limbs
    A button falls from my blouse
    Where will it all end?

MARTHA Sex, sex! That's all the young think about is sex!

CONNIE Can't talk about art, can't talk about sex!

MARTHA You think it's so smart being frank and open about
everything.

CONNIE (*Repartee. To annoy.*) Two old men, two old men on a
park bench. Says one to the other, 'What do you like
best, sex or Christmas?' 'Christmas,' says the other
old man. 'Happens more often!' –

MARTHA Can we agree not to talk about sex, please?

CONNIE   Two old men, two old men on a park bench. Before
          them runs a young man chasing a young woman.
          Says one to the other: 'Can you remember the days
          when we used to do that?' 'Very well,' says the other
          old man. 'Only I can't remember why.'

MARTHA   Please, please! I've asked you! If you want me to
          keep you company can we agree not to talk about
          sex?

CONNIE   (*Cod German, but not too heavy.*) You vant about sex
          vee talk shouldn't. You vant about life and literature
          vee talk shouldn't. You vant about mine farter
          vee talk shouldn't. I sink vee somesing verrrrry
          significant here hef.

MARTHA   On second thoughts, 'Where will it all end?' is not
          a good last line. The last line of a haiku should be
          linked to the image created by the other two.

CONNIE   Example.

MARTHA   Oh, I don't know. I can't make them up that quickly.

CONNIE   I'll give you an image. The sea. Loneliness.

MARTHA   Ah. The sea, the sea! Er – swimming. The last swim.
          'We took our last swim.'

CONNIE   (*Tapping and counting.*) Five. Good.

MARTHA   Don't stand over me.

CONNIE   Come on! Don't stop to complain. You're inspired.
          'We took our last swim.'

MARTHA   We took our last swim
          The sea was big enough –

CONNIE   Only six syllables in that middle line.

MARTHA   The ocean was big enough.

CONNIE   Better.

MARTHA   We took our last swim
          The ocean was big enough…

          The ocean was big enough…

          Er…

          We took our last swim
          The ocean was big enough

Long pause.

But salt tastes linger.

CONNIE   (*That was sad.*) Oh, Mother.

MARTHA   Well they do, they do. (*Beat.*) Remember, half of you is me.

SCENE 15

CONNIE's room.

Although in CONNIE's room, it is MARTHA's scene. She's in light. CONNIE in shadow. A listening figure.

MARTHA   (*Talking over her shoulder.*) Most women are married to men who bore them. Have you noticed that? They sit around in pubs, restaurants, social gatherings, with faces announcing to the world that they deserve more from life.

Men confuse that bored look with female mystery. It challenges them. Up they trot. 'I understand,' they say. But they don't. Within five minutes of their conversation it's painfully obvious they don't. They bore.

But 'he' understood. 'Women have the power to give or deny happiness,' he once said, 'and through that power we are manipulated.' He hated being at anybody's mercy.

1 couldn't bear him.

And he was full of opinions. He knew who was a great writer, a great painter, a great composer. He could actually say Bach was boring. Passionately say it. It mattered to him. Me – I was exhilarated by them all, Bach, Mozart, Mahler. Well, perhaps not Mahler so much. Too solemn. Still, that's just my taste. When you're that great, dismissive opinion seems irrelevant. Presumptious! Absurd! But he insisted: opinions made you a person. 'It's a guarantee of your freedom,' he'd yell at me. Always impatient. Him and his circle.

Frightening lot they were. Non-stop talkers.
Opinions on this, opinions on that. How can people
have so many opinions about the world? You'd
think it was such a vast and complex place they'd be
confused most of the time. Not that lot. Solutions for
and opinions about everything and anything.

Not me. Nothing much changes about human beings
I always think. And the world we live in seems to
be shaped by scientists and inventors not by people
with opinions. You take the opinion that everyone
should work. Work dignifies people! The work ethic!
Along comes the silicon chip and suddenly we have
– the leisure ethic! The opinion changes! Everyone's
demanding more leisure for all.

What was it about him that I hated? What really was
it? Even now as I think about him my teeth clench.
He had an air. He had – an air.

SCENE 16

Cabaret club.

*CONNIE performing. MARTHA in shadows in the
background.*

CONNIE Two old men, two old men on a park bench. Says
one old man to the other: 'A woman without a man
is like a fish without a bicycle.'

(*Yelling back as though one of the audience.*) 'Yeah! But
who needs a stationary haddock?'

Or was it two old women talking about a man
without a woman?

Depends who's telling the joke, dunnit? (*Curious
about the word 'Dunnit'?*)

Dunnit! Dinnit! Innit! Wannit! Gissit! Gerroff!

(*Yelling as though one of the audience.*) Gerroff the stage,
yer stupid wench. We're 'ere to be amused not
edumicated.

Beautiful to be alive is it not?

Don't go away, ladies and gentlemen. Stay with it.
Hang on to your pints because this evening is an
evening packed and planned, picked and plotted,
designed and divined especially for you with the
most brilliant joke-churners, story-mourners and
warning-brakers ever to weather this bar-pub's
weather-beaten boards where they will suckle fools
and chronicle small beer as Iago said. You all know
who Iago was, don't you? He was de one who made
a fool of de black man.

No, seriously, folks, let's not be intellectual about
humour. Let's not be intellectual about anything if
it comes to that. As the man says – we're here to be
amused not edumicated.

I believe the world's divided into those who know
and those who don't know, with those who think
they know coming a close second and *really* fucking
things up. So drink deep and pass out because, here
to open our show is –

SCENE 17

CONNIE's room.

CONNIE and MARTHA.

MARTHA   If I said to you, 'All money is worth twice its value',
what would you think I meant?

CONNIE   I thought you loathed talk of money.

MARTHA   Not as much as I loathe poverty.

CONNIE   You're not poor. All those stocks and shares.

MARTHA   What 'all those'? I wish they were 'all those'. I'm
trying to make them 'all those'.

CONNIE   (*Turning it over.*) 'All money is worth twice its value.'

MARTHA   Poverty says: FAILED!

CONNIE   (*Still turning it over.*) 'All money is worth twice its
value.'

MARTHA   A constant reminder. Poverty – failure.

CONNIE   It's meaningless.

MARTHA   It's meaningless because you don't understand its
         meaning.

CONNIE   Help me understand.

MARTHA   The condition of poverty is also the condition of not
         being rich. You're not only a failure, you're also not
         a success. Unhappiness is more than unhappiness,
         it's also not being happy. Each state is two states.
         Thus – the state of affairs in which you only have
         £10,000 in the bank earning you £1,000 a year
         interest is at the same time the state of affairs in
         which you don't have £100,000 in the bank earning
         you £10,000 a year interest.

CONNIE   She has gone mad. Mother has gone mad. It is sad
         about Mother, she was once happy, she was once
         content, she –

MARTHA   The Big Bang has exploded. The system for dealing
         in stocks, shares and currencies has changed.

CONNIE   She does not even make sense any longer.

MARTHA   I mean to survive.

CONNIE   I am worried about her.

MARTHA   You don't want a lecture, do you?

CONNIE   Yes. Lecture me. I love lectures.

MARTHA   Lectures are oppressive.

CONNIE   The only lecture that's oppressive is an oppressive
         lecture. When it's not oppressive it's informative,
         stimulating and full of other people's enthusiasms. I
         love other people's enthusiasms.

MARTHA   Oh, you're so confident. Nothing threatens you.

CONNIE   Everything threatens. I just try not to let it
         overwhelm. Lecture me

MARTHA   The Big Bang – a mini-lecture by Martha
         Mankowitz.

CONNIE   Did you marry him because you thought Mankowitz
         sat prettily with Martha?

MARTHA   Are you serious or not?

CONNIE   The Big Bang – a mini-lecture by Martha
          Mankowitz.

                    But MARTHA is now hesitant. In the silence a thought
                    occurs to CONNIE. She giggles. Tries to suppress the
                    giggle. Silence.

MARTHA   Well?

CONNIE   To have a name like Mankowitz when you hate Je –

MARTHA   (*Determinedly interrupting.*) The Big Bang – a
          mini-lecture.

          In the money streets of London known as the City,
          the mode of buying and selling shares used to be
          as follows: there was a purchaser, a stockbroker,
          and a jobber; I asked my stockbroker to purchase
          shares for me. He sent his dealers running among
          the jobbers in the Stock Exchange looking for the
          cheapest price. The jobber quoted to the dealer, the
          dealer phoned the broker, the broker advised me.
          When the Big Bang came the stockbroker became
          the jobber as well, and carried his own selection of
          shares.

CONNIE   Bang!

MARTHA   But – problem: whereas before my stockbroker
          could shop around for me he now becomes the
          shop. I have to buy the shares he's already bought at
          the price which will give him profit. If I want choice
          then I will have to do the shopping around. How
          will I judge?

                    Pause. MARTHA is obviously waiting for something.

CONNIE   (*Understanding.*) How will you judge?

MARTHA   I'm training myself to be a Chartist.

                    Pause. MARTHA again waits.

CONNIE   (*Obliging.*) What is a Chartist?

MARTHA   I'm glad you asked. Come with me.

                    (*They move to MARTHA's office and the charts.*)

          To buy shares which will go up in value and provide
          me with a profit I have to be able to interpret a

company's performance. There are – roughly speaking, you understand – two ways to do this. I can study company reports, accounts and balance sheets, and try to know the personalities involved. That's the conventional approach and those who pursue it are called Fundamentalists.

CONNIE   Now Fundamentalists threaten me.

MARTHA   Or I can read charts – the graphs of the price movements of shares. The readers of charts are called Chartists.

CONNIE   Not too happy with people who make charts either.

MARTHA   See here? The charts of three new companies in which I'm interested: Central Cement, Viennese Restaurants, and National Gardens. The world is building and entering a period of increased leisure. Cement, food, gardens.

CONNIE   Shouldn't they be called 'opportunists'?

MARTHA   To read a chart you must understand four main rules about patterns, trends, resistance and support levels. Is the trend up, down or sideways? Cement is generally up. Food and gardens are stable. They have support levels. That is to say their low points, bottom peaks, haven't broken down below a certain level. Someone has confidence enough to keep buying them to prevent them dropping too low. When they drop below a consistent level, you sell. Conversely, if a row of peaks at the same level is penetrated on the upside it means there are more buyers than sellers, the buyers have taken over and then you buy.

CONNIE   And did you?

MARTHA   I've watched these charts for a year and made imaginary purchases and sales. If they hadn't been imaginary I could have made…who knows what I could have made! But even to have read them right has been thrilling.

CONNIE   You amaze me.

MARTHA (*Intoxicated.*) The City is in upheaval. Mergers! Head-hunting! The poaching of expertise! Giants merging to become monoliths. Middle-sized firms merging to become giants. Small ones shiver and cross their fingers, hoping that somehow the world won't change –

CONNIE – not too much anyhow.

MARTHA But it will! The finger-crossers will go to the wall. Nothing will be the same again.

CONNIE And if you make a lot of money – what?

MARTHA 'What'? 'What' you ask?

CONNIE I ask.

MARTHA I will be the defiant possessor of a 'fuck-you' fund.

CONNIE A what?

MARTHA A 'fuck-you' fund. Independence! Books, travel, voluntary work, good deeds. No more atrophying afternoons and early nights. Good deeds and independence.

CONNIE You astound me.

MARTHA I can't wait.

CONNIE You astonish me.

MARTHA I mean to survive.

CONNIE I am thunder-clapped.

MARTHA And the key to survival is understanding the nature of money.

CONNIE Which is worth twice its value.

MARTHA Just so.

CONNIE It is sad about mother, she was once happy, she was once content, a simple soul –

MARTHA That's it! Simple! You both thought me simple. You and him. Well, let me remind you, Jesus Christ was a simple soul.

CONNIE (*Incredulous.*) But Jesus Christ wanted us to give our money away, not bank it at ten per cent.

MARTHA You will never, never, never understand!

SCENE 18

CONNIE's room.

CONNIE facing her toys.

CONNIE   She's right. I will never understand.

No. Not true. I understand. I just – don't know what to do. Give up your toys, Connie, give them up.

SCENE 19

CONNIE's room.

CONNIE and MARTHA shelling peas.

CONNIE   What would you do if he walked in here right now?

MARTHA   He couldn't. I made him give up the key.

CONNIE   If he knocked, rang the bell?

MARTHA   I wouldn't hear it.

CONNIE   If he banged, thumped, begged?

MARTHA   He wouldn't come near me.

CONNIE   Suppose.

MARTHA   Why should he? He despised me. What would he expect?

CONNIE   Never mind him. You. What would you do, feel, say?

MARTHA   I'd say nothing, feel nothing, do nothing.

CONNIE   That's not true.

MARTHA   Why ask if you're not going to believe me?

CONNIE   It can't be true. You may say or do nothing but you'd feel something;

Pause.

MARTHA   Rage. I'd feel rage.

Pause.

CONNIE   (*About to ask for something.*) Mother?

MARTHA   Worried about the tone of that.

CONNIE   I need to borrow some money.

MARTHA   See! Money! I heard money in that tone of voice.

CONNIE   Perceptive.

MARTHA   'He' never thought so.

CONNIE   (*Returning to original request.*) About a hundred and fifty pounds.

MARTHA   Don't be absurd. You know perfectly well I don't have that kind of money. I can manage twenty-five.

CONNIE   I always pay you back.

MARTHA   I wish you wouldn't ask.

CONNIE   Make it a hundred and twenty-five then.

MARTHA   You know how I hate discussion about money.

CONNIE   You could have fooled me.

MARTHA   I can go up to fifty.

CONNIE   I've got two important dates coming up.

MARTHA   I know your dates.

CONNIE   A hundred?

MARTHA   Cancelled at the last minute on a whim. Sixty is all I can manage.

CONNIE   These are dead certs, What about eighty-five?

MARTHA   Dead certs! Ha! (*Beat.*) Seventy!

CONNIE   Eighty?

MARTHA   Seventy-five and that's my final.

CONNIE   You're my saviour.

MARTHA   Where will you find the other seventy-five?

CONNIE   (*All innocence.*) What other seventy-five?

MARTHA   (*Slowly understands.*) You're a real scheming little Je –
             She holds back in time.

CONNIE   Little what?

MARTHA   You're like your fa – like 'him'.

CONNIE   Like my father was what?

MARTHA   He would never come out with what he wanted.

CONNIE   Was he a real scheming little Je –?

MARTHA   Never direct. Always circuitous.

CONNIE   (*Feeding her.*) Devious?

MARTHA Devious!

CONNIE Dissembling?

MARTHA Dissembling!

CONNIE Sly, treacherous, blood-sucking?

MARTHA Nothing threatened him either. He had an air…

CONNIE Ridiculous, depraved, greedy?

MARTHA – an air. He had – an air…

CONNIE Presumptuous, audacious, arrogant?

MARTHA Yes! Yes yes yes! Arrogant! Audacious!
Presumptuous! All that! And more…an air, an air…

She can't define it.

CONNIE I believe the world is divided into those who think
and those who hate thinkers.

MARTHA The world is divided into them and us and that's
the only division that counts. The only damn and
bloodying division that counts.

Long pause.

CONNIE Mother, talk to me about when I was a little girl.

*Pause. MARTHA doesn't want to talk about anything.
CONNIE feels contrite about goading her mother.
Wants to make her feel more comfortable with her
thoughts.*

Artists are a bit like Jews. They not only behave
as though they're in possession of the truth they
actually feel the need to impart it. (*Beat.*) And
nobody much likes them either.

MARTHA It's 'him' I hate, not the Je –.

CONNIE (*Gently.*) Say it. Say the word. You'll feel better.

MARTHA makes a huge effort to collect herself.

MARTHA You were spoilt. You were adorable and he spoilt
you. As soon as you were born you couldn't take
your eyes off one another. No matter what you were
doing – eating, crying, waking from sleep, as soon
as you saw him you stopped, stared and smiled.
It was uncanny. And he talked to you non-stop. I

fed you, changed you, made sure you had pretty clothes but he talked to you like an adult. No baby noises or words for his daughter. Real words and long sentences. And stories you couldn't possibly have understood. He wouldn't ever allow you to be a little girl. He made you stand before your time and walk before you could crawl. You could say 'claustrophobic' before you could say 'sweetie'. 'Sceptical' before 'Mummy'. It was all wrong. We have our stages. Growing up must go through stages. 'Allow her to be childish,' I warned him. 'Let her play with dolls.' He wouldn't. No fantasy. He deprived you of fantasy and fear.

CONNIE   That's not true. I developed a strong sense of fantasy…

SCENE 20

CONNIE's room.

CONNIE in light. MARTHA in the background, a shadow.

CONNIE   …and all I have is fear.

Fear of time passing, of loss, of you dying, 'him' dying without me ever seeing him again. Of growing old, ending alone. I fear that no one will laugh, that no one ever laughed, that there's nothing to laugh at.

Do I have to start again, Mother? Could I? Look at my face. The skin is hardening. I see lines. I feel lumps. I see blotches. I feel terror. Oooo…

…hold me, comfort me. It goes. I feel it going. No anchor, me.

No anchor. Anchor me, Mother.

I promised talent, once. Once I was a force. Anchor me. It goes.

O God, who art in heaven and promised meaning, don't let me go. Don't let me splinter and shatter. Hold me. Comfort me. Anchor me anchor me oh how it goes.

Pause.

There were these two women on a beach listening
to a concert on their transistor radio. One grey, the
other greyer. Early morning. Hardly crowded. Quite
hot. The sea dotted with sailing boats. Said the grey
to the greyer: 'Yes, I think it's very much one of
those modern concertos. Strindberg or someone.'

Pause.

Definition of Jewish genius: a boy with average
intelligence and two parents.

Pause.

Georg Lichtenberg said: 'It's impossible to carry
the torch of truth through a crowd without singeing
someone's beard.'

Pause.

Who *was* Georg Lichtenberg?

SCENE 21

CONNIE's room.

CONNIE and MARTHA. Sounds off.·

CONNIE   What's that?

MARTHA   What's what?

CONNIE   Sounded like a key in the front door.

MARTHA   No one has a key to the front door.

CONNIE   Daddy?

MARTHA   I made him give it back to me.

CONNIE   That was distinctly a key in the front door. (*Knock on
the door. The women are terrified.*) Who is it?

> *The door is flung open. JOSHUA stands before them, a
> man of enormous spirit, intelligence, gaiety.*

JOSHUA   The prodigal son returns! The war is over! Let us
turn our swords into ploughshares. For remember:
when God wanted a son he crawled up the skirts of a
Jewish girl!

MARTHA enters a hysterical outburst which begins, continues and ends at the same high, intense level as though she has become possessed. JOSHUA is incredulous. CONNIE is distressed. But it's an outpouring that cannot be stemmed and must run its course.

MARTHA (*Screaming.*) Ahhh! No! Tell him to go! Do you hear how he comes with offence? Look at him. He walks into everyone's room that way, as though he were born there, as though he can say anything anywhere anytime. We agreed. You promised. My home, my decisions, my privacy. Not everybody wants you around. Not everybody thinks God chose you to be their neighbour. Tell him to go. Tell him I can't bear anything about him – his arrogance, his opinions, his irreverence. No reverence for anything, only what he thinks, what he wants, what he believes. Him! Him! Him! Don't laugh at me. Do you hear his laughter? Do you hear his superior laughter? So superior, so confident, so happy, so eager, so interested, so talkative, so fucking full of his own fucking self. Listen to me. He makes me curse. He's made me decadent. He's never respected me. Destroyer of innocence, lecher, devil! Tell him to go. Tell him the world wasn't made for him. Tell him people want to be left alone. He disturbs everyone. Everyone feels unsafe, threatened. Look at him looking at me. His eyes mocking me. He always mocked me. Some of us have our own beliefs, some of us don't care what you believe. We care about our own little thoughts. Yes! Little to you, precious to us. Look at him! Full of contempt and derision. One day someone will gouge his cockiness from his eyes. Tell him that. Tell him to go. Before it's too late. Tell him he's an old man who's been in the world too long. Tell him he doesn't belong in this house. Tell him I can't breathe when he's in the room. I never know what I feel when he's in the room; I don't know what to do with my hands, where to look, what to say: Listen to me, my words are all jumbled. I'm screaming. He makes me scream. As soon as I see him I go into shock, I become unnatural, I hate myself. Tell him to go. Tell him to go. Tell him to go go go. I can't stop screaming. Tell him to go.

   Blackout.

Act Two

SCENE 1

CONNIE's room.

CONNIE and JOSHUA. MARTHA in her office.

CONNIE   She says she's not coming out till you leave.

JOSHUA   I'll cook her a meal.

CONNIE   'And tell him I don't want one of his smelly tasting meals,' she said.

JOSHUA   I bought her favourite wine.

CONNIE   'And if he's bought my favourite wine tell him to drown in it,' she said.

JOSHUA   Irrational as always.

CONNIE   'And tell him I'm not being irrational.'

JOSHUA   She'll come.

CONNIE   Irresistible, are you?

JOSHUA   She's a woman of second thoughts. Third, fourth and fifth thoughts to be precise, if one can be precise about your mother.

CONNIE   There was nothing imprecise about that outburst.

JOSHUA   Distressed you?

CONNIE   I've never heard her like that before.

JOSHUA   I've had it since the day we married.

CONNIE   Why did you stay?

JOSHUA   I have 'an air' about me, 'an air…an air…'

CONNIE   Which she can't name.

JOSHUA   Why do *you* keep coming back?

CONNIE   Elgar, Turner, George Eliot, the Lakes, fair play… 'One half of you is me,' she keeps saying. 'Remember! One half-of you is me.' (*Pause.*)

JOSHUA   My grandmother was the largest lady in her Polish village.

CONNIE   (*Music-hall.*) The largest lady in her Polish village?

JOSHUA   The Jewish community had never produced such a large lady. She could lift a man in each hand by the scruff of the neck.

CONNIE   And frequently did?

JOSHUA   And frequently did! They say, the story came down to me, that she insisted upon two husbands.

CONNIE   And got them?

JOSHUA   And got them! And when the pogroms came every village in the district suffered except hers.

CONNIE   The Cossacks were terrified of being raped! (*They are convulsed by laughter.*)

MARTHA   (*From her room.*) Judas!

        The laughter dies down.

JOSHUA   'The first truth', says Buddha, 'is that all life is suffering.'

MARTHA   (*From her room.*) Judas!

        Pause.

CONNIE   I believe the world is divided into those who were born when God was around and the rest of us who were born when he was on holiday. –

JOSHUA   I believe the world is divided into those who manage to get discounts on everything and the rest of us who have to pay the full price.

CONNIE   Dad, can you lend me a hundred and fifty pounds?

        Special burst of laughter from JOSHUA.

        A hundred then?

        They both laugh.

        Tell you what, I'll go easy on you. Make it seventy-five.

        JOSHUA takes out his wallet and carefully lays out seven five-pound notes, two one-pound notes, some loose change.

JOSHUA   Thirty-seven pounds fifty-three pence. All the money I have in the world.

CONNIE Ah!

JOSHUA (*Trying to suppress laughter.*) Sad, isn't it?

CONNIE (*Trying to suppress laughter.*) Yes.

JOSHUA But it's even worse than that.

CONNIE Worse?

JOSHUA I've been forced to resign my post.

CONNIE Forced to? I thought that couldn't happen unless you seduced a student.

JOSHUA I did.

CONNIE It's not true.

JOSHUA She was brilliant. You know how I find brilliance irresistible. Nineteen years old. She knew everything. I had nothing to teach her. Except one thing.

CONNIE Dad, is this true?

JOSHUA No. She seduced me. (*They continue laughing.*)

CONNIE Dad. We do not make jokes about seducing nineteen-year-old girls when we're fifty-six.

JOSHUA Fifty-five.

CONNIE (*Warning.*) Dad!

JOSHUA Nothing happened. I couldn't make it. She tried everything. She sang to it, tickled it, honeyed it, oiled it, got down on her knees and prayed to it. Nothing.

She played music to it, stripped to it, danced to it, whistled, even told hair-raising stories. Nothing!

She whacked it, she shook it, she cursed it, she blew it, she threatened, chanted mantras, salt-and-peppered it – wept. Nothing!

CONNIE is convulsed.

Imagine! We were caught not doing it! In my rooms at college. Among all that medieval oak panelling. The most uncomfortable rooms in Cambridge. (*Beat.*) Thirty seven pounds fifty-three pence, and a £25,000 overdraft secured by a job I no longer have.

(*Through his laughter.*) Ah well, as the philosophers have observed: we're all dying one way or another.

CONNIE   That's life, innit? (*Beat.*) Innit? Dinnit? Wannit!
         Gissit! Gotcha! Gerroff!

         MARTHA enters.

MARTHA   (*To CONNIE.*) Judas! (*Referring to JOSHUA.*) And him!
         Why is he here?

CONNIE   Oh, Mother, stop this.

MARTHA   You don't know what it's costing to be in the same
         room with him. Ask him. Why is he here?

CONNIE   Why are you here?

JOSHUA   (*To MARTHA.*) I want you to invest in my project.

CONNIE   (*To MARTHA.*) He wants you to invest in his project.

         MARTHA can't believe such audacity.

MARTHA   He must be mad.

CONNIE   You must be mad.

         SCENE 2

         MARTHA's office.

         MARTHA and JOSHUA. CONNIE in her room.

MARTHA   He must be mad.

JOSHUA   Not mad, romantic.

MARTHA   He doesn't respect me, why is he asking me for
         help?

JOSHUA   We need each other.

MARTHA   Why should I need someone who doesn't respect
         me?

JOSHUA   Come, sit with me, be friends.

MARTHA   He's pretended to respect me. Only ever pretended.

         *JOSHUA makes the effort he has always had to make
         to control his exasperation with her.*

JOSHUA   What are these charts?

         MARTHA, despite herself, is pleased he's asked.

MARTHA   I'm studying the market.

JOSHUA   With charts?

MARTHA Doesn't he know about them? Isn't he supposed to know everything?

JOSHUA I thought one studied the stock market by looking at personalities and balance sheets.

MARTHA There are other ways, you study the performance of the shares themselves.

JOSHUA And you worked out how to do all this?

MARTHA And then make predictions. What am I talking to him for?

JOSHUA And you key in information every day?

She nods.

And you make a mark every day?

MARTHA From the *Financial Times*.

JOSHUA Have you done today's?

She reaches for the pink sheets. Scans. Marks. Stops halfway.

MARTHA It's me who's mad, talking to him again.

JOSHUA Martha! I'm not a 'him'.

MARTHA Showing him, explaining –

JOSHUA I'm in the same room.

MARTHA – tolerating his presence, his existence –

JOSHUA Aren't you at least interested to know what my project is?

MARTHA I don't care about his projects.

JOSHUA We could make a fortune.

MARTHA He's always had hare-brained projects for making a fortune.

JOSHUA Martha, you have to acknowledge me.

MARTHA I just want him to go. Please, God, make him go away. (*CONNIE enters.*)

CONNIE Two Jews, two Jews. About to be executed. The Nazi captain, a civilized man, sensitive, a lover of Wagner virtue heroes children dogs and the Alps, not being without pity, and mindful of tradition, asked the Jews if they had a last request before being shot. The

first Jew asked for a cigarette and was given one.
The second Jew thought a second and then – spat in
the captain's face. At which the first Jew spluttered,
choked on his cigarette, went pale and whispered,
'Hymie, Hymie, do me a favour, don't – make
trouble!' –

JOSHUA In my version the second Jew asked if he could learn
to play the violin.

MARTHA Jews! Jews! Always jokes about Jews.

CONNIE (*In an Irish dialect.*) Two Irishmen, two Irishmen.
About to be executed. The British captain, a
civilized gent, sensitive, a lover of brass bands horses
Darjeeling tea Sunday mornings and his mother,
not being without pity, and a stickler for tradition,
asked the Irishmen if they had a last request before
being shot. The first Irishman asked for a pint of
Guinness. The second Irishman thought a moment
and then – spat in the captain's face. At which the
first Irishman coughed, spluttered, choked on his
Guinness and went red in the face crying out, 'Jasus!
Seamus! Do me a favour, don't make trouble!'

    Pause. Silence. Nothing.

'Jasus! Seamus! Isn't it trouble enough we have?'
(*Still nothing.*)

Jasus! Seamus! Haven't yers got me into enough
trouble?' (*Pause.*)

Not the same, is it?

MARTHA And why is it, I wonder, that when a Jew tells a
Jewish joke it's called Jewish humour but when
anyone else tells it it's anti-Semitic?

JOSHUA Because when a Jew tells a Jewish joke it's Jewish
humour but when anyone else tells it it's anti-
Semitic.

MARTHA There! He *looks* for trouble.

JOSHUA (*Ironically*) Can't get enough of it!

MARTHA And because he looks for it he attracts it.

JOSHUA   That's really what you wanted, that I shouldn't ever make trouble.

MARTHA   I wanted respect.

JOSHUA   That I should be invisible.

MARTHA   His air, his air…he has an air…

JOSHUA   An air of what? What air? What, what, what, you foolish woman, what?

MARTHA   Fear! He has no fear!

JOSHUA   (*Incredulous.*) Fear? Why should I have fear?

MARTHA   People without fear have no respect.

JOSHUA   Interesting.

MARTHA   He's mocking me again.

JOSHUA   People without fear have no respect. It is interesting.

MARTHA   He mocks me, and my thoughts jumble.

CONNIE   (*Warning.*) Dad!

MARTHA   He always mocked me.

JOSHUA   *You* speak to your mother.

MARTHA   He was contemptuous

JOSHUA   I don't understand the woman.

MARTHA   His voice was loud –

JOSHUA   And I *have* tried.

MARTHA   – he spent money before he earned it.

JOSHUA   How have I *not* tried!

MARTHA   He quarrelled with friends, wrote letters to the press, the Prime Minister –

JOSHUA   I called the fraudulent frauds, the faint-hearted cowards, the lickers of arses arse-lickers.

MARTHA   – and to the Pope.

CONNIE   The Pope?

MARTHA   Yes! The Pope, the Pope! He wrote to the Pope!

CONNIE   You actually wrote to the Pope?

MARTHA   At last Rome held an ecumenical council agreeing to forgive the Jews for the Crucifixion, and your father, your wise, witty father wrote announcing the creation of a Jewish ecumenical council to decide whether to forgive the Christians.

JOSHUA It's called irony.

MARTHA It's called irreverence.

JOSHUA I screamed at the pompous, the complacent, the tyrannical, the opportunistic – I screamed and I stirred and I made trouble because sometimes trouble had to be made.

MARTHA Like seducing the innocent?

JOSHUA I have my weaknesses.

MARTHA Is it any wonder he's thrown out of everywhere?

JOSHUA I think it's time to tell a funny story.

MARTHA I have a background. I have a heritage. It must be respected. Tell him it must be respected.

JOSHUA There were these thick Irishmen…

CONNIE Jonathan Swift.

JOSHUA Oliver Goldsmith.

CONNIE Oscar Wilde.

JOSHUA Yeats, Synge.

CONNIE Bernard Shaw, Sean O'Casey, Brendan Behan…

Beat.

JOSHUA Did anyone ever laugh at that joke?

CONNIE Not in the clubs where I played, they didn't.

MARTHA Neither of you. No respect. None at all.

SCENE 3

CONNIE's room.

CONNIE and JOSHUA. MARTHA in her office.

JOSHUA You at least will ask about my project.

CONNIE A book on the difference between what people say and the way they say it?

JOSHUA More than that. More, more than that. A book about the national characteristics revealed by language.

CONNIE Worrying.

JOSHUA Hopefully.

CONNIE What will you call it?

JOSHUA Suggest a title.

CONNIE Hidden Meanings?

JOSHUA Excellent! Splendid! But my book is only the beginning. I want to construct a machine.

CONNIE God help us. Science fiction?

JOSHUA Mock not my future. Let me explain. Just as there are only a handful of basic plots in literature, so there are only a handful of basic emotions in literature and personas in life. And each basic emotion and each persona has its own identifiable melody which the voice sings: love, hate, happiness, sadness, yes? The sanctimonious, the arrogant, the demagogue and so on. And because sometimes people utter *words* which are modest but in the *melody* of arrogance; or they utter words of love but in the melody of hate; or they offer words of respect but in the *melody* of contempt, and most people can't hear the *melody* so they're fooled and misled by the *words.*

CONNIE So?

JOSHUA So, my machine will be sensitive to the melodies and will show up as a colour on a screen. The melody of sanctimony – green. The melody of demagogy – red. The melody of arrogance – blue.

CONNIE The melody of seduction – pink.

JOSHUA The melody of mockery – yellow.

CONNIE The melody of false modesty – brown.

JOSHUA The melody of intimidation –

CONNIE – grey, grey, grey!

JOSHUA Everyone will have my machine attached to the TV set. No politician, journalist, diplomat, actor, prize-winning novelist or born-again priest would be safe.

CONNIE   A lie detector!

JOSHUA   No! A 'distinguisher'! To make distinctions. Very important to make distinctions. A lie detector tries to detect what you feel. Feelings are not to be trusted. My machine will distinguish between what's honestly intended and what's dishonestly intended. Not by registering feelings but by identifying melodies. (*Beat.*) You ask your mother to invest.

CONNIE   Me?

JOSHUA   Appeal on my behalf.

CONNIE   When I can't even appeal on my own behalf?

JOSHUA   One half of you is her, she said.

CONNIE   But the other half is *you*, dammit!

JOSHUA   She was left a great deal of money, your mother. Began after the steam engine was invented. The age of empire: philanthropy, long novels, a new sense of who belonged where in what place. I need her.

CONNIE   If you need her, be good to her.

JOSHUA   I trusted her, I advised her, I tried to love her but I am who I am what I am that I am. She couldn't suffer it.

CONNIE   And how am I expected to help her suffer who you are what you are that you are?

JOSHUA   It would help her feel benign.

CONNIE   I'm hearing a melody.

JOSHUA   It would help her set up the relationship she really believes is right and proper.

CONNIE   I'm hearing a melody louder than words.

JOSHUA   She believes the world is divided into those who need to be conferring favours and those who have no alternative but to beg them.

CONNIE   And the melody is of self-pity.

JOSHUA   Self-pity?

CONNIE   You thought you were identifying a fact about human behaviour. But the way you sang it revealed you were sorry for yourself. Powerless.

JOSHUA   Powerless? What are we talking about power for? The knowledge that my neighbour is a fool gives me power.

CONNIE   Wrong! That gives you superiority. There's a distinction

JOSHUA   Your father's daughter.

CONNIE   Superiority is the *knowledge* you have over the fool. *Power* is when you can prevent the fool from murdering you.

       Pause.

JOSHUA   They planted a bomb outside a Jewish old people's home in Copenhagen.

CONNIE   How brave. (*Beat.*) Anybody killed?

JOSHUA   Injured merely. Nothing much: A leg here, an arm there. (*Beat.*) The Danish government protested, 'But we have been critics of Israel…'

CONNIE   And the Jewish community?

JOSHUA   Those who never attend synagogue want to fill it. Those who attend regularly say, 'Hush… be invisible.'

       Pause.

CONNIE   God's already invented a distinguisher. It's called 'woman'.

JOSHUA   Woman?

CONNIE   Men only listen to words, women listen to the melody of words. There's millions of us about.

JOSHUA   But flawed! Inaccurate! Unreliable! Like everything God invented.

CONNIE   Still, it was his first go.

JOSHUA   No excuse! You're not sure how to do something? Leave it to somebody else.

CONNIE   (*Sadly.*) Who else was there, Josh?

Pause.

JOSHUA   It must be possible to get at the truth of human intention.

CONNIE   Technology won't lead you to the truth.

JOSHUA   I need to try. I need her help, I need your help to get her help. Ask her…

Pause.

CONNIE   I believe the world is divided into those who know the world is divided and those who don't know the world is divided.

JOSHUA   Or don't care, dammit, don't care!

SCENE 4

MARTHA's office.

MARTHA and CONNIE.

MARTHA   Tell him to ask me himself.

CONNIE   You just want him to beg.

MARTHA   I want him to face me.

CONNIE   His face angers you.

MARTHA   If he wants my help he must learn the art of normal social intercourse.

CONNIE   The art of social hypocrisy you mean.

MARTHA   We are talking about large sums of money.

CONNIE   The truth is expensive.

MARTHA   I have to hear from him the detail of his plans.

CONNIE   You know he won't have detailed plans. A man like Dad has a track record. His books, his honours, his standing in the world. The big foundations fund people not blueprints.

MARTHA   I am not a big foundation.

CONNIE   He's on to something important, Mother, possibly even lucrative.

MARTHA   I'm a small investor. I need facts and figures.

CONNIE   Think of the glory you'll reap.

MARTHA   I'm a pragmatist.

CONNIE   Think of your epitaph.

MARTHA   I'm Protestant and pragmatic.

CONNIE   'Mammon helps Truth.'

MARTHA   'Innocence exploited by Cunning' more like.

CONNIE   At least declare you're prepared to help in principle.

MARTHA   I will declare nothing. Tell him to ask me himself.

SCENE 5

MARTHA's office.

MARTHA and JOSHUA. The middle of a conversation. CONNIE in her room.

JOSHUA   Will you or will you not help me?

MARTHA   Nor did he ever like my father.

JOSHUA   I didn't ever like the image you had of your father. Otherwise I liked him. After my fashion.

MARTHA   I'll never forgive him the time he carne for dinner and remained silent a whole evening. Deliberately. Rudely. Embarrassingly.

JOSHUA   Your father was a kind man, an intelligent man but he never talked with you, only at you. He asserted his ideas, didn't offer them. Disagreement was unthinkable. Even small contributions. You had to exist in his space, his world, at his speed, with his laws, his references, his choice of subject, his beginnings, his ends, for his was the kingdom, the power and the glory. It was not that he was angry if you introduced other values, other perspectives. He was bewildered. Hurt. One day I decided to stop hurting him.

MARTHA   He insulted him instead. With silence.

JOSHUA   You mean I should've said 'amen' now and then?

MARTHA   And he expects me to keep him while he writes his absurd book and assembles his absurd machine?

This man without respect, with his sarcasm, his mockery…?

JOSHUA I do not mock. Mock is one thing I do not ever do. It's an English habit. I just have difficulty being reverential about some things.

MARTHA Some things? Everything!

JOSHUA No. Some things. You never listened to me carefully enough.

MARTHA And did he ever love me?

JOSHUA I'm at your mercy. Stronger than love.

MARTHA Did he imagine I wanted him to crawl to me? That I married him for that?

JOSHUA I think you married me to be your guest. I think you married me as one opens the front door to a visitor one wants to impress with one's interiors, one's culture, one's good manners, one's magnanimity. I think you married me that way. That's the way I think you married me.

MARTHA And he expects me to keep him knowing he thinks that about me?

JOSHUA You can afford it. It's your responsibility.

MARTHA Afford or not afford, I will decide my responsibilities.

JOSHUA You have an inheritance you don't know how to use.

MARTHA My inheritance is my inheritance.

JOSHUA One I contributed to.

MARTHA Ha!

JOSHUA But you were too grudging to acknowledge it.

MARTHA He nags for attention.

JOSHUA It embarrassed you.

MARTHA He whines for praise.

JOSHUA Talk about money was bad taste. Expressions of passion were bad taste.

MARTHA Listen to his shrill self-serving.

JOSHUA   Enthusiasm, appetite, energy, ideas, touch, loud laughter, generosity, second helpings – all, all bad taste.

MARTHA   Guttural, strident, ostentatious.

JOSHUA   You, mean, thin-lipped, tight-arsed, unimaginative, sanctimonious, hypocritical, gold-plated bitch, will you or will you not help me?

MARTHA   I will not. I will not. Oh, will I will I not! (*Tense silence.*)

JOSHUA   One day I found myself peeing in the loo during the interval of a production of *King Lear*. And I looked up as is the wont of loitering urinists and read the following graffiti: 'God is love – as all bunglers are!'

   MARTHA screams and screams and screams as though the intolerable incomprehensibility of this man is driving her mad.

SCENE 6

CONNIE's room.

CONNIE, toy telephone in hand. MARTHA and JOSHUA in MARTHA's office.

CONNIE   You still there, God? I have this father and mother and one is and one isn't and one does and one doesn't so I don't know if I am or am not, do or do not. Know what I mean?

   She positions herself regally in order to play God. Looks around, slowly.

   (*Booms out.*) Not only do I not know what *she* means, I never know what anybody means!

   She returns to the phone.

   Sorry, God. I keep being blasphemous I know but – can't resist it. You understand, don't you? I'm my father's daughter and it's my profession to joke and my nature to be irreverent and – oh, I don't know.

   It – was – all – simple – once.

Long, long pause.

Not true. It was never simple.

SCENE 7

CONNIE's room.

CONNIE and JOSHUA. MARTHA in her office.

JOSHUA   Do you think she finds me indigestible?

CONNIE   I think she finds you incomprehensible.

JOSHUA   I think she's like the second child who one day realizes her father was someone else's father first.

CONNIE   Pity the third child.

JOSHUA   Poor Jesus.

CONNIE   Poor Ishmael. (*Pause.*)

JOSHUA   And yet how often the third child is the most beloved.

         Pause.

CONNIE   I think you should have been a rabbi.

JOSHUA   My belief in God cannot be relied upon.

CONNIE   Rabbis don't believe in God, they just use him to control unmanageable Jews.

JOSHUA   What would you know! Only half of you is Jewish. And the wrong half at that.

CONNIE   Doesn't stop me feeling unmanageable. You're indigestible, I'm unmanageable.

JOSHUA   My father *wanted* me to be a rabbi. He said, 'Son,' he said, 'the world respects a scholar. You will never want for bread if you become a scholar.' The Enlightenment had passed him by so for him there was only one kind of scholar – a Talmudic one! I – wanted to study language. 'Language? Language is something you use, not study.' 'But, Daddy,' I said…

CONNIE   You called him 'Daddy'?

JOSHUA   I called *him* 'Daddy' and my mother 'Mummy' right up until they died. I was nearly fifty years old.

CONNIE   'But, Daddy', I said…'

JOSHUA   'But, Daddy,' I said, 'the history of nations is in their language and how it was formed and how it evolved.' He was amazed.

     Pause.

CONNIE   Josh, talk to me about when I was a little girl.

JOSHUA   There was the time you tried to milk a bull.

CONNIE   I never did!

JOSHUA   We used to go on holiday each year, for about four years running, to a little farm sublet by one of your mother's brothers from his 2,000 acre estate – for a not inconsiderable rent, I might add. You were ten years old and you'd seen the farmer's wife sitting on a stool with a pail between her legs pulling at something hanging, so you got a stool and put a pail between your legs and you found something hanging and you pulled!

CONNIE   And he kicked.

JOSHUA   He kicked! You pull a bull's ding-dong he gets confused. He say – 'Who dat dere? Who dat dere pulling my ding-dong when I ain't ready to have my ding-dong pulled?'

     CONNIE in fits of laughter.

Fortunately the pail was in the way. (*Pause.*)

(*Quiet.*) I remember we took you to concerts and theatre and on long journeys to foreign parts. You liked puddles, I remember. (*Pause.*)

'The first truth,' says Buddha, 'is that all life is suffering.' (*Sad smiles.*)

Do we really accept that? Really, really accept that? (*Pause. The question hangs in the air.*)

CONNIE   Daddy, I'm sorry I was none of the things you wanted me to be.

JOSHUA   *Wanted* you to be? *Wanted*? Only one thing I wanted you to be – free. Independent. Dependent upon no one. Not a husband for your keep, not a country

for your identity, not a group for your cause, nor
an ideology for your fulfilment. I wanted you to
learn your way out of prisons. To be nobody's slave,
nobody's guest. You make people laugh. I'm not
complaining.

CONNIE   Only they don't laugh and I am.

JOSHUA   You want to know about laughter? Let me tell you
about laughter. Laughter comes from the Jews. Why
the Jews? Because we're a nervous people. When
you invent God you make people uneasy. When
you then say he's chosen you to bear witness to the
beauty of his creation and to guard justice you make
people feel indignant. 'We have our own Gods,
we have our own justice.' But does the Jew listen?
He can't! When you've invented God no other
authority can really be taken seriously. And so the
Jew questions all authority. People don't like that.
They burn you for it. Isn't that enough to make you
nervous? Nervous people laugh. And that doesn't
help either.

(*Looking up.*) You there? I'm talking to you. We've
got problems down here. You sure you put the
parts together in the right order? (*To CONNIE.*)
He even questions the authority he claimed was
unquestionable. What can you do with such a
people? And they write funny books about it all.

Look at the Bible, the largest collection of jokes in
the world.

The Book of Job. To prove Satan wrong God lets
him play dice with Job's fortunes. A man who had
everything – beautiful wife, lovely children, wealth,
a house in the country on the West Bank, and then,
all of a sudden, wham! He loses everything. His wife
dies, his children all die, his car, his hi-fi, his washing
machine – everything repossessed! And he's struck
down with herpes. It's enough to make you nervous.
So what does Job do? If he were a Christian, faith

would be enough. But for a Jew nothing is enough. He has to go to the top.

(*Looking up.*) You there? I'm talking to you. I've got problems down here. I'm an upright man, I take a little here give a little there. Is this just? Look at me. I'm a mess.

And what does God do? He laughs back. He shows Job a big fish, a leviathan he calls it. 'Can you hook it?' God asks. 'It's a big fish;' says Job. 'How can I hook it?' 'Right!' says God. 'How much more difficult to hook me!' 'He's doing a Hamlet on me,' says Job. 'Very funny!' What could be funnier? And he's right.

The Jew can't help it, he questions authority with laughter. It's a nervous tick.

Take Einstein. Einstein questioned authority with laughter. You know how it is. You meet a Jew on the stairs and you ask him if he's going up or he's going down and he says, 'Well, it depends. Everything's relative!'

Take Freud. Freud questioned authority with laughter. 'Ernest,' he said to his biographer, Ernest Jones – another Jewish habit, talking to your biographer – 'Ernest, I'm half convinced by socialism.'

'How come, Herr Doktor?' Ernest knows the Herr Doktor is a thorough conservative. 'Well,' says Freud, 'I've been reading Trotsky on socialism' – Trotsky, another funny man who questioned authority – 'I've been reading Trotsky and he says that in the first phase of the transition to socialism there will be big problems: upheavals, misery, large-scale disaster. But in the second phase the promised land for us all, paradise on earth, utopia! Well, Ernest, I am convinced about the first half.'

No, don't laugh. This Jewish humour, this laughing at authority, it causes such irritation. You're not supposed to laugh at the misery they bestow on you. It's unnatural. It causes a great deal of misunderstanding, better known as anti-Semitism. And what *is* anti-Semitism? It's hating Jews more than is necessary. It's enough to make you nervous. Especially when you're never certain whether you've got an audience out there or a lynch mob.

CONNIE   A lynch mob, a lynch mob! That's my problem, I'm telling jokes to a lynch mob.

SCENE 8

Between Cabaret club and MARTHA's office.

JOSHUA in CONNIE's room. Fade in first on CONNIE in the Cabaret Club.

CONNIE   Kafka! Kafka! You take Kafka. Kafka questioned authority with laughter. He was talking to his biographer, Max Brod – they all have biographers these funny men – and Kafka as usual was being gloomy and pessimistic. Dark, he was a dark, dark man. And Brod says, 'Frank,' he says, 'you're being more depressing than usual. The way you talk. Is there no hope?' And Kafka says, 'Who says there's no hope? Of course there's hope, Max. An infinite amount of hope...but not for us!'

(*As one of her audience.*) Bloody hell!

All right then. There was an Englishman, Irishman, Scotsman and this Jew. No. There was a Norwegian, Dane, Swede and this Finn. No. There was a Russian, Hungarian, Czech and this Pole.

(*Yelling* as *one of the audience.*) Make up yer mind, yer silly cow.

How about – there was this Finn, this Pole and this Jew?

(*Yelling.*) They shouldn't 'ave bloody women telling bloody jokes.

Women never was funny. (*Fade in on MARTHA.*)

MARTHA   I don't mean to be what I am, say what I say. He
           drives me to it. Draws it from me. And when it
           comes I don't know where it comes from.

CONNIE   So God finally found this bloke called Moses on top
           of a mountain tearing his hair out 'cos his family
           down below were dancing naked round a golden calf
           and doing all sorts of rude and wicked things and
           he said to Moses, 'I'm *giving* them away' and Moses
           said, 'Good! I'll have ten!' (*Beat.*) Pity! Thought
           you'd like that one.

MARTHA   (*Getting to her knees.*) Dear Lord Jesus, pray for me.
           Send me a sign. Teach me what to think, how to
           behave. Explain it to me. We suffered too, didn't we?

CONNIE   I had a Jewish grandmother – yes, you heard!
           We've all got our crosses to bear. And this Jewish
           grandmother used to say to me, 'You can live a long
           time, learn a lot and still die a fool.'

MARTHA   Why does he want to destroy me? I didn't want to
           hate him. Hate is not my nature.

CONNIE   There's a certain kind of English mentality which
           turns very nasty if you don't take its flippancy
           seriously. Know what I mean?

MARTHA   I *wanted* to love him.

CONNIE   The kind of mentality that buys two-seater cars so
           they can't give friends lifts home.

MARTHA   But I loathe him. With a passion.

CONNIE   So, she nudges her neighbour across the wall and
           says, 'My old man, my old man, 'e's the only man I
           know 'oo's risen to the depths!'

MARTHA   No one to talk with.

CONNIE   (*Yelling as though one of the audience.*) Gerroff! You've
           never told a good joke and never will tell a good
           joke.

MARTHA   If there's no one to talk with, you talk to yourself.

CONNIE   Gerrout! Gerrup! Gerroff!

MARTHA   Cigarette. Need a cigarette. Tried to give up; Can't.
         (*She finds one. Lights it. The pleasure of inhaling is
         immense.*)

         What I feel is not what I want to feel, know what I
         mean, angel? Focus, focus! I can't focus while he's
         around.

CONNIE   All right then, try this.

MARTHA   Who is angel?

         (*A sound grows. Of protesting jeering voices.*)

CONNIE   I believe the world's divided into the conscious and
         the unconscious.

MARTHA   I'm angel.

CONNIE   The givers and the takers.

MARTHA   My father called me 'angel'.

CONNIE   The winners and the losers.

MARTHA   'Angel,' he said, 'beware of everything beyond these
         shores.'

CONNIE   The submissive and the domineering.

MARTHA   'Beyond these shores nothing is predictable.'

CONNIE   The sick and the healthy.

MARTHA   'There has to be predictability.'

CONNIE   Those who need God and those who don't.

MARTHA   My father knew. My father warned – 'he will be
         unpredictable'.

         Crescendo of voices ends abruptly.

CONNIE   'I must remember,' said Florence Nightingale, 'that
         God is not my secretary!' (*Beat.*) *She* couldn't have
         been Jewish then! (*Fade out on CONNIE. MARTHA
         reaches for her phone.*)

MARTHA   Connie? Connie? Please come back. If I shout a bit
         it's because I hurt a bit, I'm confused a bit. You've
         nothing to be afraid of from me. Remember – half
         of you is me. (*Puts down phone. Pauses. Dials again.*)
         Hello, God? Is it true that you are a Je – that you're
         Je – Je – Je –

The word sticks in her throat. She gags on it.

SCENE 9

CONNIE's room.

CONNIE and JOSHUA.

JOSHUA Did you speak to her again?

CONNIE I did.

JOSHUA And?

CONNIE She doesn't like being called a gold-plated bitch.

JOSHUA Did I call her that?

CONNIE 'Mean, thin-lipped, tight-arsed, unimaginative, sanctimonious, hypocritical, gold-plated bitch.'

JOSHUA I couldn't have said all that.

CONNIE In one breath. She wrote it down.

JOSHUA No hope then.

CONNIE But she is a woman of second thoughts.

JOSHUA There is hope then?

CONNIE Do you know what it's *like* having the two of you knock around inside me?

JOSHUA Take what's best, my darling, the rest reject. What makes you think she may have second thoughts?

CONNIE I'm talking about me!

JOSHUA Talk.

CONNIE I'm a mess.

JOSHUA So was Job.

CONNIE I tell Jewish jokes for a living.

JOSHUA But God adored him and I adore you.

CONNIE Adoring me doesn't help.

> *Knock on the door. CONNIE opens it. MARTHA enters with a birthday cake and six lighted candles in one hand, a bottle of champagne and three glasses in the other. CONNIE and JOSHUA are astounded.*

MARTHA Cakes and champagne for the family.

JOSHUA   I exist for her! There *is* hope.

MARTHA   (*To JOSHUA.*) Couldn't let your birthday go by
          without a little celebration.

JOSHUA   But it's not my birthday.

MARTHA   It *was* on at least one day this year.

JOSHUA   And I'm not six years old.

MARTHA   Six is for sixty, silly.

JOSHUA   I'm not sixty, either. I'm fifty-five.

MARTHA   We're all ancient members of an ancient race. We're
          celebrating that, then.

JOSHUA   It's poisoned!

MARTHA   If you stop to think about any day you'll always
          find a reason to celebrate it. The day you met your
          husband. The day you moved into the house. The
          Lord's Day. The first rose is out. Midsummer's Eve.
          Your monthlies are finished. A hostage is released.
          The Lord's Day – oh! I've already said that, haven't
          I? Anyway, it could be cakes and champagne every
          day. If one could afford it.

JOSHUA   All lunacy has logic.

MARTHA   Of course I can't really afford it.

CONNIE   I'm glad we're a family, mother.

MARTHA   I know your father has these fantasies of my vast
          wealth hidden in banks around the world but for
          all the wealth I know about they might as well be
          hidden in banks. Now Joshua, blow.

JOSHUA   It'll explode. As I blow it'll explode and she'll have
          solved all her problems. In one blow!

MARTHA   Come. I want you both to taste the cake and tell me
          what it's made of.

JOSHUA   Martha, I'm not understanding.

MARTHA   Oh well, you can't expect to understand everything
          in this life.

JOSHUA   You're showing one face and hiding another,
          Martha.

MARTHA   That's the trouble with you people –

JOSHUA   'You people'?

MARTHA   You educated ones. Don't be so sensitive. You always want to understand everything, explain everything. You're all scientists, linguists, professors – of psychology or biochemistry or genetics. Genetics! There! You'll end up filling the world with monsters. Leave it alone. Mystery. Let there be mystery –

JOSHUA   – and darkness. How about some medieval darkness around the place while we're about it?

MARTHA   (*Peeling free the champagne foil.*) And opinions! You've always got to have opinions. Stop tampering with the world. Eat cakes and drink champagne. Celebrate the days. Blow!

> *He hesitates. Closes his eyes. Crosses himself. Clasps his hands in prayer. Mumbles a little, then blows. The cork pops.*

(*Pouring.*) Had no faith in your Adonai? (*To* CONNIE.) Did you know I can recite the prayer for wine. In the days when we trusted and loved one another he taught me.

> *She raises her glass. Recites.*

Baruch atah Adonai
Eloheinu melech haolam
Boreh pri hagofen.

> *They clink glasses. She drinks. The others follow, though* JOSHUA *waits for* CONNIE *to drink first.*

Do you know why we clink our glasses? All over the world people clink their glasses before they drink – why?

> *Pause.*

Don't we know? My clever darlings don't know? Or do we think it's useless information? Ah, well, it's been Martha's role in life to be a fund of useless information.

The ancients had for years loved wine. Every sense was gratified but one. No one talked about it. It became a taboo subject – like not mentioning that one's beautiful, intelligent, happy child had an arm missing. Until one day glass was invented and like the silicon chip it changed all living thereafter.

It was the court jester during the reign of Rameses III – no! That can't be so. The Egyptians hadn't learned that laughter at oneself could heal. Or had they?

JOSHUA (*Admiringly.*) Keep going, Martha, keep going.

MARTHA Do you think every civilization had Jesters to help them through life? I digress. Wherever, whenever, whoever, said: 'How good it is that we have wine to gratify so many senses. We can look at it, we can smell it, we can taste it, and to make it we must touch it. But how sad that we cannot *hear* it.' At which the court jester, inspired as only court jesters can be, clinked the glass of the pharaoh or the emperor or the duke, and said, (*Clinks JOSHUA's glass.*) 'Health to all your senses, Lord!'

    She drinks.

CONNIE That was a very beautiful story, Mother.

MARTHA Martha not so useless after all? Good. Now. (*Cuts the cake.*) It's a new recipe and I shall be very disappointed if you guess all the main ingredients.

    She hands each a slice. Neither eats.

    I suppose I should be used to your humour by now.

CONNIE (*Eating.*) Well, half of me is her. I'm safe.

JOSHUA Don't bank on it.

    CONNIE chokes. Staggers around. Falls.

MARTHA Come now, dear. The death of children is not game for ridicule.

CONNIE (*From her prone position.*) Butter, eggs, flour, for sure. Then – er – honey?

MARTHA Couldn't miss that.

    MARTHA drinks quickly. She will become drunk soon.

CONNIE   Now there's an interesting question. What's not game for ridicule?

MARTHA   You haven't finished guessing the ingredients of my cake.

CONNIE   Who, if anyone, or what, if anything, is too sacred to be ridiculed?

MARTHA   Joshua?

JOSHUA   Oh – er – walnuts. I taste walnuts. (*To* CONNIE.) Everything must be game for ridicule.

MARTHA   Connie, he says walnuts. What do you say?

>   *A subtle conflict ensues. JOSHUA becomes excited by the topic. MARTHA fights for CONNIE's attention.*

CONNIE   Oh – er – almonds. Honey and almonds. (*To* JOSHUA.) Everything?

MARTHA   What else?

CONNIE   Is the martyr game for ridicule?

MARTHA   I mean, there is one very special spice which sets it off.

CONNIE   The freedom fighter? The missionary? The educator? Those in pain?

MARTHA   I did take the trouble to bake a cake…

CONNIE   (*Biting.*) Cinnamon.

MARTHA   (*Giggling.*) Nothing so ordinary.

JOSHUA   Yes! All of them are game for ridicule if they can be seen to be in love with or intoxicated by: the martyr her sacrifice, the freedom fighter his anger, the missionary his zeal, the educator her cleverness, and those in pain their suffering.

MARTHA   I'll give you a clue. It comes from –

JOSHUA   I'm a puritan. I believe everything has to be earned, and all those who engage in altruism and agony should do so with reluctance. Anyone caught enjoying it should be punished with ridicule.

MARTHA   I really am surprised you didn't get it at once, Connie.

CONNIE walks to a note on her wall.

CONNIE (*Reading.*) 'Wherefore I perceive that there is nothing better than that a man should rejoice in his own works; for who shall bring him to see what shall be after him?' Ecclesiastes, chapter 3, verse 22.

MARTHA It's a spice often referred to in the Bible.

JOSHUA In my opinion all opinions are provisional! Even Eccles– (*MARTHA snaps.*)

MARTHA Opinions! He has to have opinions about everything! Puritan? Huh! I'd say he was. Not an ounce of fun in him. Takes himself so bloody seriously. Too clever by half! He'll have a fall one day which will break his bloody neck, and serves him right.

CONNIE Mother!

MARTHA Serves them all right. I'm sick of being nice and tolerant and baking cakes.

CONNIE Mother!

MARTHA It's happening again. He didn't go and it's happening again.

CONNIE Please, Mother.

MARTHA His air…

JOSHUA I feared it wouldn't last long.

MARTHA …he has this air…

JOSHUA I'm having an intelligent conversation with my daughter.

MARTHA *His* daughter, *his* conversation, *his* intelligence. It suffocates me.

JOSHUA What suffocates you?

MARTHA (*Struggling to name it.*) His air…

JOSHUA Air! Air! What air, you foolish woman, you? What air?

MARTHA (*At last.*) He has no fear of God.

JOSHUA Fear of God? Why should I fear God? I invented him!

MARTHA There! That! That's it! Did you hear him?

CONNIE   Mother, I am going mad with all of this. Mother –

MARTHA once more goes out of control into hysteria.

MARTHA   Mother! Mother! Don't 'mother' me. I'm not your
mother.

He's your father, though. And can't you tell it! The
way you stick together. You. You and him. All of
you. Keeping to yourselves. Cosy. Exclusive. Private.
Private jokes, private conversations, private plots
for this and that. You'd like to take over this house,
wouldn't you? Find some way of getting me out of
the place I was born in, grew up in, welcomed him
into. Eh? I bet that's what you're plotting to do. Take
over. I bet you arranged – Oh, my God!

Why didn't I see it before? Of course! Fool! Trusting
bloody fool. You arranged to come together, didn't
you, at the same time? You've been scheming behind
my back. Why? Why?

CONNIE   Cardamom. You've put cardamom in the cake. What
a clever idea.

MARTHA   It's happening again. He didn't go and it's happening
again. I can't breathe, I don't know where to put
myself, I don't know what to do with my hands,
I don't know what to say, I'm not making sense,
I'm screaming again, I'm screaming, I can't stop
screaming.

*MARTHA is drunkenly weeping. Inconsolable. She lays
her head in CONNIE's lap.*

Why didn't he go? I've never understood. He's
got his own little flat now, hasn't he? I've never
understood any of it, any of it, never understood…

*They watch her simmer down. She moans softly, as
though trying to comfort herself. It is a long pause.*

JOSHUA   (*Realizing it, as though for the first time.*) She will never
have any peace.

Slow fade.

By the Same Author

Wild Spring

Break My Heart

Barabbas (*15 minute play for TV/stage*)

Denial

Groupie

Longitude

Letter to Myself (*For a 13 year old actress*)

Amazed & Surprised (*15 minute radio/stage play*)

Phoenix Phoenix Burning Bright

The Rocking Horse Kid (*For radio*)

Short Stories

Six Sundays in January

Love Letters on Blue Paper

Said the Old Man to the Young Man

The King's Daughters

Essays and Non-fiction

Fears of Fragmentation

Distinctions

Say Goodbye, You May Never See Them Again (Wesker text, primitive paintings by John Allin)

Journey Into Journalism

As Much As I Dare (autobiography)

The Birth of Shylock and the Death of Zero Mostel (Diary)

For Children

Voices on the Wind

When I Was Your Age

Novels

Honey

Opera Librettos

Caritas

Grief

Poetry

All Things Tire Of Themselves – a collection of 45 poems.